GROWING UP IN THE WILD

Dr. Tony Hare

Checkmark Books™
An imprint of Facts On File, Inc.

Animal Life Cycles

Published 2001 for Facts On File
for sale in North America only
by Marshall Cavendish Books
An imprint of Times Media Private Limited
A member of the Times Publishing Group
Times Centre, 1 New Industrial Road
Singapore 536196

For information contact:

Checkmark Books
An imprint of
Facts On File, Inc.
11 Penn Plaza
New York NY 10001

Library of Congress Cataloging-in-Publication Data
Hare, Tony
Animal life cycles : growing up in the wild /
Tony Hare.
p. cm.
ISBN 0-8160-4595-X (hardcover)
ISBN 0-8160-4596-8 (pbk.)
1. Animal life cycles.

Printed and bound in Singapore

CONTENTS

INTRODUCTION

Animals are confronted with countless hurdles every day of their lives and each of them employs innumerable strategies in their struggle to survive. Yet whether they rely on speed, strength or cunning, all animals have one common goal — reproduction and with it the continuation of their species.

Animals reproduce in a variety of ways. Most mammals develop in their mother's womb. When born, the offspring are well-formed and, in many species, are up and about within hours of birth. A small number of animals, however, do not follow this system. In marsupials, or pouched animals such as the rat kangaroo, the baby grows in the mother's womb for four to five weeks before wriggling from the birth opening to the teat in its mother's pouch. In contrast, the platypus is one of three species of egg-laying mammals.

Animals devote a lot of time and energy to raising their offspring. In many cases, the mother cares for the newborn animal entirely on her own, but responsibility is shared by both parents in some species, notably among many monkey species, dogs and foxes. In extreme cases, care is left predominantly to the male, such as in the titi monkey species.

Ranging from the common hamster to the endangered giant panda, *Animal Life Cycles* introduces the life patterns of some 70 species of mammals. Carefully selected to represent a lifestyle that is successful in its particular environment, each animal profile offers comprehensive information on reproduction, birth, parental care and growth. *Animal Life Cycles* also discusses the strategies that these animals have developed, their interaction with other members of the same species and the amazing solutions in their struggle for survival.

Dr. Tony Hare

AFRICAN WILD DOGS

Many wild dog packs spend most of the year roaming in search of prey, but they cannot breed on the move, since the pups need the shelter of a secure den. This limits the hunting scope of the pack just when they need to be most certain of their food supply, so they must choose the right time and place. Packs breed in response to local conditions, so in areas where prey animals migrate, the dog packs in each area will breed at different times.

When a female comes into heat, she quickly attracts the attention of the males. Junior males may mate with her before she ovulates, but the dominant male usually fathers the pups, attending the female closely during her fertile period and denying the others access to her. At 70–75 days, the gestation is the longest known among dogs, but for two-thirds of this period the fetuses remain small, only growing rapidly during the final three or four weeks of the pregnancy. This enables the female to stay active for as long as possible before she dens.

Bringing up the pups

A typical breeding den is a burrow dug and abandoned by some other animal, such as an aardvark or a hyena, deep enough to maintain a stable temperature. After the pups are born, the mother spends the first few days with them in the den, and even when she emerges, she stays nearby while the rest of the pack hunt. The adults bring her food, regurgitating it on demand, and when the pups start to take solid food at the age of three to four weeks, they bring meat for them, too. Both mother and pups rely on the other adults to keep them supplied, and it is doubtful whether a breeding pair on their own would be able to raise a litter to maturity. From about seven weeks subordinate adults may stay at the den to guard the pups while the mother hunts with the rest of the pack, and these helpers beg food alongside the pups.

At about two months old the pups begin to acquire their rangy adult shape and coloration. Their games become more earnest as they start to sort out who's who, and they begin tagging along behind the pack as it sets off to hunt. Initially an adult may lead them back to the den, but in time they are allowed to feed directly from the kill. The adults always move aside to allow the pups to feed, although they take care to eat as much as possible before the pups catch up. At about ten weeks the pack abandons the den and returns to the nomadic life, but it will be several months before the young recruits learn the art of hunting for themselves.

COMING OUT
When the pups are three or four weeks old, their mother forsakes the den and starts to suckle them outside (above).

PULLING RANK
Like all the pack, the pups receive their fair share of a kill, after which the alpha female will readily steal the surplus from their mouths (above).

FROM BIRTH TO DEATH

AFRICAN WILD DOG

GESTATION: 70–75 DAYS
LITTER SIZE: 2–19, AVERAGE 7–10
BREEDING: MATE WHEN PREY BECOMES SEASONALLY ABUNDANT
WEIGHT AT BIRTH: 14 OZ (400 G)
EYES OPEN: 3 WEEKS
FIRST LEAVE DEN: 3–4 WEEKS
HUNTING WITH PACK: 12–14 MONTHS
SEXUAL MATURITY: 12–18 MONTHS
LONGEVITY: RARELY UP TO 10 YEARS

Illustration Carol Roberts

GROWING UP

The life of an African wild pup

FEED ME

By about five weeks old, the pups are begging food from all the adults in the pack. The adults respond tolerantly enough, often playing with the pups and allowing them all kinds of liberties.

A HUMBLE ACT

The pups incite adults to bring up food by licking at their lips (left). This act becomes central to the dogs' social life, with juniors using it as a gesture of submission to their superiors.

in SIGHT

FAMILY PLANNING

Occasionally a wild dog pack will rear two litters at once. If prey is abundant, there is less pressure to concentrate the whole pack's resources on one litter, and the alpha female may tolerate breeding by one of the subordinate females. More usually, though, the harsh economics of life in the wild dictate otherwise, and if a subordinate produces pups, they are quite likely to be killed and even eaten by the alpha female.

Luckily such extreme measures are rarely necessary, for subordinate females seem to have their breeding instincts suppressed while they remain under the influence of the alpha female. It may be that psychological pressure leads to a reduction in hormone levels, preventing ovulation; alternatively there may be some chemical factor, possibly in the dominant female's urine. Either way, the alpha female usually gets her way.

TUG-OF-WAR

The alpha female wrestles a pup from a younger mother who has also bred a litter (below).

AMERICAN BLACK BEARS

Black bears usually mate between June and mid-July, or a little later in northern areas. Now males wander the range in search of females; if they meet a rival, particularly in the vicinity of a female, a fight may break out. The female remains in estrus until she has been mated; males and females spend little time with each other even at this time, usually mating and then parting again.

Birth will take place when the mother is in her den during the winter sleep, where the tiny cubs are protected during their first few months. To achieve this timing, the fertilized egg is not implanted in the female's uterus until around October, often when she is already denning, and true gestation takes eight to ten weeks from this time. If, by any chance, the female has not put down sufficient fat reserves to nourish her and the potential litter, the egg does not implant but simply gets reabsorbed into her body.

THE FERTILIZED EGG ENTERS THE UTERUS, PERHAPS DIVIDES A FEW TIMES, THEN FLOATS FREE FOR A FEW MONTHS

POCKET-SIZED CUBS

In January or February, the female gives birth to up to five, but usually two or three, cubs, rousing herself just sufficiently to bite through the umbilical cords. The cubs are incredibly tiny, weighing less than 1/500th of the mother's weight. They are blind, helpless, and covered in such fine, sparse hair that they actually look naked. For the next few weeks, they simply nestle into their sleeping mother's fur and suckle her rich milk. Their eyes open at 25–30 days old.

At first, the cubs' hindquarters are so weak that if they want to move around the den, they have to pull themselves along by their forelegs. They develop fairly rapidly, however, and by the

FROM BIRTH TO DEATH

AMERICAN BLACK BEAR

GESTATION: 220 DAYS INCLUDING DELAYED IMPLANTATION
LITTER SIZE: 1–5, USUALLY 2 OR 3
BREEDING: MAY–JUNE
WEIGHT AT BIRTH: 8–10 oz (248–312 g)
EYES OPEN: 25–30 DAYS
FIRST WALKING: 5 WEEKS
WEANED: 6–8 MONTHS
INDEPENDENCE: 13–14 MONTHS
SEXUAL MATURITY: 4–5 YEARS IN FEMALE, 5–6 YEARS IN MALE
LONGEVITY: HARD TO ASSESS, BUT 26 YEARS RECORDED

MATING
is one of the few times that males and females meet — and then only briefly. Come autumn, the female retires to her den, where she will later give birth.

EARLY SUMMER
heralds the breeding season, when sexually mature males compete aggressively to secure their mating rights.

YOUNG ADULTS
set out in their second spring to live life on their own. Times can be tough, as they must defer to mature adults at prime feeding sites.

Illustrations Joanne Cowne

GROWING UP

The life of a young black bear

IN THE SPRING *the new family emerges from the den, the cubs now fully developed. They stay close to their mother, who protects them from marauding adult bears. Time is spent nursing, sleeping, and playing rough-and-tumble games with one another.*

THE FOLLOWING *winter the cubs once more den with their mother, but they disperse the next spring to find and establish their own territories.*

AMAZING FACTS

- **A female American black bear may be mated by several bears during the weeks she is in estrus.**
- **A human baby having the same weight proportion as the American black bear to its mother at birth would weigh only about 5 oz (140 g).**
- **Most female bears produce one cub in their first litter and two or more in later seasons.**
- **American black bear cubs in the same litter may display different coat colors.**

time they are five weeks old, they are strong enough to walk. By the time the mother awakens, her cubs are fully furred, miniature bears, ready to accompany her and examine the world around them.

The female is fiercely protective of her young at this time, and they are indeed vulnerable. It is, in fact, adult male bears—black and brown (grizzly)—that present the greatest danger. The cubs also fall prey to pumas, bobcats, and eagles. Their mother tries to protect them by leaving them in a sheltered nest, either in the undergrowth or a hollow tree, while she goes off to forage for food. She, after all, is in a weakened state after her sleep and must get sufficient food so that she can nourish her cubs.

THE TWO MONTHS AFTER THEY FIRST LEAVE THE DEN ACCOUNT FOR THE GREATEST MORTALITY AMONG CUBS

The cubs nurse frequently from the mother until they are six to eight months old. She usually lies on her back or her side while they suckle, but sometimes she simply sits back on her haunches and the cubs perch in her lap. Although weaned by the autumn after their birth, the cubs generally spend the following winter with their mother in the den. The next spring, the female may forcibly evict them from her territory—particularly any young males—as she once more seeks a mate.

Their first year alone is a dangerous time for young black bears. They are harassed by adult bears, especially at prime feeding spots; they are consequently attracted to places where the feeding is easy, such as garbage bins and dumps. Here, they may often be shot as nuisances. ■

ANTEATERS

Giant anteaters and tamanduas both mate in the southern autumn (March to May), timing the event so they give birth in the spring, when they can rely on many months of abundant food. The actual courtship and mating has never been scientificially described and remains something of a mystery. This is partly a reflection of inadequate research, but it also reflects the anteaters' distinctly casual attitude toward the whole business.

THE FEMALE GIANT ANTEATER *gives birth standing up, using her tail for support.*

PASSING SHIPS

As solitary, seminomadic creatures, anteaters do not enjoy a rich social life. In general, both males and females forage and sleep alone, within their own home ranges. There is no evidence to suggest that males fight for access to females, or that either sex indulges in elaborate courtship procedures. Males and females seem merely to run across one another, mate, and then part—although it is probable that males are attracted by the scent of females in breeding condition.

PARASITIC NEMATODES

Parasitic nematodes, also known as roundworms, are some of the most abundant animals on the planet with over 15,000 known species.

This worm is elongated and tapered at both ends. It is found in every living environment, including plants, and on many animals.

Unusually though, female tamanduas are, in fact, the only mammals known to suffer from infestation with parasitic nematode in their ovaries.

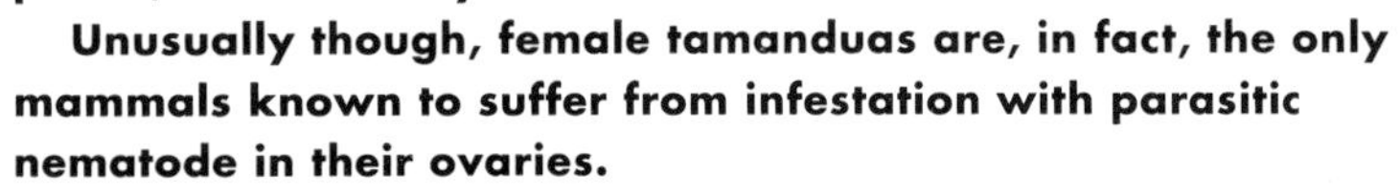

All illustrations Barry Croucher/Wildlife Art Agency

The sexual habits of the silky anteater are even more mysterious, mainly because it lives in the forest canopy, beyond the range of casual observation. But radio tracking indicates that it is more territorial than its larger relatives, with each individual apparently defending its own patch of forest against neighbors of the same sex. The range of each male incorporates that of three females, suggesting a deliberate attempt to monopolize them, but there is no direct evidence of this.

In giant anteaters the gestation is around 190 days, while that of the tamanduas is 130–150 days. The giant anteater gives birth standing upright, propped on her hind legs and tail like a three-legged stool; and the single newborn baby immediately crawls up her fur and onto her back. Fully furred, the young giant anteater is an exact miniature of its mother, and as it rides upon her back its color pattern merges into hers so the two are almost indistinguishable.

By contrast a young tamandua is usually quite different in shade, so it is relatively conspicuous as it clings to its mother's fur.

A young giant anteater relies on its mother's milk for six months, but it may ride on her back for a year or more, feeding alongside her when she cracks into an ants' nest. It is mobile at about the age of four weeks, but if she wanders off it will call her with shrill whistles until she returns. Eventually—up to two years after birth—the young anteater achieves independence. By this time it is fully grown and on the verge of sexual maturity, and its mother may be pregnant again.

PRIMITIVE REPRODUCTION

Jany Sauvanet/NHPA

Female anteaters have reproductive and excretory functions both situated in a single chamber. Unlike other mammals, they also have a simple uterus (a single uterine cavity rather than a two-chambered branching organ). The placenta is discoid in shape and is shed at birth. Female anteaters and tamanduas bear only one young at a time and suckle it for six months.

The reproductive life of the silky anteater *(above, with young)* is still largely a mystery.

GIANT ANTEATER *(below) carrying young piggyback style. The mother alone bears the responsibility of raising the offspring.*

Caring for Their Young

The tree-dwelling tamanduas and silky anteaters also carry their young on their backs but often park them in secure corners while they feed. A silky anteater will make a nest in the fork of two branches and place her infant in it while she works on an ant colony. Then she gathers up the baby for the next stage of her night patrol.

Silky anteaters are quite unlike the larger species in that the father helps with raising the young. The parents take turns carrying it, and once it is weaned they both feed it on semidigested insects, regurgitated on demand. As it grows it becomes more adventurous, wandering off while the parents are feeding. For some weeks it feeds within part of its home range, but then it strikes out into the forest to claim a space of its own. ■

ANTELOPES

Nursing mothers and young calves need plenty of food and so calving among antelope is timed to coincide with the most productive seasons. In grasslands, this is the wet season, when the rains bring on a fresh growth of grass. However, in rain forests and tropical wetlands, plant growth is continuous and timing is less important.

The swamp-dwelling sitatunga, for example, breeds throughout the year, although each female produces only one offspring about every 12 months. Similarly, the nyala can breed at any time of year, but births tend to peak during the spring and autumn. Little is known about the shy bongo. Births are said to occur in December and January in the wild, although in captivity bongos have given birth in April and August.

MATING AND BIRTH

The eland, though, has distinct breeding seasons in some areas. In Zambia, for example, calves are born in July and August. Like other spiral-horned antelope, eland produce one offspring at a time. It weighs 49–79 lb (22–36 kg) at birth and continues to suckle for four or five months. Males become sexually mature at four years, females at three years. Captive eland have lived for over 23 years.

Among most of the reduncines, breeding may also occur at any time, but the birthrate often peaks at certain times. For example, in Uganda most waterbuck give birth during the two wet seasons, in August and in November and December. The kob population of the Boma region of Sudan produces young mostly at the end of the rainy season in November and December and the

TONGUE FLASHERS

Male impala have developed an unusual form of foreplay prior to mating. As a dominant male approaches females or rival males, he opens his mouth wide and flicks out his tongue rapidly several times. The response of females to this tongue flashing is to bunch together. On the other hand, males see it as a challenge, to which they react either by fleeing, or by replying with the same display, thus indicating their willingness to accept the challenge to combat.

MALE *impalas form herds for courtship and breeding purposes and gather together 15-25 females for mating (above). They spend the rest of their time defending their territory.*

YOUNG IMPALAS *are placed in a crèche with adults in attendance and on constant alert for predators (above). The lambs are weaned at five to seven months and become sexually mature at 13 months.*

Johnathan Scott/Planet Earth Pictures

A wildebeest and new calf (left). The single calf will be born in February–May. This is a vulnerable time for both, so the calf will be up and standing within minutes.

Color illustrations Nick Pike/Wildlife Art Agency

GROWING UP

The life of a young impala

MATING
occurs at any time of year. It is immediately preceded by an elaborate ritual performed by the male, who will need all his fat reserves for the breeding effort.

GIVING BIRTH
A single young is born six to seven months after the rutting period. Newborn impalas are highly likely to be taken by predators at this time. In fact, the mortality rate is over 50 percent.

reedbuck of the Kruger National Park in South Africa mostly between December and May.

The reedbuck of this region live in groups consisting of a mated pair and their young. Male and female separate for three or four months when the female gives birth. She keeps the calf hidden for two months, visiting it for just 10–30 minutes each day to feed it. The bond between mother and calf is broken just before the birth of the next calf, which takes place some nine to 14 months later after gestation of about eight weeks. Females reach sexual maturity between nine and 24 months. One captive reedbuck lived for 18 years.

Mating and birth among wildebeests and hartebeests is highly seasonal—wildebeest calves are born within two or three weeks of the onset of the rainy season. In South Africa this occurs between November and January, while in the Serengeti it takes place in January or February. Females usually produce a single calf after a gestation period of eight to nine months. The calf can stand within 15 minutes of being born and is weaned by the time it is nine months old. Females become sexually mature between one and three years, depending on the size of the herd. Females belonging to large herds tend to mature earlier.

Impalas breed throughout the year, although there are generally two peaks of mating and birth, particularly in South Africa; in equatorial regions, breeding is more continuous. A female impala (ewe) produces a single young (lamb) after a gestation period of six to seven months. The lambs are weaned at five to seven months and males breed at 13 months. Impalas are known to live to over 13 years old in the wild, and a captive impala has reached the age of 17 years.

Addax also breed at any time but mostly in winter or early spring. Oryx and gemsbok do not have special breeding seasons. Gemsbok come into season immediately after giving birth and produce offspring about every nine months. The Arabian oryx produces one calf about once a year under favorable conditions. Gestation takes about eight months, the young are weaned at about 42 months, and the potential life span of oryx and gemsbok seems to be about 20 years. ■

FROM BIRTH TO DEATH

IMPALA
GESTATION: 6–7 MONTHS
LITTER SIZE: 1
BREEDING: ANY TIME, WITH PEAKS IN SPRING AND AUTUMN
WEIGHT AT BIRTH: 8.6–12.1 LB (3.9–5.5 KG)
WEANING: 5–7 MONTHS
LONGEVITY: 13 YEARS

BLUE WILDEBEEST
GESTATION: 8–9 MONTHS
LITTER SIZE: 1
BREEDING: FEBRUARY–APRIL IN SOUTH AFRICA; APRIL–MAY IN THE SERENGETI
FIRST WALKING: 6 MINUTES
WEANING: 9 MONTHS
LONGEVITY: 18–20 YEARS

ARMADILLOS

The life cycles of many species of armadillos and pangolins remain sketchy. This is partly because many of the species are studied little in the wild. At least in the case of pangolins, it is also because they are notoriously difficult to keep in captivity, particularly outside the tropics, due to their very precise dietary requirements.

Secretive breeders

There is little information about armadillo mating behavior, although it seems likely that scent marking is important in alerting males to the presence of a sexually receptive female.

Armadillos are unusual among the majority of mammals in that they display delayed implantation. This is the process whereby the single egg, having been fertilized by the male, lies in the female's uterus for a period of time (in this case several months) before becoming embedded in the uterine wall where development can take place. This method of reproduction allows the adults to mate at a time that is convenient for them, but delays the development of the offspring, enabling the young to be born during the spring growing season when food is plentiful and the climate more amenable.

Even more unusual, several identical young of the same sex are produced from a single egg. Usually two to four young are produced in this way, but as many as twelve have been recorded.

At birth, armadillos are fully developed, having fully formed and hardened claws but, at least in some species, with the eyes and ear flaps closed (these open after three to four weeks in three-banded armadillos). When the young are at this vulnerable stage of development, they remain inside the burrow for protection and are suckled by the mother. Armadillo young also have soft, leathery skin, which soon hardens, and the young armadillos are able to walk within a few hours of

COURTSHIP
Armadillos seem to court somewhat secretly! Though little is known about armadillo breeding habits, it is thought that the female scent marks the area to alert males that she will be receptive.

STRIKING OUT
After a few weeks the young armadillo is weaned and leaves the nest to start foraging for insects.

COMING OF AGE
Adolescent armadillos become sexually mature when they are between six and twelve months old.

Alan Root/Survival Anglia

Traveling by tail is the only way to go for a young African tree pangolin (above).

birth. Captive young six-banded armadillos are known to take solid foods at one month old.

Pangolins share a not dissimilar life cycle with armadillos. The young are born in burrows, or, in the case of the arboreal species, in cavities in trees. They seem to be born at any time of the year, with a single young, rarely two, being produced.

Their scales are soft at birth but start to harden by the second day. Giant pangolins are born with their eyes open. And even though they cannot yet support their own weight, they are very active: at one day old they will have scrambled to their mothers' tails where they will cling with their own prehensile tails. The young of Cape pangolins are kept folded up in the coiled body of the mother. Young pangolins grow rapidly and soon double in size and weight. Weaning of the young is thought to take place at about three months.

TAIL RIDE

Female pangolins use the base of the tail to transport the young. When carried by the mother, the young pangolin usually sits across the tail, which is held clear of the ground and clings tightly with its sharp claws. If alarmed, the mother will curl into a protective posture and the youngster will find protection under the mother's stomach, further sheltered by her tail.

The role played by the male pangolin in the rearing of the young is unclear, but both male and female have been found sharing a burrow with the offspring. ■

GROWING UP

The life of a young armadillo

QUADS
Common armadillos give birth to four young of the same sex. Other species have between one and four young.

TOUGHENING UP
The soft, pink, leathery skin of a newborn armadillo soon hardens.

Illustrations Barry Croucher/Wildlife Art Agency

FROM BIRTH TO DEATH

COMMON ARMADILLO

GESTATION: 120–140 DAYS
LITTER SIZE: 4 (OF ONE SEX)
BREEDING: MATING TAKES PLACE JULY–AUGUST, BUT IMPLANTATION IS DELAYED UNTIL NOVEMBER
EYES OPEN: AT BIRTH
WEANING: A FEW WEEKS
SEXUAL MATURITY: 6–12 MONTHS
LONGEVITY: 12–15 YEARS IN CAPTIVITY

CAPE PANGOLIN

GESTATION: 140 DAYS
LITTER SIZE: 1 (SOMETIMES 2 IN ASIAN SPECIES)
BREEDING: ANY TIME OF YEAR
WEIGHT AT BIRTH: 10–14 OZ (280–392 G)
WEANING: 3 MONTHS
SEXUAL MATURITY: 2 YEARS
LONGEVITY: OVER 11 YEARS RECORDED IN CAPTIVITY

BADGERS

European badgers have been known to mate at any time from February to October, yet the cubs are always born in February. This is because, in common with many other mustelids, there is a delayed implantation of the fertilized egg in the wall of the uterus. Generally, the egg is implanted in December. This delay has many benefits. It gives the adults plenty of chance to mate, the cubs are suckled when the female is still fat from her autumn feasting and is also spending the most time in the sett, and they are weaned when food is most abundant. They have plenty of time to grow and store fat for the coming winter.

Mating in badgers is a vigorous affair accompanied by a deep, throaty purring from the male and softer grunts from the female. It typically takes place at night outside the burrow, and can last for up to an hour. It is actually the act of mating that induces the female to ovulate.

Jason Venus/Biofotos

A female European badger nursing her three-week-old cubs (above).

Cubs are born in a specially dug chamber near an entrance to the sett to insure good air circulation. The fastidious mother fills it almost full of dry bedding to insure a cozy nest, as February can be very cold, particularly in northern climates. While the cubs are being reared, she regularly removes the bedding and replaces it anew.

There are up to five—usually two—cubs in a litter. They are born blind and tiny, weighing only 2.6–4.8 oz (75–135 g) and measuring about 5 in (13 cm). Their thin coats of silky, silvery hair have faint black stripes; it is possible to see the dark spots on their otherwise pink skin. Soon after their eyes open they begin to explore their underground home,

MUTUAL GROOMING
is important for reinforcing bonds — and a useful method of removing parasites.

YOUNG ADULTS
soon learn about the nighttime scents and sounds of the forest — what they can eat and how to find it.

THE YOUNG
may stay with their mother through the snows of winter but, come spring, she will drive them away to a new life elsewhere.

Illustrations Evi Antoniou

GROWING UP

The life of a young badger

THESE MONTH-OLD CUBS *are just about to open their eyes. Not all cubs survive — many die during the first eight weeks, or during the few months following weaning.*

WHEN CUBS FIRST EMERGE *from the sett, it is usually well after dark and they press together, keeping close contact with the mother, who constantly reassures them with a quiet purring noise.*

FROM BIRTH TO DEATH

EUROPEAN BADGER

GESTATION: 8 WEEKS FROM IMPLANTATION OF EGG
LITTER SIZE: 1–5, USUALLY 2
WEIGHT AT BIRTH: 2.6–4.8 OZ (75–135 G)
EYES OPEN: 5 WEEKS
FIRST WALKING: 6–7 WEEKS
INDEPENDENCE: 14–18 MONTHS
SEXUAL MATURITY: 12–15 MONTHS
LONGEVITY IN WILD: 10 YEARS (19 YEARS RECORDED)

AMERICAN BADGER

GESTATION: 6 WEEKS FROM IMPLANTATION OF EGG
LITTER SIZE: 1–5, USUALLY 2 OR 3
WEIGHT AT BIRTH: NOT KNOWN
EYES OPEN: 4–6 WEEKS
FIRST WALKING: NOT KNOWN
INDEPENDENCE: 10–30 WEEKS
SEXUAL MATURITY: 6–12 MONTHS
LONGEVITY IN WILD: 14 YEARS

but they do not venture outside the sett until they are eight to ten weeks old.

They usually stop suckling when they are about three months old, but may feed sporadically for another month. During this time, the female regurgitates semidigested food to wean them on to solids. As the summer goes on, the cubs get bolder and indulge in lively games, although never far from the burrow. Cubs that survive often remain with the female in the same burrow all winter.

At one year old, the cubs measure about 30 in (76 cm) long with a full coat of long, thick hair. Females can mate in their first autumn, thereby giving birth when they are just one year old. Males are usually sexually mature at one year.

American badgers follow a similar pattern of reproduction to their European cousins, although

> AT EIGHT MONTHS OLD, THE CUBS ARE TOUGH LITTLE ANIMALS, WELL ABLE TO STAND UP FOR THEMSELVES IF NEED BE

they tend to mate later in the year—in August or September. Two to five young are born usually in April, but sometimes as late as June in high-altitude areas. Weaned within two to three months, they leave the mother by late summer.

Honey badgers are one of the few badger species in which delayed implantation does not occur. They may mate and give birth at any time of the year, gestation lasting about six months. Commonly only two cubs are born, in a grass-lined chamber in the burrow.

Little is known about the mating habits of other badgers, although it is thought they all have delayed implantation. The true gestation in the hog badger is thought to be six weeks or less. ■

BEAVERS

Adult beavers usually pair for life. Mating, which takes place in the water, occurs in January or February in both species of true beaver.

After a gestation period of 100–110 days, three or four young are born, although there may be up to six in the European and up to eight in the Canadian beaver. The female gives birth in the lodge and the young, known as kits, are highly precocious when born. Fully furred, with eyes open and teeth already cut, they can swim within a few hours of birth, although their dense fur and light body weight make them too buoyant to dive. Also, their glands have not yet begun to secrete the oily substance needed to render their coats waterproof at this stage, and so their mother anoints them with secretions from her own sebaceous glands by simply rubbing her fur against theirs.

In fact, young beavers often show a marked reluctance to enter the water initially, in spite of the fact that they will soon be more at home here than on dry land. Quite often, when the kits are about one week old, the mother has to pick

LIVELY LITTER
The kits are fully furred at birth, with their eyes open. Although eager to investigate their snug surroundings, they still lack the courage to take a plunge (above).

DRIVEN FROM HOME
Beavers form close family bonds, and the young adults are reluctant to leave. The parents have to bully the young into departing (right), since they themselves must start preparing for the next litter.

Jen & Des Bartlett/Bruce Coleman Ltd.

The adults spend an inordinate amount of time caring for their young. Although much of a beaver's skill is based upon pure instinct, there is still a great deal to be learned by copying from elders and betters (left).

Illustrations Robin Budden/Wildlife Art Agency

GROWING UP

The life of a Canadian beaver

WATERPROOFING
It takes a while before the kits' sebaceous glands start to function. To prepare them for the water, the female rubs her own oily secretions against their coats (above).

WATER BABIES
The first encounters with the lake and the shore can be somewhat traumatic for the kits, accustomed as they are to the cozy fug of the lodge. It is left to their mother to take a firm hand in launching them bodily into the water, and onto dry land (above).

them up in her forearms and throw them into the tunnel from the lodge to make them take their first swim. This seems to trigger the sebaceous glands into operation, and before long the young animals are diving and playing in the water at every opportunity.

A FAMILY RESPONSIBILITY

The kits suckle from the mother until they are at least six weeks old, and sometimes for up to three months. Before they are fully weaned, however, they have begun to take solid food, brought to them by all other family members, particularly the male. In fact, in the first week or so after the birth, solid food is brought to the female as well so that she does not have to leave her kits at all at this time. This is one of the few times where the family acknowledges a pecking order, with the female taking the dominant position. She spends quite some time grooming herself while in the lodge, leaving her babies in a heap on one side of the chamber. As soon as she moves over to them, they greet her with high-pitched squeaks, anxious to suckle. She has only four teats, so if there are more kits than this, they have to wait their turn, which they do with great impatience.

All members of the family assist in looking after the kits, and the adult male has a strong sense of paternal care, which is unusual in a rodent. Should one of the babies fall into one or another of the floor entrances before it is ready to dive, the father will often be the one to rescue it, nudging it back to the safety of the living chamber.

When the kits have their first foray onto dry land, it is often in the arms of the mother, who may walk erect, holding one in her forepaws. Sometimes she also gives them a ride on land on her tail. If they get tired on their early swimming forays, she is generally close by to give them a lift through the water on her broad back. Autumn, when the kits begin learning to feed on bark, is a difficult time and the mortality rate is often quite high. If they survive their first year, however, they have a fair chance of living a good ten years or more.

INDEPENDENCE

The kits stay with their parents for up to two years. Although this seems like a long time, they have a lot to learn, for they must be skilled in the ways of building if they are to survive on their own. This they learn by watching their parents and older siblings at work and eventually joining in. Sexual maturity is reached as the animals approach two years old, although they are unlikely to mate until a year or more later. Around this time the parents become aggressive toward their young, finally pushing them out altogether. They rarely disperse far from parental territory—perhaps only some 10 miles (16 km) or so—but it has been known for a beaver to establish a new territory more than 62 miles (100 km) away. ■

FROM BIRTH TO DEATH

TRUE BEAVERS

GESTATION: 100–110 DAYS
LITTER SIZE: 1–8 IN CANADIAN, 1–6 IN EUROPEAN
LITTERS PER YEAR: 1
WEIGHT AT BIRTH: 1 LB (450 G)
WEANING: 6–12 WEEKS
SEXUAL MATURITY: 18–24 MONTHS
LONGEVITY: AT LEAST 10 YEARS IN THE WILD; UP TO 35 IN CAPTIVITY

MOUNTAIN BEAVER

GESTATION: 28–30 DAYS
LITTER SIZE: 3–5
LITTERS PER YEAR: 1
WEANING: 6–8 WEEKS
SEXUAL MATURITY: 2 YEARS
LONGEVITY: 5–10 YEARS

BROWN BEARS

Brown bears mate from May or June to July, and it is at this time of year that males start searching around their territories for receptive females. As female brown bears generally only mate every three years, they are in comparative short supply, and angry fights may break out between competing adult males at this time.

It is the act of mating that induces ovulation in the female, so she will mate several times while she is in estrus, sometimes with just one male, but usually with two or three. For this reason, a male may often attempt to hide a receptive female away for a week or so, keeping her away from other males and mating with her as many times as possible. A male will try to mate with several females during the spring mating season.

Delayed implantation

Like some other mammals, bears experience a delayed implantation of the fertilized egg into the wall of the uterus. Implantation occurs in October or November—that is, after the female has fed herself up in the autumn and has actually begun her winter sleep. (A pregnant female generally enters her den earlier in the winter and emerges later in the spring than other bears.) True gestation begins with implantation of the egg, and the tiny cubs, weighing no more than 12–24 oz (340–680 g), are born about three months later, while the female is still asleep in the den.

A litter may contain up to four cubs, but usually two or three. Tiny, naked, blind, and helpless, they remain in the den for a few months, feeding on their mother's rich milk. Next to polar bears, the milk of brown bears is the richest of all bears' milk, and contains up to 33 percent fat. It is also rich in protein, so the cubs gain weight rapidly.

The female bear is not feeding at this time, which is another reason why she must put on sufficient weight during the autumn and why it is important that she expend no energy in any other way. When she emerges from the den with her cubs—now fully furred and wholly recognizable

GROWING UP

The life of a young brown bear

MATING
occurs from May to July. Once the male has found a receptive female, there is a brief courtship before mating occurs. The implantation of the egg is delayed until the late autumn.

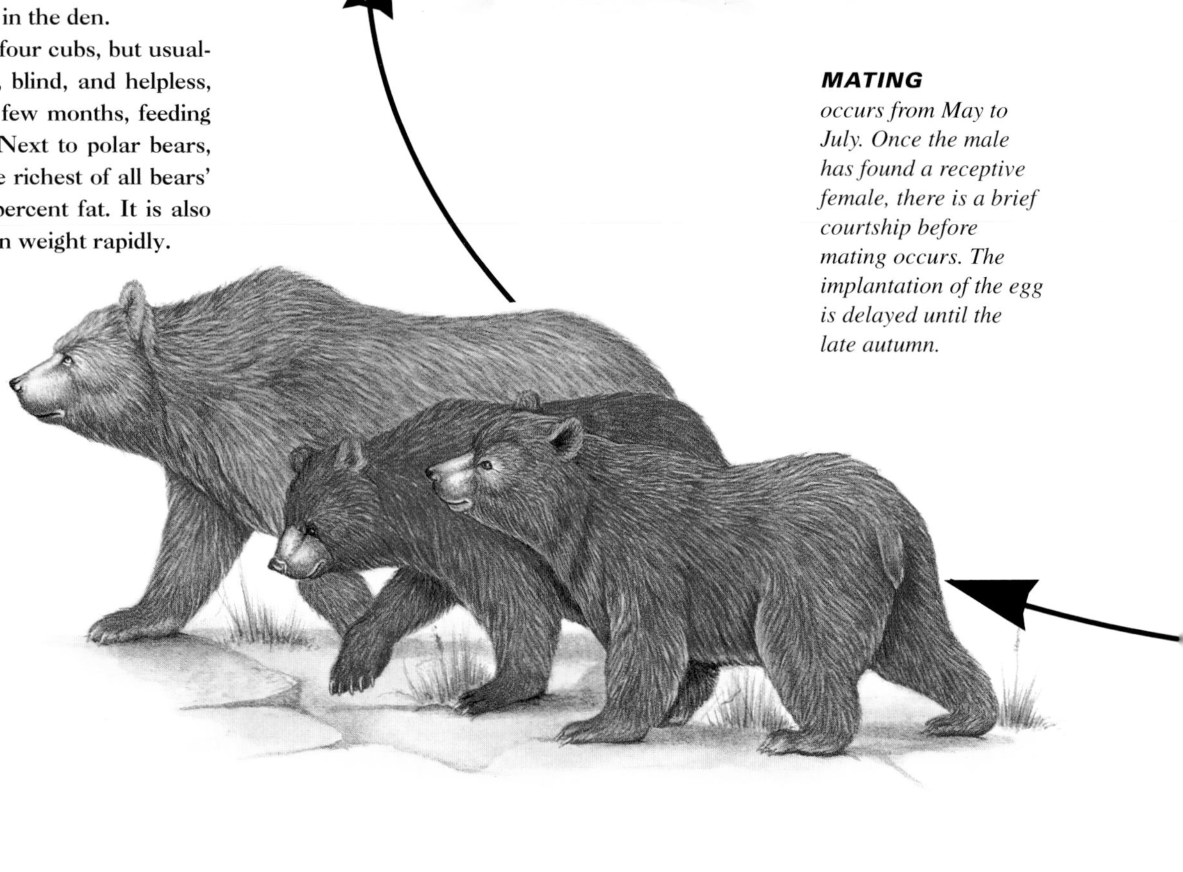

THE YOUNG
stay with their mother for over two years. After this time, the female young may stay nearby, but the males leave to establish their own range.

WHY ARE BEAR CUBS SO TINY?

All bears give birth to cubs that weigh only a tiny fraction of their own body weight. This is because they are born—and develop—when their mother is sleeping. In most mammals, a pregnant, and then nursing, female needs to feed on richer food than at any other time of her life. In addition, for the first few months of their lives, the female bear must also provide her cubs' only nourishment—still while she is not feeding. Although we can only speculate, it is likely that the female conserves more energy with a shorter pregnancy and her ability to produce small cubs with independent thermoregulation.

L. Lee Rue/Frank Lane Picture Agency

THE DEN
is either a natural hollow tree or a specially dug burrow. The young, born in early spring, are nearly naked and helpless.

IN LATE SPRING
the mother emerges from her den, together with her cubs. Though playful, they remain close by her side.

as baby bears—she will keep them close to her and guard them fiercely. Adult male brown bears are one of the main predators at this time of the cub's life. Besides providing the adult with a nutritious meal, there are two other possible reasons for this. First, by killing young males, an adult male reduces the number of brown bears likely to compete for females in the future; and second, without a litter, the female will come back into estrus the following year, thereby providing another opportunity for mating.

LEARNING THE ROPES

Provided that they survive, the cubs will stay with their mother for at least the next two years, learning how to forage and hunt by following her closely. Play-fighting teaches them the skills they will need for survival on their own.

Although they are usually weaned at about five months old, brown bear cubs may go on suckling occasionally from their mother right up to the time that the family disperses. This probably helps to maintain the strong bond between a female and her cubs. When the time comes for them to leave, the female offspring will often stay nearby, but young males may wander widely, as far as 60 mi (100 km) from their birthplace. ■

FROM BIRTH TO DEATH

BROWN BEAR

MATING SEASON: MAY–JULY

GESTATION: 80–226 DAYS, BUT IMPLANTATION OF EGG IS DELAYED UNTIL OCTOBER–NOVEMBER. BORN APPROXIMATELY 80 DAYS POST-IMPLANTATION.

LITTER SIZE: 1–4

WEANED: ABOUT 5 MONTHS, BUT MAY GO ON SUCKLING OCCASIONALLY FOR UP TO 2 YEARS

LONGEVITY: 15–34 YEARS IN THE WILD; UP TO 50 YEARS IN CAPTIVITY

Illustration Evi Antoniou

CAMELS

The breeding season for vicuñas and guanacos can be a time of considerable aggression as males compete with one another for females. The dominant male of a vicuña herd has his work cut out: He is busy chasing after his females and anxious to catch them when they are receptive to mating; at the same time he is nervous about leaving the other females in the herd in case some trespassing male should try to steal them away.

Vicuñas mate in March and April, and, after a gestation period of 11 months, a single young is born. Within a matter of weeks of giving birth, the female will mate again, even though she is likely to go on suckling her young for 8 more months.

WITHIN A FEW WEEKS OF GIVING BIRTH, FEMALE VICUÑAS ARE READY TO MATE AGAIN

When camels and llamas mate, they generally do so lying down; females give birth standing up, and, unlike most mammals, they do not lick their newborn offspring. Most give birth to a single young—twins are very rare—that is well developed at birth. A vicuña foal, for instance, is able to stand and walk within 15 minutes of birth. It will stay close by its mother's side until it is at least 8 months old, leaving her only to play with the young of the other females in the herd.

The fact that vicuñas give birth each year, whereas most other lamoids give birth every other year, probably explains why the dominant males are so fierce in their protection of good grazing territories. This way they can be sure that there will be enough food for all the newborn young. It may also explain why the dominant male begins to chase young males out of the herd at 8 months old and females when they are no more than a year.

NERVOUS WITHDRAWAL

The guanaco's mating season is rather longer, taking place from November to February. The gestation period is between 11 and 12 months. After the female has given birth to her young—called *chulengo*—she is quite

JUST A FEW HOURS OLD, *the newborn camel is too weak to stand and is dependent upon its mother in every way.*

MATING *among camels is unusual for mammals, as the male mounts the female from behind when she is lying down.*

in SIGHT

DISEASES OF THE DESERT

Camels can fall victim to a number of diseases that often spread quickly within a camel herd. One of the most dangerous and, unfortunately, common of these is jarrah, a form of mange. This spreads quickly, often attaining epidemic proportions, and brings death in little over a month if left untreated.

Another ailment is manhus, a disease of the lungs. Before the introduction of modern veterinary practice, this could have a mortality rate of 50 percent.

Like any other creatures inhabiting a difficult environment, camels suffer cuts and bruises from stones, rocks, and thorns, but these usually heal quite quickly.

GROWING UP

The life of a young Bactrian camel

THE MOTHER SUCKLES *the young foal on her rich milk. Females produce up to 1.59 gallons (6 liters) a day.*

YOUNG BACTRIAN CAMELS *trail behind their mother in search of food. Foals feed on easily digestible food such as tender grass.*

Illustrations Jo Cowne with thanks to Colin Fountain/Cotswold Wildlife Park

FROM BIRTH TO DEATH

BACTRIAN CAMEL	LLAMA
GESTATION: 13 MONTHS	**GESTATION:** 10 MONTHS
LITTER SIZE: 1	**LITTER SIZE:** 1
BREEDING: MATING OCCURS IN JANUARY AND FEBRUARY	**BREEDING:** SEASONAL; BETWEEN SPRING AND EARLY SUMMER
SEXUAL MATURITY: 5 YEARS	**SEXUAL MATURITY:** 1–2 YEARS
LONGEVITY: UP TO 50 YEARS	**LONGEVITY:** 20–25 YEARS

DROMEDARY	GUANACO
GESTATION: 12 MONTHS	**GESTATION:** 11 MONTHS
LITTER SIZE: 1	**LITTER SIZE:** 1
BREEDING: SEASONAL	**BREEDING:** NOVEMBER TO FEBRUARY
SEXUAL MATURITY: 5 YEARS	**SEXUAL MATURITY:** 6–12 MONTHS
LONGEVITY: UP TO 50 YEARS	**LONGEVITY:** 20–25 YEARS

nervous for a few weeks, withdrawing to the cover of the forest at the slightest hint of danger.

Guanacos are one of the few ungulates that nurse two generations of offspring simultaneously. This only occurs for a few weeks, however, before the dominant male chases off the previous year's offspring. The female will attempt, almost always in vain, to prevent him from doing so.

Camel courtship

Old World camels mate throughout the year, although births tend to coincide with the maximum plant growth in an area. These camels have a gland on the back of their necks which produces a secretion that seems to be sexually stimulating to both male and female. During courtship, the animals rub this secretion onto their own humps and also over their partner's, intertwining their necks as they rub their heads together.

BIRTHS AMONG OLD WORLD CAMELS TEND TO COINCIDE WITH THE TIME OF OPTIMUM PLANT GROWTH

Males also possess a peculiar physical feature at the back of their mouths. Known as a *palu*, this can be inflated so that it extends outside the mouth like a pink rubber balloon. This is displayed when the male is sexually aroused.

Gestation in camels lasts between 12 and 13 months. Again, the single young is well developed and covered in fur at birth, and will move about freely by the end of its first day. Human owners usually wean a foal when it is about one year old, but it will not be fully grown for another four years.

Old World camels usually live longer than their South American counterparts. It is not unusual for a dromedary to reach 50 years of age, while it is unlikely that a lamoid will live even half as long. ■

CAPYBARAS

Capybaras and coypus are well developed at birth—able to see, move about, and even begin foraging for food. But there are significant differences in the development of the young, linked to the contrasting social structures of the two species.

Capybaras in tropical areas breed at any time of the year, but reach a peak at the start of the wet season in early May. Those in the more temperate regions of southern Brazil and Argentina breed once a year, at the wettest part of early spring.

Mating takes place in the water, although it is initiated on land. A male approaches a sexually receptive female, who leads him on an elaborate pursuit in and out of the water. This stage may last more than an hour before the female lets the male mount her in the water.

Male and female return to the group during most of the gestation period, which lasts about 150 days. A few hours before birth the female leaves the group and enters ground cover nearby. Litter sizes range from two to eight, with four being the average. The mother returns to the group a few hours after the birth. The newborn young are highly active. This advanced state of development is likely to help them adjust to the mobile lifestyle of the roving group. As a result, the offspring follow their mother to the group after a few days.

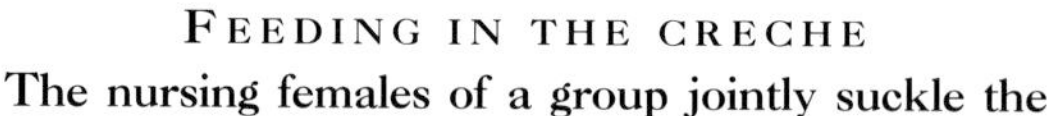

FEEDING IN THE CRECHE

The nursing females of a group jointly suckle the offspring of their group. Lactation usually lasts for about 16 weeks, during which time the young

LIVELY YOUNG
Each litter contains up to 12 young coypus. They are precocial (able to move around freely without help): Their eyes are already open, and they have a thick coat of fur.

GROWING UP

The life of a young capybara

MATING
Capybaras breed during the rainy season, or all year-round in the tropics. They mate in shallow water.

ADULT CARE
Although active, the young are still protected by their mother or another adult for up to six months (below).

GROWING UP

The life of a young coypu

PARENTAL BURDEN
As her young are still highly vulnerable, the mother carries them about on her back (above).

SWIMMING LESSONS
It is only a matter of days before the young join their mother on her foraging trips (below).

Press-Tige Pictures/Oxford Scientific Films

A young coypu (above) remains with its mother for six to ten weeks, learning how to groom and feed.

SECLUSION
The mother leaves the main herd to give birth in a thicket. As in the coypu, the young are born with their eyes open (left).

become introduced to the grasses and other foods that make up the adult diet. The young become integrated into the group's pattern of grazing excursions and resting periods. All the while they emit a purring sound, which implies either contentment or a locating signal to their mother—or possibly both.

LARGE AND HUNGRY LITTERS

Coypus normally live in pairs rather than in groups, so the mother has none of the "child care" provisions afforded to her capybara counterpart. There is a September–October (spring) mating peak in the more temperate regions of the coypu's South American range, but mating is nonseasonal in many regions. Females are in heat every 25–30 days, and may produce 2 to 3 litters each year. After mating, the female feeds heavily for the 130-day gestation period. She can give birth to 10–12 offspring, but 3 to 6 are much more common. She is in heat again within a day or two.

The newborn young can follow their mother when they are only a few hours old. Unusually, the mother's nipples are high up on her flanks and nearly on her back; this allows them to suckle while the mother is swimming.

The timing of sexual maturity depends on the birth. Coypus born in the summer attain it in 3 to 4 months, while those born in the autumn take almost twice as long. They find a mate and pair up soon after reaching sexual maturity. ■

FROM BIRTH TO DEATH

CAPYBARA	COYPU
GESTATION: 148–156 DAYS	**GESTATION:** 128–132 DAYS
LITTER SIZE: 2–8	**LITTER SIZE:** 1–12; USUALLY 5–6
BREEDING: NONSEASONAL IN TROPICS (PEAK IN APRIL–MAY AT START OF WET SEASON)	**BREEDING:** NONSEASONAL BUT A SEPTEMBER–OCTOBER (SPRING) PEAK IN COLDER PARTS OF RANGE
WEIGHT AT BIRTH: 3.3 LB (1.5 KG)	**WEIGHT AT BIRTH:** 8 OZ (225 G)
EYES OPEN: AT BIRTH	**EYES OPEN:** AT BIRTH
WEANING: 16 WEEKS	**WEANING:** 6–10 WEEKS
FORAGING: 1 WEEK	**FORAGING:** WHEN WEANED
SEXUAL MATURITY: 18 MONTHS	**SEXUAL MATURITY:** 3–8 MONTHS
LONGEVITY: 8–10 YEARS IN WILD	**LONGEVITY:** 6 YEARS

Illustrations Robin Budden/Wildlife Art Agency

CEBID MONKEYS

The social patterns of cebid monkeys strongly influence their reproductive and developmental behavior. At the most basic level, small-group species maintain pair bonds and the young are looked after to some extent by both parents. Larger-group species, on the other hand, are more promiscuous and the mother has primary responsibility for infant care, although she can get willing help from other group members.

SOCIAL ADVANCEMENT
Soon the offspring starts to climb and explore on its own, making contact with other members of the troop and making "friends" among both young and old (left).

Courtship is a slower, more involved affair among monogamous monkeys than it is among those species that do not establish lasting pair bonds. A newly forming pair of titi monkeys may spend many days examining and sniffing one another, sitting close together, grooming and entwining tails before mating. In capuchins and howlers, courtship is brief and to the point. A female approaches a group male, or occasionally one from a neighboring troop, and makes mouth gestures to which he replies in kind if interested. They then mate and soon after separate. A female woolly spider monkey announces her readiness to mate with special calls, attracting any number of males with whom she may mate.

Gestation in cebid monkeys lasts from four to seven months, and births take place in the trees. Only very rarely are twins born. The newborn infant immediately clings to its mother's fur, quickly finding for itself the most secure site on which to be carried, which may be on the back, the belly, or in the groin. Several weeks may ensue before the tiny youngster is ready to clamber off the mother when she rests, and tentatively take hold of the branch or clamber onto another body in the troop.

Illustration Joanne Cowne

AT TWO MONTHS
of age the infant is more active, regularly clambering off its mother and onto siblings who come to help. At this stage the youngster is carried lengthwise (above).

Development of young is generally more prolonged in the larger species. A young titi is weaned at about five months and may be sexually mature in three years, while a young male howler is nursed for eighteen months and may not reach maturity until its eighth year.

Older siblings as well as parents are allowed to handle and groom infant titis, night monkeys, and sakis at least after the first weeks of life, but it is the young of polygamous species that tend to have the most varied social interaction. Female companions of a mother squirrel monkey help care for and carry an infant while she forages. By its seventh month, a

GROWING UP

The life of a young brown capuchin

MATING
in the brown capuchin is initiated by the female, who gestures and calls to a male with eyebrows raised (above). After a period of close physical contact, they mate.

PIGGYBACK
For the first month of its life, an infant capuchin clings across its mother's back, seldom moving from this position except when ready to be suckled (left).

Adrian Warren/Ardea

Sakis live in small family groups, in which the female is responsible for rearing the young (above).

young ouakari may still be dependent on its mother, but nevertheless spends much time playing with other monkeys and is sometimes carried by males.

In its early years, a monkey seems to have plenty to learn. Much of the behavior it will employ in adult life to find food and shelter, move through the trees, react to danger, assert itself socially, and find a mate appears to be acquired rather than innate. Some of the learning comes from exploration of its immediate surroundings, while a great deal of the rest comes from play—not just with peers in the group but also with older animals. ■

inSIGHT

FATHER CARE

Males of many monkey species take an interest in their young, but in titi family groups the father takes primary responsibility for caring for the youngest offspring. An infant titi spends more time in paternal care than with either its mother or its siblings. It is the father that usually carries the infant unless it is being suckled, and after nursing the youngster soon starts to cry out for him again. He grooms it most readily and rushes to protect it when heavy rain falls, high winds blow, or any other danger threatens.

FROM BIRTH TO DEATH

BROWN CAPUCHIN

BREEDING: NONSEASONAL, ALTHOUGH BIRTH PEAKS MAY OCCUR IN RAINY SEASON
GESTATION: 150–160 DAYS
LITTER SIZE: 1
LITTER FREQUENCY: USUALLY ONCE EVERY 2 YEARS
WEIGHT AT BIRTH: 9–10 OZ (250–290 G)
FIRST SOLID FOOD: 2 MONTHS
WEANING: 6–11 MONTHS
SEXUAL MATURITY: 2–6 YEARS
LONGEVITY: UP TO 40 YEARS IN CAPTIVITY

CHEETAHS

When ready to mate, a female cheetah makes her intentions very plain. As she nears sexual receptivity, she busily inspects and sniffs all likely scent marks in her home range and leaves her own urine marks as often as once every ten minutes. Eventually, males that overlap with her range, and perhaps some wanderers too, detect the signs and home in, yelping as they approach. Sometimes the female yelps back and walks toward the male, the couple getting down to mating without further ado.

But it is often not as simple as this; there may be some ritual approach then fleeing by the female, sometimes accompanied by heightened aggression in the male. Frequently, a number of males—up to six in some cases—congregate close to the female, and the rivalry leads to much threatening and some fighting. In the end, though, it is usually a dominant, territorial male that has the chance to mate. There have been sightings of a female being mated by several males in succession.

After bouts of copulation over a day or two, the sexes part company. Three months later, and weighted down so much that hunting can be difficult, the female finds a suitable place to give birth. Lairs are often well concealed in dense vegetation, such as within marshes or under bushes among rocks, providing protection as well as shelter for the cubs.

FRAGILE FORMS
Though hidden in the lair (above), newborn cheetahs often fall victim to other carnivores against which their instinctive hissing and spitting is pitiful defense against large predators.

EAGER TO LEARN
After several weeks cubs start to follow their mother when she hunts, rushing avidly to join her when she has killed and learning to eat meat (above).

K. & K. Anamann/Planet Earth Pictures

The cub's mane, which looks a bit like a bunch of dried grasses, helps to conceal the tiny creature from its many enemies. It may also be a device to regulate body heat (left).

GROWING UP

The life of a young cheetah

SHAPING UP

At two weeks, cheetah cubs have opened their eyes and have erect ears (above). They also have charming spotted coats and a fluffy gray mantle, the last traces of which are still visible a year later.

SAFEKEEPING

Parasites and odors quickly build up in the lair, forcing cautious mothers to move nests every few days. Each cub is carried carefully to the new home, one at a time (above).

Litter sizes vary considerably, from just one to as many as eight cubs, but larger litters are soon significantly reduced by high cub mortality. The blind, uncoordinated and helpless newborn young are highly vulnerable to predators and other hazards, especially since their mother's high energy needs for lactation may force her to emerge on regular long-distance hunting forays. But even when the youngsters are ready to leave the lair and start following her on hunting trips at about six weeks of age, their inexperience, higher visibility, and poor running skills mean that life for them is still fraught with myriad dangers.

BEREAVED MOTHERS

It is by no means uncommon for a mother cheetah to lose all her cubs to a single predator. A marauding lion, for example, may chase off the parent before crushing each of a litter in turn in its jaws. In situations when this has occurred, females have been known to linger around the lair for several days, regularly checking the site as if for signs of life and sometimes uttering mournful cries. Even though they go out on hunting trips, they may still return to the vicinity of the lair to sleep at night. It is as though the mother cannot accept that her litter has perished.

Not until about three months of age, when they are fully weaned, do cubs acquire the skills that start to tip the survival scales in their favor. Play becomes very important at this stage. In chasing one another and their mother, pretend stalking, pouncing, and wrestling, cubs develop their strength and coordination and start to hone their predatory skills. No longer a distracting liability for their mother, they learn to sit tight while she hunts.

HUNTING SKILLS

At about six months of age, the cubs may be given the chance to practice on live prey. Mother cheetahs bring back live gazelle fawns from time to time, and let the growing cubs chase and paw at the poor creature for a while. But the hunting skills of a cheetah take many months to master; at twelve months a young but well-grown animal may be able to capture a fawn or a hare, but probably still needs its patient mother to administer the killing bite. Many cheetahs are still learning the ropes by the time they are forced into independence in their second year, and since they are lone hunters, the danger of starvation is very real even at this late stage of development. ■

FROM BIRTH TO DEATH

CHEETAH

BREEDING: NONSEASONAL, BUT BIRTH PEAKS MAY BE ASSOCIATED WITH THE CHANGING SEASONS

GESTATION: 90–95 DAYS

LITTER SIZE: 1–8, AVERAGE 3

WEIGHT AT BIRTH: 6–11 OZ (170–311 G)

EYES OPEN: 4–11 DAYS

CUBS LEAVE LAIR: 6 WEEKS

WEANED:: 3 MONTHS

INDEPENDENCE: 13–20 MONTHS

SEXUAL MATURITY: 20–23 MONTHS

LONGEVITY: UP TO 12 YEARS IN THE WILD

Simon Turvey/Wildlife Art Agency

CHIMPANZEES

GROWING UP

The life of a young chimpanzee

In the wild, female chimps start to breed when they are about 12 years old, though they will mate only when they are in heat, which happens about every four to six weeks. This condition lasts for two or three weeks, during which time the pink skin of her rear swells as a signal that she is ready to mate. A female in heat may mate several times a day, and the males compete for the right to mate with her.

Helpless babies

Usually, a receptive female forms a pair bond with a single dominant male toward the end of this period, and the two will tend to keep away from other chimpanzees at this time. It is during this time that the female is most likely to conceive, and, by keeping her clear of rival males, the dominant male insures that he will be the father of her offspring. After about 235 days a single baby is born. Though on rare occasions twins may be produced, their survival prospects in the wild are poor.

> ALTHOUGH A FEMALE CHIMP IS OFTEN FERTILE FOR A LONG TIME—ABOUT 25 YEARS—SHE IS LIKELY TO PRODUCE NO MORE THAN FIVE YOUNG IN HER LIFETIME

Newborn chimps are almost wholly dependent on their mother. They cling to her belly fur, and this remains their favored position until they are about five months old, after which they start to ride piggyback. By the age of three, young chimps are

AMAZING FACTS

PHYSICAL FEATS

Although chimpanzees are usually gentle, an adult male chimpanzee, with its broad muscular chest and strong arms, has the strength of three men and is capable of considerable feats. During fights or territorial disputes, it can pick up and hurl large boulders or branches at rivals with seeming ease.

A group of males attacking an intruder or making a foray into alien territory is a frightening sight. They can kill other animals by smashing them against the ground or by stamping on them, and inflict terrible wounds using their sharp canine teeth.

BABY CHIMPANZEES *are helpless; they remain dependent on their mothers for up to seven or eight years, though weaning occurs during the third year.*

MALE CHIMPS BEGIN *exhibiting sexual behaviors toward females at three to four years of age but do not reach puberty until about seven. Males do not attain full integration into normal social hierarchy until midteens.*

YOUNG MALES FIGHT *for dominance. Their displays include chases, physical attacks — hitting or stamping — and screaming.*

YOUNG CHIMPS RIDE *on their mothers' backs as soon as they are able, at around five to seven months. By the time they are four years old, they will travel mostly by walking alongside their mothers.*

CHIMPS PLAY *with other young chimps and with their mothers from the age of about eight months.*

Illustrations Chris Turnbull/Wildlife Art Agency

Gerry Ellis/Nature Photography

LOOK AND LEARN

Just like children, chimps learn a great deal by imitating older chimps, which is a much more efficient process in terms of the species' survival than trial and error. Living in groups gives chimps an excellent opportunity to watch and learn from others, so new tricks and techniques can be passed on to the next generation. Sometimes special skills are developed within particular groups.

Young chimps also learn through play. Like many young mammals they indulge in mock fights and tumbles, safely honing the skills which they will later use for real in hunting and fighting. Young chimpanzees start to prepare sticks at the age of two or three and use these in their play. Later, they will copy their elders and use them to fish for ants and termites.

weaned, but they are not fully independent until they reach about seven or eight. A female is able to conceive and produce offspring for about twenty-five years, though in practice she usually has no more than about five young during her lifetime.

Male chimpanzees are sexually very precocious. They begin mounting females by the time they are two years old, but they do not establish their full courtship rituals until they reach the age of about four. Then they will grab the attention of a receptive female by shaking branches, stripping leaves from trees, and standing near to her with their hair erect. If the female is ready to mate, she adopts a squatting posture in front of the male, who then mounts her from behind.

The behavior of pygmy chimps is less well known, as they are rare and therefore difficult to study. However, recent research has shown them to be even more sexually active, at all ages, than common chimpanzees. Pygmy chimps also show great variety in their sexual exploits, and, unlike common chimps, they sometimes mate face-to-face. They even seem to kiss each other in a very human way.

SEXUAL PROMISCUITY

Pygmy females remain sexually active throughout most of their pregnancy and when feeding their young. This extended period of sexual activity is another attribute chimps share with humans. It is yet undetermined, but increased sexual activity might contribute in some way to social bonding and overall group cohesion.

To date, scientists have no clear idea why these distinctive behavioral differences should exist between two such closely related species. ■

DEER

Mating in deer occurs during what is known as the rut—the period during which females come into heat and are served by the males. In most cases males compete for the females, but the extent to which they do this varies between species.

In caribou, for example, the rut takes place during late October and early November and the bulls serve the cows indiscriminately, without forming harems. Only if two bulls meet by chance is there aggression, and even then any sparring is very brief.

A roe deer buck generally mates with just one doe, whom he appears to court. In July or August he marks out an area by fraying young trees and scraping the ground with his antlers, sometimes marking the scrapes with scent from glands on his forehead. He then chases the doe, weaving a figure-eight pattern on the ground. Although the doe appears to be driven by the buck, the chase is followed by mating.

Among moose the breeding season, which

Although bull caribou rarely fight with each other, they do display to their prospective mates by thrashing the undergrowth with a side-to-side movement of the antlers.

The young of caribou are born in early June, while the herds are on their spring migration. Most of the calves are born within a fortnight of one another, which has several advantages. If they are born too early, they cannot survive the harsh weather and if they are born too late, they will not be strong enough to survive the following winter. And if all the cows have calves, the herd travels more slowly and there is less danger of some being left behind and falling prey to wolves and bears.

Manfred Daneger/NHPA

BEFORE GIVING BIRTH, *the doe may chase off young left from the previous year.*

YOUNG DEER *are especially vulnerable to predators, such as this golden eagle.*

CARIBOU MATING *Females give birth in spring in areas that will provide rich summer pasture.*

GROWING UP

The life of a young deer

AT BIRTH,
the fawn is born with its eyes open. The mother licks it clean and encourages it to its feet.

THE FAWN
lies hidden in the undergrowth until it is able to run alongside its mother. She visits regularly to feed it.

All illustrations Barry Crouder/Wildlife Art Agency

occurs in September and October, is marked by fighting between the bulls. They spar with their antlers, doing one another little or no damage, but the winners mate with more cows than the losers. Bulls bellow for the cows, and on hearing their answering calls, crash through the undergrowth to find them.

More territorial behavior is shown by fallow deer bucks. In October, each buck stakes out a small area that temporarily becomes his territory. He marks this by fraying tree trunks and marking them with scent from his facial glands, and scraping the ground with his antlers and urinating in the scrapes. He warns intruders to keep away by barking and prancing about on stiff legs. Fights occur only occasionally and are seldom serious, combat usually consisting of sparring with the antlers or boxing with the forelegs. Only if a senior buck is threatened by a close rival does a serious fight occur.

Normally, a younger buck signifies submission by giving a loud grunt and running away, and by the end of the rut an order of precedence will have been established. The younger bucks tend to have territories downwind or uphill of the older ones, who rush about trying to keep as many does as possible in their territories.

Red deer behave in a similar way. In October, the stags undergo a dramatic change of mood. They wallow in peaty bogs or muddy pools and roar or "bell" to each other and to the hinds. The hinds, which are sexually mature at three years old, are then rounded up into harems in areas about 100 ft (30 m) across, each dominated by a mature stag. The stags patrol their harems endlessly, roaring defiance at other stags and often engaging in fights. These fights are not merely sparring matches—foreheads clash and the antlers are used to inflict wounds. During a fight it is not uncommon for a

FROM BIRTH TO DEATH

RED DEER
GESTATION: 231–238 DAYS
NO. OF YOUNG: 1 (SOMETIMES 2)
EYES OPEN: AT BIRTH
FIRST WALKING: 2–3 HOURS
WEANING: 8–10 MONTHS
SEXUAL MATURITY: 15–28 MONTHS
LONGEVITY IN CAPTIVITY: OVER 20 YEARS

FALLOW DEER
GESTATION: 230–240 DAYS
NO. OF YOUNG: 1 (OCCASIONALLY 2)
FIRST WALKING: 1 HOUR
WEANING: 3–4 MONTHS
SEXUAL MATURITY: 18–30 MONTHS
LONGEVITY IN CAPTIVITY: 25 YEARS

ROE DEER
GESTATION: ABOUT 280 DAYS
NO. OF YOUNG: 1 OR 2
FIRST WALKING: 1 HOUR
WEANING: 3 MONTHS
SEXUAL MATURITY: 18 MONTHS
LONGEVITY IN CAPTIVITY: 17 YEARS

MOOSE
GESTATION: 240–270 DAYS
NO. OF YOUNG: USUALLY 2
FIRST WALKING: 3 DAYS
SEXUAL MATURITY: 2 YEARS
LONGEVITY IN CAPTIVITY: UP TO 20 YEARS

BOTH SEXES OF CARIBOU HAVE ANTLERS. THE LARGE BROW TINES ARE THOUGHT TO BE AN ADAPTATION TO PROTECT THE EYES FROM TWIGS AND STEMS OF BUSHES

in SIGHT

RED ROAR

F. Millington/Planet Earth Pictures

During the rut, red deer stags spend much of their time roaring at one another. A stag wishing to challenge another for possession of a harem approaches and begins to roar, and the incumbent stag roars back. Often the contest ends there or soon afterward, without a fight actually taking place. The reason for this can be seen in the cost of actually fighting. A mature stag fights about five times during the rut, and each time he does so, he risks considerable injury. In one study, it was found that 23 percent of stags were injured during the rut each year—up to 6 percent permanently. Thus any strategy that enables stags to establish dominance without fighting is an advantage. Stags appear to try to outdo their rivals in the frequency of their roars, and it has been shown that stags who can roar most often also tend to fare better in fights.

third stag to sneak swiftly into the harem and mate with one of the females, only to be chased off again as soon as the fight is over.

Gestation varies from about from 160 days in musk deer, 180 days in such species as muntjac, tufted deer, and white-tailed deer, to 280 or more days in roe deer and sambar. Roe deer take so long because implantation of the developing embyro is delayed until December in order that the young may be born the following May or June, when food is most plentiful.

Newly born deer are extremely vulnerable to predators and thus deer tend to be secretive about birth. A female roe deer produces her one or two (very occasionally three) fawns deep inside a thicket, and only brings them out after about a fortnight to rejoin the buck. The family group stays together at least until the end of the following winter, and male calves grow their first antlers, simple unbranched prongs, in February of their second year. Antlers increase in complexity until the fourth year, when they reach the full extent of their growth. In moose, the gestation period varies between 240 and 270 days and each cow normally produces two calves, except the first time, when she produces only one. For the first three days the calves are unable to walk very much and the mother has to remain in close attendance. After about ten days the calves are able to run with their mother, and they remain together for two years.

CARIBOU CALVES, WHICH WEIGH ABOUT 9 LB (4 KG), CAN RUN AFTER HALF AN HOUR AND CAN OUTRUN A HUMAN AFTER FOUR HOURS

Red deer produce their calves about 235 days after mating. Each hind chooses a secluded spot among the bracken and usually has a single calf. It can stand within a few minutes of being born and is able to run alongside its mother within a few hours. It is weaned after about nine months, but remains with the hind until the autumn of the following year. Young red deer become sexually mature between 15 and 28 months and may live for over 20 years. ■

1.

All illustrations Robin Budden/Wildlife Art Agency

1. At the start of the contest, stags roar at each other for several minutes.

2. The two stags walk alongside each other until one turns to face the other.

3. The combatants lower their antlers, ready for combat.

4. The stags push strenuously, each trying to push the other rapidly backward.

AMAZING FACTS

William S. Paton/Planet Earth Pictures

- Mud wallowing is usually done to keep cool and/or to remove parasites.

- When danger threatens, fallow deer fawns freeze instinctively, making themselves almost invisible. Meanwhile the doe bolts in an attempt to draw a possible enemy away from her offspring.

DHOLES

Male canids are unusually attentive fathers. For many mammals the paternal role begins and ends with courtship and mating, and the male maximizes his dynastic chances by impregnating as many females as possible. Among typical dogs and foxes, however, the male tries to make the most of each mating by working to ensure the survival of the pups that result. This involves a lot of time and energy, so he cannot generate too many families or he would be worn out. Accordingly, he tends to form a semipermanent pair bond with his mate. From a human point of view this may seem virtuous, but it is only a strategy. For a canid, male or female, looking after the family is just a way of securing the dynasty.

The raccoon dog is as conscientious as any. In northern Japan raccoon dogs mate in March or April, when they emerge from their winter hibernation, and immediately settle down to living as a pair. The four to eight young are born in a nursery burrow after a gestation of about two months, and the male brings food for their mother while she suckles them. As soon as the pups begin to take solid food, after a month or so, he brings food for them too. Eventually both parents share the job, foraging separately and carrying food back to the den. By the end of summer the pups are sufficiently well developed to forage for themselves and the family breaks up, although the pair bond may persist for several years.

In the dhole the pattern is more complex. Mating takes place within the social context of the pack, and if either of the previous season's dominant pair shows signs of weakness, there may be a revolution,

PATERNAL RIGHTS
The male often becomes lodged inside his mate for a long period after mating (above). This actually benefits him, as it prevents other males from intruding and making their own bid for paternity.

PUP FIGHTS
are a mixture of play and real aggression (below); these lessons teach youngsters how to stand their ground against rivals, and also how to hunt.

Like any other pups, young raccoon dogs (below) engage in lively rough-and-tumble games.

Darek Karp/NHPA

in SIGHT

WET NURSES

Occasionally two or more female dholes may appear to breed in the same den, but this is unlikely: Among social canids such tolerance is very rare. One explanation for den-sharing may be "phantom pregnancies" caused by hormonal imbalance. Although only one female in the pack actually gives birth, two or three may produce milk, and even suckle the pups of the alpha female.

GROWING UP

The life of a young dhole

THE BIRTH
occurs in the safety of a den below ground. At least three or four pups are born (above).

FEEDING TIME
There is little rest for the alpha female until her hungry pups (left) are fully weaned.

Robin Budden/Wildlife Art Agency

resulting in a subordinate or two moving up into "alpha" position. These new top dogs will then assert their dominance over the others, although defeated animals often leave to found new packs elsewhere.

Once the hierarchy has been resolved, the alpha pair mate. The whole pack moves into a suitable nursery den, which may be an abandoned porcupine burrow or similar hole, well disguised among dense vegetation, and after a two-month gestation five to ten pups are born. The mother relies on the alpha male and the rest of the pack to bring her food while she suckles the pups, and they do so by swallowing meat at the site of the kill and carrying it back to the den in their stomachs, regurgitating it on demand. Eventually they provide the same service for the pups until they are old enough, at about seven months, to begin hunting with the pack.

Meanwhile the family may have moved the den two or three times, either because they feel threatened or because the original den has become riddled with parasites. Normally several dholes guard the den site when the others are hunting, but they cannot defend against fleas. On their part the pups engage in their own battles for status, squabbling violently to establish a hierarchy of their own. They also play more peaceably, both among themselves and with the adults, chasing and ambushing one another in clear rehearsal for the more serious chases they will undertake when they become fully fledged hunters.

In the more remote parts of Australia dingoes may get a similar start in life, but usually the breeding pattern seems to be more like that of the raccoon dog, with young dingoes leaving their parents within the year to seek territories of their own. A breeding pair is less conspicuous than a pack, and the dingo, having been persecuted for two centuries, appears to have learned this lesson the hard way. ■

The female dingo suckles her litter on her feet, in the manner of a wolf (below).

FROM BIRTH TO DEATH

DHOLE	**DINGO**
GESTATION: 63 DAYS	**GESTATION:** 63 DAYS
LITTER SIZE: 4–10, AVERAGE 6	**LITTER SIZE:** 3–10, AVERAGE 5
BREEDING: MATE IN AUTUMN TO WINTER, GIVE BIRTH LATE WINTER TO EARLY SPRING	**BREEDING:** MATE IN AUTUMN, GIVE BIRTH LATE WINTER
EYES OPEN: 14 DAYS	**EYES OPEN:** 8–9 DAYS
FIRST LEAVE DEN: 3 MONTHS	**WEANING:** 2 MONTHS
HUNT WITH PACK: 7 MONTHS	**FIRST LEAVE DEN:** 3 MONTHS
SEXUAL MATURITY: 1 YEAR	**INDEPENDENCE:** 1 YEAR
LONGEVITY: 10 YEARS OR MORE IN THE WILD	**SEXUAL MATURITY:** 1 YEAR
	LONGEVITY: 10 YEARS OR MORE IN THE WILD

Gerard Lacz/NHPA

EARED SEALS

Although sea mammals such as whales and manatees pass their entire lives in water, having severed all links with the land, seals give birth and suckle their pups on land, and often mate onshore as well. The choice of a breeding site is a very important one, on which the future of many thousands (perhaps millions) of animals depends. For this reason, it is not left to chance. Both males and females are genetically programmed to return to the place of their birth to breed.

Eared seals have an annual cycle that begins just before the start of the breeding season, when males come ashore to establish their territories. A few weeks later, shortly before they are ready to give birth, the females come ashore. Studies of marked northern fur seals have shown that they try to return to the exact site of their own birth—to within a few feet. Mothers-to-be jostle with their sisters and maybe their own mothers for the same area on the beach.

Five times larger than females, male northern fur seals *(Callorhinus ursinus)* might easily be mistaken for a separate species. During the breeding season the males are an unpleasant sight. Bloodshot eyes rolling, neck dripping with blood from half a dozen wounds, in a state of crazed aggression, they attempt to control the beach. The stakes are high. Only the strongest get to breed and pass on their genes.

The most successful males are those that manage to establish a territory in the center of the breeding beach, where the natural concentration of females is thickest. If a bull can lay claim to a few square yards here, his worries are partly over. The females will come to him. However, he will be surrounded on all sides by belligerent rival males, some with established territories of their own and others intent on engaging him in battle in order to drive him off his patch. To survive the breeding season, a male must be in his prime. Few males are powerful enough to command a territory before they are nine years old, and among northern fur seals, males last an average of one-and-a-half seasons. Older "has-beens" and juvenile males are relegated to traditional hauling grounds (where there are no females) nearby.

Birth is not a complicated procedure, for the pup is a convenient torpedo shape and slithers into the world, head or tail first, quite easily. It starts

DELAYED IMPLANTATION

After mating, the fertilized egg develops into a hollow ball of cells called a blastocyst. This lies dormant in the seal's womb for about four months until the most crucial stage of feeding the previous pup is over. Then the blastocyst implants itself into the wall of the womb and begins to develop normally. Delayed implantation allows seals to give birth on land, then mate immediately afterward. Unlike other seals, Australian sea lions give birth every eighteen months, which suggests a longer pregnancy.

BEACH MASTERS
Only the strongest males earn the name of beach master. They are the ones to establish a "harem" and are able to breed.

WEANING
The length of time pups take to be weaned depends on the species. The time varies from four months to a year.

SUCKLING
In many species the female suckles the young for about a week, then goes to sea to feed herself. She returns at intervals of five or six days. Other species feed the pups much more often.

GROWING UP

The life of a young seal

FROM BIRTH TO DEATH

NORTHERN FUR SEAL

GESTATION: 51 WEEKS
LITTER SIZE: USUALLY 1
WEIGHT AT BIRTH: 10–12 LB (4.5–5.4 KG)
WEANING: 3–4 MONTHS
SEXUAL MATURITY: MALES 5–6 YEARS; FEMALES 3–7 YEARS
LONGEVITY IN THE WILD: UP TO 30 YEARS

CALIFORNIA SEA LION

GESTATION: 50 WEEKS
LITTER SIZE: USUALLY 1
WEIGHT AT BIRTH: 13.5 LB (6 KG)
WEANING: 1 YEAR
SEXUAL MATURITY: MALES 9 YEARS; FEMALES 6–8 YEARS
LONGEVITY IN THE WILD: NOT KNOWN (30 IN CAPTIVITY)

WALRUS

GESTATION: 15–16 MONTHS
WEIGHT AT BIRTH: 140 LB (63 KG)
WEANING: 2 YEARS
LONGEVITY IN THE WILD: 40 YEARS

MATING
Immediately after each female has given birth, the beach master will mate with her.

Simon Turvey/Wildlife Art Agency

suckling within a few hours, and initially the mother seal stays by its side.

The Antarctic fur seal and the northern fur seal pups get barely a week's attention before their mothers leave to go fishing. They return once every five or six days to suckle their offspring with a highly concentrated form of milk. The pups put on weight rapidly and are ready to be weaned by four months old. As soon as the pups reach 40 percent of their adult size, the mothers lose interest and the pups are abandoned to catch their own food.

Sea lions and fur seals, which give birth in warmer waters, suckle their offspring for much longer. There's plenty of food just offshore so their absences from the breeding beach are short. The mothers have a stronger bond with their pups and appear to be more caring. ■

ELEPHANTS

The cooperation of individual elephants within a herd sees baby elephants successfully into their teens, young adults into maturity, and adult females into ripe old age.

When a male is ready to mate, he will become very aggressive. During this time, a bull will fight with other bulls, sometimes to the death, to win the chance to mate with a female. Mating is preceded by much touching, rumbling, and twining of trunks. The bull mounts the cow from behind with his front legs stretched along her back. Then the herd breaks into a noisy frenzy, called the mating pandemonium. If another bull is nearby, this will call him to the scene, but he must then fight to mate with the cow. The strongest bull will be the last to mate. He stays with her for a few days to keep other bulls at bay.

MATING IS A SOCIAL EVENT, TAKING PLACE AMONG THE HERD. BULLS WILL FIGHT OTHER BULLS FOR SUPREMACY AND THE PRIVILEGE OF MATING WITH A COW IN ESTRUS

Usually a single calf is born, about 22 months later for an African elephant, or 21 months later for an Asian elephant. The calf, which weighs about 220 pounds (100 kilograms) and is about 3 feet (less than a meter) tall, can usually stand on its

MUSTH

Steve Turner/OSF

Musth (pronounced *must*) is an unexplained and little-studied phenomenon where an elephant's temporal glands—situated on each cheek between the eye and the ear—periodically secrete a dark, strong-smelling fluid. These glands are rarely active in Asian female elephants, although they are in African females. Musth is usually linked with the urge to mate, but elephants also reproduce outside this time. Musth bulls are extremely aggressive and many keepers have been killed by musth bulls in captivity.

PLAYTIME
Young calves love to play. Through these games calves establish their social status within the family group.

THE NEWBORN CALF
takes its first wobbly steps, staying close to its mother. She remains in constant touch with the baby, gently reassuring it with her trunk.

THE BULL MOUNTS
a female in heat, supporting his weight on his hind legs as mating takes place. An excited commotion then breaks out among the rest of the herd.

Alan Male/Linden Artists

THE BABYSITTER

A young female acts as a babysitter for a calf to protect it from danger. Here the female stands in a defensive posture at the approach of a hungry lioness.

Sonia Boulton/ICCE Photolibrary

ELEPHANT GRAVEYARDS

Legends often tell of secret places where elephants go to die. There is no evidence that these "graveyards" exist, but why, then, have piles of elephant bones been found in certain places? There are several possible explanations. In times of drought, dying elephants often migrate to swamps and rivers in search of water and food. Several may starve there or may be too weak to climb out of the mud again. Or they may be sites of mass slaughter by hunters: In the past, African tribesmen drove herds of elephants into a deep gorge and killed them for meat.

FIGHTING RIVALS

When they have the urge to mate, adult bulls become very aggressive. They will fight with any other bull they meet, wrestling with their trunks.

own within half an hour. It is totally dependent on the care it receives from the rest of the herd.

The calf suckles from two teats between its mother's front legs and continues to do so until it is about two years old. It will try to pick at grasses after a few months, but baby elephants find it difficult to manage their trunks at first.

Male calves need twice as much food as females in order to reach maturity, and because of this bull calves are the first to die in times of food shortage.

Young calves often play together, developing the skills they will need as adults, such as butting heads and charging. Playing continues for longer with male calves than females and is used to establish rank among the males.

Sticking Together

Young females usually stay with their families for the rest of their lives, helping to care for the calves. In this way they learn how to care for their own young. These babysitters will fiercely defend the calves in their care against rhinos, lions, cheetahs, hyenas, and leopards.

Elephants may reach the grand age of sixty-five or seventy before they die. Other herd members will stay close by to comfort a dying elephant and will guard the body for hours afterward. ■

FRUIT BATS

The length of time it takes from mating to birth varies greatly; usually the smaller the animal, the shorter the amount of time. With fruit bats it can take over six months before the gestation period is complete, which is an incredibly long time for such relatively small animals—and it is even more incredible for an animal that relies on flight to obtain its food.

At birth a flying fox young is well developed. It is born fully furred and with its eyes open. In the Indian flying fox the newborn baby can weigh as much as 8.8 oz (250 g), almost one-third the adult female's own weight. Not surprisingly most flying foxes give birth to only a single offspring, although in the rousette fruit bat twins do occur. The newly born bat clings tightly to the mother and feeds from her breast at will. Despite the huge size of her baby,

SEXUAL MATURITY VARIES AMONG BAT SPECIES BUT CAN BE ANYWHERE FROM SIX MONTHS TO TWO YEARS

the female flying fox must carry her offspring with her on the nightly search for food. However, once the female has arrived at her feeding site, she will often unhook her young and leave it hanging from a nearby branch while she collects fruit.

For the Indian and gray flying foxes this will continue for two to three weeks. As it grows, the youngster rapidly becomes too heavy to carry, and the female will leave it behind, clinging to the tree. This is a dangerous time for the young flying fox, for if it should fall from the tree, it would become easy prey for any passing predators. On her return, after circling a few times, the mother locates her own offspring even though there may be hundreds

THE FIRST MOMENTS

A baby fruit bat is helpless and totally dependant on its mother at birth. It clings to its mother constantly until it is ready to fly. It can even feed while its mother is in flight, fastening on to her nipple with needlelike teeth. The females of some bat species have false teats that the baby bat can cling to when it is not feeding.

THE MATING GAME

The male bats mount females from behind, using wings and thumbs to hold the females still.

GUIDED BY SMELL

The fruit bat locates fruiting trees and then crushes the fruit for its juices.

All illustrations Evi Antoniou

GROWING UP

The life of a young fruit bat

BABY FRUIT BATS
They are born large, alert, and with their eyes open. This gives the bat a good chance of survival early on.

FROM BIRTH TO DEATH

INDIAN FLYING FOX

GESTATION: 140–160 DAYS
LITTER SIZE: 1
BREEDING: JULY–OCTOBER
WEIGHT AT BIRTH: 7–10 OZ (200–280 G)
EYES OPEN: AT BIRTH
FIRST FLIGHT: 2–3 MONTHS
WEANING: 5 MONTHS
INDEPENDENCE: 6–8 MONTHS
SEXUAL MATURITY: 18–24 MONTHS
LONGEVITY: USUALLY 12–15 YEARS IN THE WILD; UP TO 31 YEARS 5 MONTHS IN CAPTIVITY

ROUSETTE FRUIT BAT

GESTATION: 110–130 DAYS
LITTER SIZE: 1 (TWINS EVERY THIRD OR FOURTH YEAR)
BREEDING: JUNE–SEPTEMBER
WEIGHT AT BIRTH: 1–1.4 OZ (30–40 G)
EYES OPEN: AT BIRTH
FIRST FLIGHT: 4–5 MONTHS
WEANING 4 MONTHS
INDEPENDENCE: 5–6 MONTHS
SEXUAL MATURITY: 5 MONTHS FOR FEMALES; 15 MONTHS FOR MALES
LONGEVITY: USUALLY 11–14 YEARS IN THE WILD; UP TO 23 YEARS IN CAPTIVITY

BATS FORAGING
The mother cannot gather food and carry her young at the same time, so she leaves it hanging in branches.

of screaming infants all trying to gain attention. This is achieved through a combination of memory, eyesight, and hearing.

A young bat grows quickly, and it will only be another two to three months before it will be able to fly and begin to fend for itself. During the weeks before this happens, the young bat will hang upside down and flap its wings. This builds up its muscles. When it is ready, it simply lets go of its roost branch and drops. Unlike a bird, if it hits the ground it will be able to climb up a tree and try again. Yet even though the young bat is now able to fly, it will be nursed for another month or so by its mother and will remain with her for a further two to three months.

At about eight months old the young bat sets up a roost of its own. However, it will continue to grow until it is one year old. Young males will remain with their mothers until they are almost two years old before leaving to join the bottom rung of the hierarchy of the lek. ■

FIRST FLIGHT
Larger fruit bat young take their first flight at three months. Even so, they continue to suckle.

GALAGOS

For the savanna-dwelling species of galago, the climate is markedly seasonal; so the lesser and the greater galagos time mating so that births take place in the wet season. During this period, a female lesser galago gives birth to up to two litters, each with one to three young. The rain forest galagos, along with the pottos, lorises, and tarsiers, have a less-precise breeding season in keeping with their more stable climate, yet birth peaks tend to coincide with certain months when food is most abundant. As in many rain-forest mammals, a single young is the norm.

COURTING COUPLES

Reproductive behavior is preceded by acts of courtship, which vary considerably in vigor. In the western tarsier it generally involves a good deal of chasing and calling. In galagos there are ritual stages of chasing, sniffing, facial licking, and long periods of mutual grooming that build up the pair

MATING

When ready for mating, a female lesser galago allows the male she has already courted to grasp her waist from behind and mount. Copulation lasts for several minutes at a time.

PIGGYBACK

After the initial period in the nest, the mother takes her young out every night, "parking" them on a branch while she feeds in one tree before moving them on to the next.

Alain Compost/Bruce Coleman Ltd.

A newborn toris is remarkably agile, and its fingers possess a tenacious grip. Nevertheless, it will be several months before it is brave enough to venture far from its mother. Until that time, it spends many a night clinging to her fur as she feeds (left).

GROWING UP

The life of a lesser galago

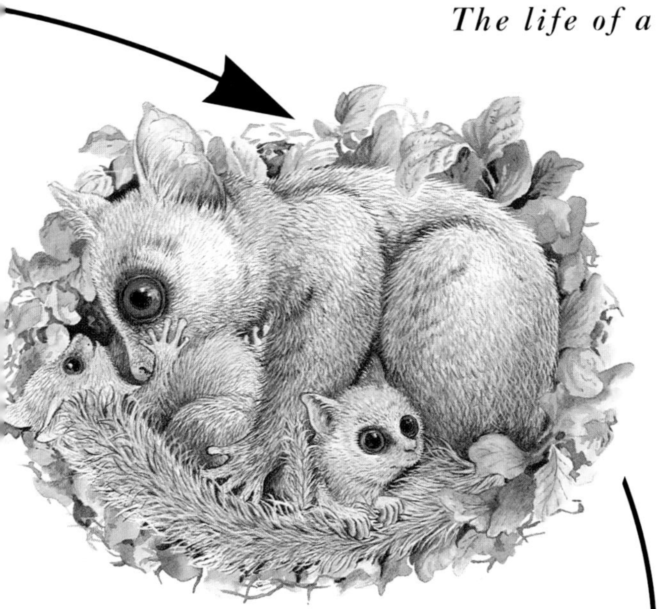

HELPLESS YOUNG
In lesser galagos, there are usually two young born in a litter (left). Their eyes are open from birth, but they are unable to move purposefully about the nest until a few days have passed.

AIR CARGO
Should predators threaten the nest, the protective mother is fully prepared to carry the young in her mouth (above), even when leaping dramatically between branches.

Illustrations Wendy Bramell/Wildlife Art Agency

BABY PARKING

As soon as an infant lorisid or tarsier can grip tightly, its mother takes it out at night and "parks" it while foraging. At each feeding site she places the young on a thin branch, to which it instinctively grips, while she busies herself nearby. In this manner she can keep an eye on the young, which is so tiny that it is unlikely to be detected by predators. But even then, the infant can make a last-ditch escape attempt by letting go and dropping to the ground.

FROM BIRTH TO DEATH

LESSER GALAGO	WESTERN TARSIER
BREEDING: USUALLY 2 BREEDING PERIODS PER YEAR	**BREEDING:** ANY TIME OF THE YEAR, BUT BIRTHS PEAK IN FEBRUARY–APRIL
GESTATION: 4 MONTHS	**GESTATION:** 6 MONTHS
LITTER SIZE: 1–3	**LITTER SIZE:** 1
WEIGHT AT BIRTH: 12–15 G (0.4–0.5 OZ)	**WEIGHT AT BIRTH:** 20–30 G (0.7–1 OZ)
EYES OPEN: AT BIRTH	**EYES OPEN:** AT BIRTH
WEANING: 10–11 WEEKS	**WEANING:** 8 WEEKS
SEXUAL MATURITY: 10 MONTHS	**SEXUAL MATURITY:** 1 YEAR
LONGEVITY: UP TO 15 YEARS IN CAPTIVITY	**LONGEVITY:** 8–12 YEARS

bond. This may take place several days before the female is physically ready to mate. In the potto, on the other hand, there is little close contact at all prior to mating.

A HEAD START IN LIFE

Gestation periods can be long for such small mammals, up to six months in the case of the tarsiers. But the advantage is that the newborn young are quite well developed and quickly begin to find their way around. An angwantibo gives birth on a branch, and the newborn must immediately climb up and cling to its mother's belly fur, where it will

> AT ONE DAY OLD A TARSIER CAN CLIMB AROUND A LITTLE, AND WEIGHS ALMOST A QUARTER OF ITS MOTHER'S WEIGHT

remain for several days. As soon as a slow loris is born it can cling firmly to thin branches. Newborn galagos are less precocious. Their eyes are only half-opened, and they can only crawl about awkwardly. Accordingly they are born in secure leaf nests or in tree hollows.

In all species, within a few days the young can cling tightly enough to accompany the mother while foraging, although she "parks" it each night (see box). By ten days, the young is becoming ever more mobile in the nest. It can climb, stand, jump, and wrestle. In the greater and needle-clawed galagos, the mother is big enough to carry an infant on her back all the time while foraging and does so when it is aged about four weeks. The same applies to the lorises and pottos.

By about six weeks the young of all species of lorisids and tarsiers have learned to move about on their own, though they keep close to their parent, and are learning to find palatable food for themselves. Weaning is shortly thereafter. After several months of foraging within its mother's range, the offspring approaches adult weight. ■

GAZELLES

Compared with some other aspects of their behavior, the breeding habits of duikers, dwarf antelopes, and gazelles are broadly similar. In tropical zones at least, breeding is not tied to any single time of the year. Nevertheless, distinct birth peaks occur, especially in savanna species, with mating periods timed so that more young are born during food flushes that coincide with one or two bouts of seasonal rains. Outside the tropics, in those regions of Central Asia that experience harsh winter cold, gazelles give birth in the spring.

In all species, courtship tends to be initiated by the male. A male duiker begins by following his partner until he has a chance to sniff her urine and discover whether or not she is about to come into estrus. If she is, he becomes even more persistent over the next few days, even turning to chasing and butting, until she becomes receptive and willing to mate. A similar pattern, differing only in details of the ritual, occurs with gazelles and dwarf antelopes. Courtship sometimes involves vocalizations, such as a growling sound produced by male dorcas gazelles.

A series of short mating sessions occur for up to a day between partners, followed by several months of pregnancy for the female. When a female gazelle is ready to give birth, she typically moves away from the herd to a concealed site where she delivers her single fawn. Though newborn duikers, dwarf antelopes, and gazelles are quite well developed, all of them spend the first weeks of life lying low in bushes or tall grass, scarcely moving unless the mothers return to suckle them. And though the mothers may be with them for no more than one or two hours per day, this concealment strategy is the youngs' best means of defense from predators during this highly vulnerable stage. In those duikers and dwarf antelopes that live in stable pairs, males may assist in parental care by being extra vigilant for predators and by responding to fawns' distress calls. But otherwise tending to the concealed youngster is done by the female.

GAINING GROUND
The male may one day acquire enough strength and experience to fight for the takeover of a territory (below).

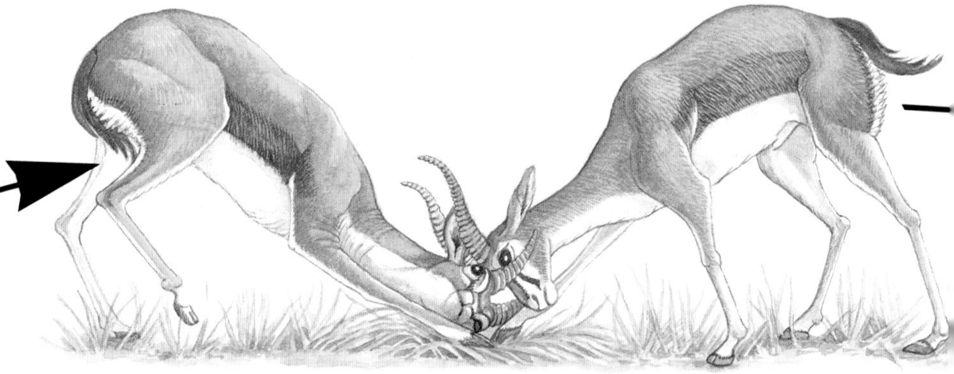

EVICTION
Before the year is out, a young male is threatened into leaving and forms a bachelor group with other young males (above).

LYING OUT

The young of duikers, dwarf antelopes, and gazelles all spend their first few weeks concealed in cover—a behavior called lying out. Lacking any odor and staying still lessens the chances of their being detected by enemies. In addition, they are hard to spot against the ground. In several of the duikers, the newborns lack the bolder colors of their parents; hence the yellow rump of the yellow-backed duiker is entirely absent for the first month of life. Both Jentink's duiker and the bay duiker are born darker brown than adults and lack, respectively, the adults' black hood and black stripe along the back.

David Keith Jones/Images of Africa

Cryptic colors and body shape combine superbly to conceal a gazelle fawn (above).

GROWING UP

The life of a Thomson's gazelle

READY TO MATE

Having avoided a male's advances until her time is due, a female Thomson's gazelle at last allows him to mount (right). Six months later she moves away from the herd to a secret refuge and gives birth to a single young.

IN THE NURSERY

For several weeks the offspring lies in hiding, moving only when summoned for milk by its mother. At several months old the young is developed enough to run with the herd (left).

At about the time of weaning, a few months after birth, fawns begin foraging with their mothers, and mother and offspring gazelles become reintegrated into a herd. The youngster is still very vulnerable, but at least it is learning how to spot danger and flee. Those young that survive the early months develop rapidly, and by the first or second year may already have reached sexual maturity.

Duikers and dwarf antelopes tend to strike out on their own during the second year; males are often forced by their fathers to leave earlier than females, which may be tolerated in the family group even when fully adult. In male klipspringers, the first signs of harrassment by the father may begin as soon as the horns start to appear, at about six months.

In gazelles, young females may remain close by their mothers for a year before taking their place within the herd. Young males, however, are apt to be displaced by territorial males as early as eight months and forced to join bachelor herds. ■

FROM BIRTH TO DEATH

THOMSON'S GAZELLE

BREEDING: YEAR ROUND. BIRTHS AND MATING PEAK DURING THE RAINS AND 6 MONTHS LATER

GESTATION: 6 MONTHS

LITTER SIZE: USUALLY 1

REJOINS HERD: 10 WEEKS

WEANING: 3–6 MONTHS

SEXUAL MATURITY: FROM 1 YEAR IN MALES AND FEMALES

BLUE DUIKER

BREEDING: THROUGHOUT THE YEAR

GESTATION: 4 MONTHS

LITTER SIZE: 1

REJOINS HERD: 4 WEEKS

WEANING: 2–3 MONTHS

SEXUAL MATURITY: FROM 1 YEAR IN MALES AND FEMALES

Illustrations Carol Roberts

GIANT PANDAS & RED PANDAS

Giant panda courtship is a fragile endeavor fraught with difficulties. To mate, the couple have to be responsive to each other, and must engage in a long sequence of vocal and scent communication. Even then, a male may suddenly become agitated or indifferent and the female may simply have a change of mind.

The mating season over most of the panda's range is between mid-March and mid-May. Female pandas come into heat only once a year for about 12

> PANDAS HAVE LITTLE TIME TO MATE SUCCESSFULLY—SOMETIMES THE FEMALE IS FERTILE FOR ONLY TWO DAYS EACH YEAR

to 25 days, with a peak of 2 to 7 days: this is the only opportunity for a pair to mate.

To mate, the female stands on all fours with her head lowered, and indicates her readiness to mate by crouching and presenting her rump to the male. The male stands behind her and mounts her, resting his forepaws on her back. Though most adult males manage to mate during a mating season, not all father young since they may mate before or after the female has ovulated.

THE TIME IS RIGHT

Giant panda cubs are born in August and September, though the gestation period varies from three to five-and-a-half months, due to a delayed implantation of the embryo. This strategy evolved in mammals living in places where there is seasonal food scarcity, so they can delay giving birth until conditions are most suitable for rearing their young.

Once she is pregnant, a female giant panda sets

SMALLEST YOUNG

Proportionately, giant pandas have the smallest young of any placental mammal—about the size of a small rat—and, at 3 to 3.5 ounces (90 to 100 grams), are only about one nine-hundredth of their mother's weight. Newborn giant panda cubs are completely helpless at birth: blind, toothless, pink, and naked, except for a sparse covering of white hair.

THE FIRST MONTH *of the young panda's life is spent being nursed by its mother in the safety of her den.*

PANDA MATING *is brief: females are fertile for only a few days.*

Illustrations Toni Hargreaves

GROWING UP

The life of a young giant panda

AFTER SIX MONTHS, *the cub can walk and climb on its mother's back. At this time, it begins to eat bamboo.*

AT EIGHTEEN MONTHS, *the young panda is left to fend for itself as winter approaches.*

BY THIS TIME, *the panda has perfected the art of climbing trees.*

FROM BIRTH TO DEATH

GIANT PANDA	RED PANDA
GESTATION: 125–150 DAYS	**GESTATION:** 90–145 DAYS
LITTER SIZE: SOMETIMES 1, USUALLY 2, OCCASIONALLY 3	**LITTER SIZE:** 1–4; ONLY 2 ARE USUALLY REARED FROM THE LITTER
BREEDING: SEASONAL; BETWEEN MARCH AND MAY	**BREEDING:** MATING IS NON-SEASONAL
WEIGHT AT BIRTH: 3–3.5 OZ (90–100 G)	**WEIGHT AT BIRTH:** 4–4.5 OZ (110–130 G)
EYES OPEN: ABOUT 7 WEEKS	**EYES OPEN:** ABOUT 18 DAYS
FIRST WALKING: 3 MONTHS	**FIRST WALKING:** 2–3 DAYS
WEANING: 9 MONTHS	**WEANING:** 6–8 MONTHS
SEXUAL MATURITY: BETWEEN 5 AND 7 YEARS	**SEXUAL MATURITY:** BETWEEN 18 AND 20 MONTHS
LONGEVITY: UNKNOWN IN THE WILD; UP TO 30 YEARS IN CAPTIVITY	**LONGEVITY:** UNKNOWN IN THE WILD; UP TO 14 YEARS IN CAPTIVITY

about finding a suitable site to give birth. This can be in a hollow at the base of a tree, in a dense thicket of bamboo, or in a cave that she lines with wood chips, bamboo stems, rhododendron branches, or saplings to keep out the cold and damp.

Twins are usual, but normally only one cub will survive. Newborn pandas are often invisible, hidden under their mother's forepaw or tucked under her chin. In their first few days, cubs will suckle from 6 to 12 times a day for up to 30 minutes at a time.

HOME PROTECTION

Apart from its long tail, which will remain about the same size as it grows, the cub resembles a miniature adult by the time it is about three weeks old. After six months, it has all its teeth except for its molars. About two to three months later, during the spring, the panda is fully weaned. However, it still needs the protection of the nest and of its mother because of the danger from predators and because it has not yet learned how to interact with adults.

The mother remains with her cub throughout the spring breeding season into summer and autumn before the cub finally sets off to fend for itself. Estrus does not occur at this time. ■

OUT OF ACTION

THE THREAT OF PARASITES

Parasites pose a serious problem to the small, fragmented giant panda populations. Roundworms are most common and can be present in such numbers that they fill the animal's intestines, making holes in the gut wall. In some areas up to 70 percent of pandas are thought to be affected, suffering retarded growth, low fertility, and, in some cases, death.

GIBBONS

Gibbons are unique among apes in being monogamous—that is in choosing a partner and then pairing with it for life. Such a system suits the gibbons' lifestyle and gives them the highest chance of survival as a species. If mating and bonding were more casual—the family group not so tightly-knit as a result—establishment of territories and thus the most efficient use of forest resources would be far harder to accomplish.

Remarkably little is known about the reproduction of gibbons in the wild. It seems that siamangs give birth from November to March, but the estrous cycle in gibbons corresponds to humans—that is they have a menstrual cycle that lasts twenty-eight days, during which they are able to conceive for about seven days.

LIFE BEGINS

Just one young is born after a gestation period of between 210 and 235 days. A single young will have a better chance of survival than, for example, twins, for from the moment of its birth—high up in the trees—it has to be able to hang tightly on to its mother's fur, with no extra support from her, as she flies through the trees daily to forage. The baby is therefore fully developed and precocious at birth,

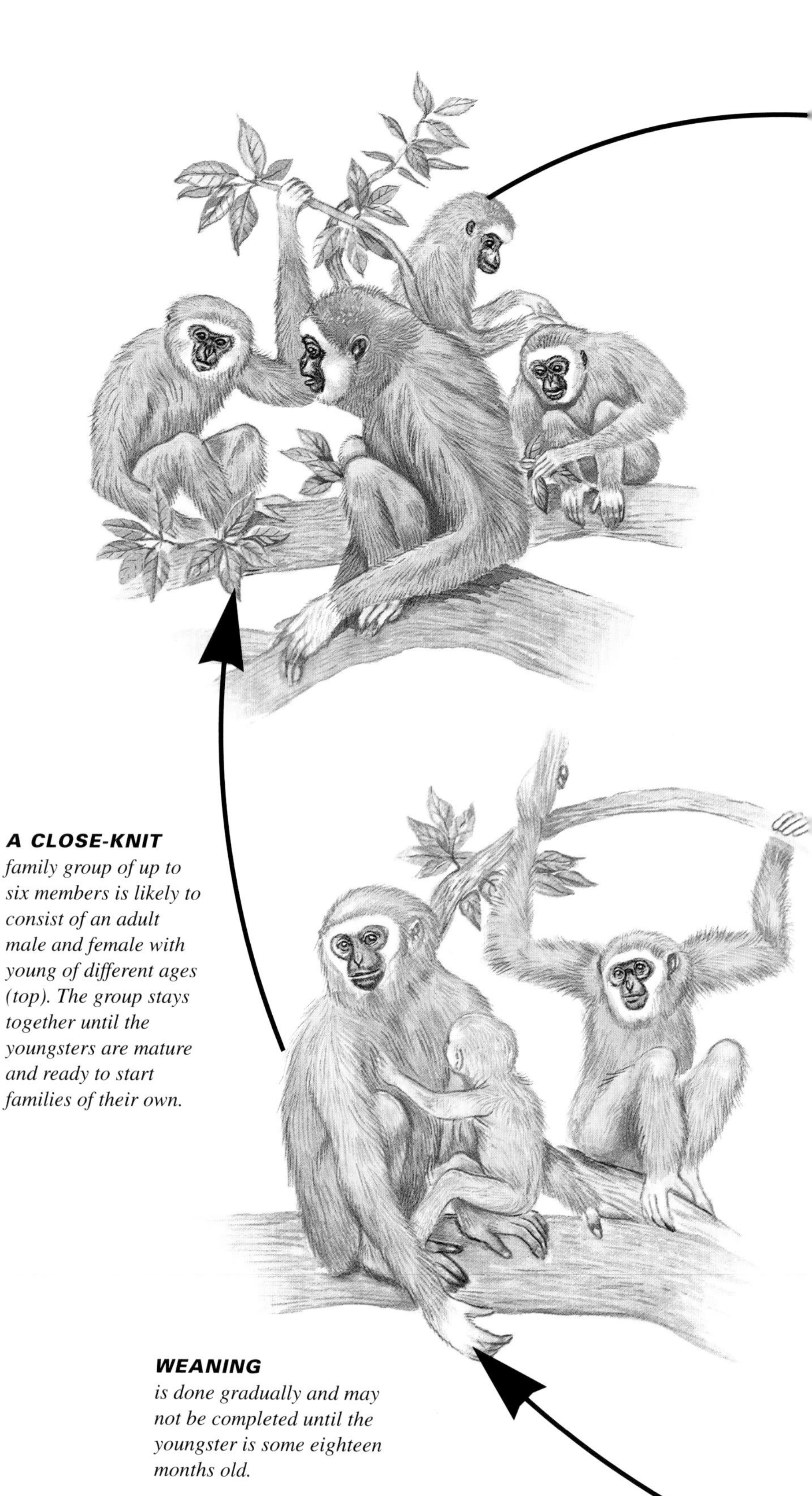

A CLOSE-KNIT *family group of up to six members is likely to consist of an adult male and female with young of different ages (top). The group stays together until the youngsters are mature and ready to start families of their own.*

WEANING *is done gradually and may not be completed until the youngster is some eighteen months old.*

The young concolor gibbon's whitish coat (below) will darken to golden or black depending on its sex.

Rod Williams/Bruce Coleman Ltd.

GROWING UP

The life of a young lar gibbon

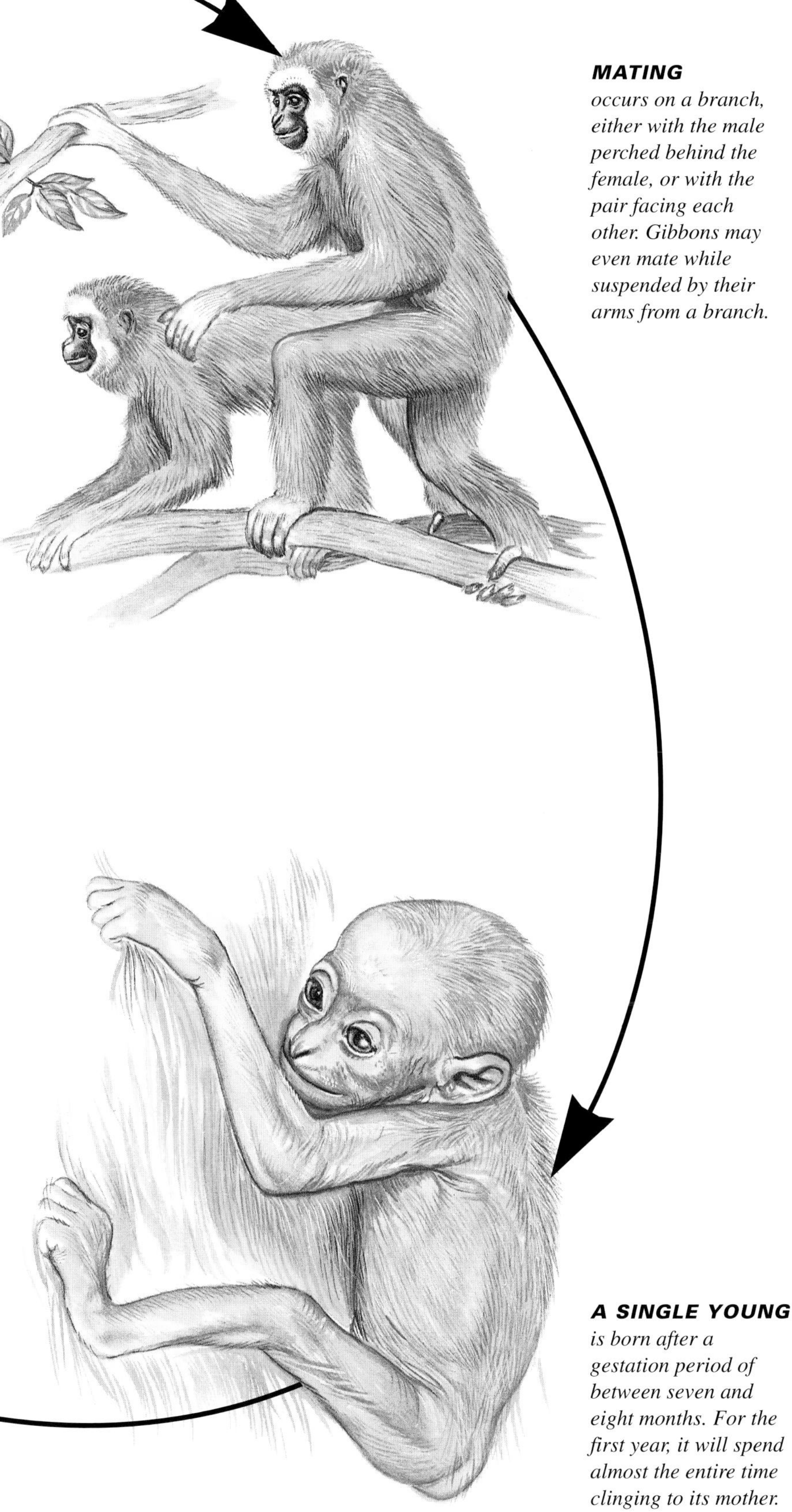

MATING
occurs on a branch, either with the male perched behind the female, or with the pair facing each other. Gibbons may even mate while suspended by their arms from a branch.

A SINGLE YOUNG
is born after a gestation period of between seven and eight months. For the first year, it will spend almost the entire time clinging to its mother.

Illustrations Peter Bull

FROM BIRTH TO DEATH

GIBBON

MATING: CAN OCCUR THROUGHOUT THE YEAR	**WEANING:** APPROXIMATELY 18 MONTHS
GESTATION: 210–235 DAYS	**PUBERTY:** 6 YEARS
NO. OF YOUNG: 1 (TWINS CAN OCCUR)	**SEXUAL MATURITY:** 7–8 YEARS
	LONGEVITY: 30–40 YEARS

although it is generally almost naked except for a cap of hair on the crown. When the mother is resting or is still on a branch, the baby will nestle into the fur on her abdomen and thighs in order to keep warm.

The infant grows up close to its parents and will remain in the group probably until it is at least six years old, by which time it will have at least one, probably two, younger siblings. Female gibbons give birth only once every two or three years, again so that attention and care can be focused on the youngest member to give it the best chance of survival. However, because of this and also the territoriality that excludes meeting with other groups, young gibbons do not interact or indulge in play-learning with their peers. While their older siblings may interact with them in a friendly way, most of their interaction is with their parents.

The young gibbon is usually weaned at about 18 months or so. However, by this time, it is usually the father that has taken over daily care of the youngster, particularly in the siamang. The young will

OF ALL THE APES, GIBBON MALES ARE THE ONLY ONES TO FULFILL A CLEAR PARENTAL ROLE

cling to the male's fur as he sets off in search of food, and from him it will learn how to swing through the trees and find the ripest fruit, and how to behave within the family group. Only at night does the father return the youngster to the mother's care.

The group remains tightly knit as the youngsters grow up. They cannot begin to fend for themselves until they are three to four years old, but, by about six years old, the young gibbons will begin to reach puberty. They will begin to interact with the male in both an aggressive and friendly manner and increasingly they have less and less to do with the female, so as not to come into conflict with the dominant male. Eventually, when they are about eight years old, young males begin to occupy the solitary space of no-man's-land between territories, where they begin to sing in the hope of attracting a mate. Solitary or subadult females do not sing; they wait to be wooed by a young male, after which they will establish their own territory and begin a family group. ■

GIRAFFES

Giraffes are able to breed at any time. In some places, however, conception appears to take place during the rainy season so that birth occurs in the dry months. In the Serengeti, most births take place from May to August. Cows reach sexual maturity at about three and a half—bulls a year later—but giraffes generally do not breed until they are four and a half and seven or eight respectively. Females can go on producing young until they are at least twenty years old.

Ritualized courtship

Quite frequently a younger bull in an area will consort with a female approaching estrus, indulging in initial courtship behavior; however, it is usually the dominant bull within the core of the range that actually mates with her. The dominant bull spends much of his time wandering the area looking for receptive females. He inspects each one by licking her tail, which encourages her to urinate. The urine runs over his lips and he responds by curling his upper lip upward—an action known as the

A mother encouraging her newborn to stand in the Masai Mara, Kenya (below).

Jonathan Scott/Planet Earth Pictures

GROWING UP

The life of a young giraffe

WITH THE HERD
The calf is ready to wander and browse with the herd from the time it is six months old, although it will not be fully weaned until well over one year old.

ADULTS
At about three years old, calves have wandered away from their mothers and their main activity is browsing. Males begin ritualized necking at about this age.

THE FIGHT TO MATE
Bulls will fight over a sexually receptive female. They engage in head-butting fights that can be extremely violent.

BIRTH
A cow gives birth to her calf standing up, the calf dropping some 6.5 ft (2 m) to the ground. It will be up on its feet and suckling within one hour.

flehmen reaction. Testing the urine probably helps him to gauge her sexual receptivity; additional courtship behavior involves him nudging her gently with his muzzle or horns, or trying to rest his neck on her back. If she is ready for mating he will slide his forelegs onto her flanks and mount her.

Giraffes have a long gestation—approximately 457 days—so cows give birth at intervals of about twenty to thirty months (the minimum recorded time is sixteen months). Usually just one calf is born, but twins are not unknown.

The female gives birth standing up, so the newborn calf has to drop to the ground. Well developed at birth, it appears to suffer no harm and is up on its wobbly legs within about 15 minutes. The 6-ft- (1.8-m-) tall calf will take its first drink within an hour.

A YOUNG GIRAFFE CAN OUTRUN A LION BUT IT GENERALLY LACKS THE STAMINA TO OUTRUN A HYENA

For the first week or so of its life, the cow keeps her calf in isolation, watching over it with a fiercely protective, maternal devotion. At this time, she never moves far from her calf, so it is always in her sight, usually lying by a bush or tree, half-hidden by the grass. If the calf is alarmed it lowers its head almost to ground level, and the markings on its coat, already present at birth, afford it almost complete camouflage. When it is three to four weeks old, the cow moves it to the company of other youngsters in a guarded crèche.

Cows are fierce in the protection of their young, although the initial line of defense is concealment—one reason why calves spend much of their time lying down in the long grass. ■

CRECHE
When the calf is a month or so old, the cow moves it into the company of other calves. The young are constantly guarded by one or two cows, while the others browse.

All illustrations Kim Thompson

FROM BIRTH TO DEATH

GIRAFFE

GESTATION: 400–468 DAYS
NUMBER OF YOUNG: 1
HEIGHT AT BIRTH: 5–6.2 FT (165–190 CM) AT SHOULDER
WEIGHT AT BIRTH: 103–154 LB (47–70 KG)
FIRST SUCKLES: WITHIN 1 HOUR
WEANED/MALES: 12–14 MONTHS
WEANED/FEMALES: 12–16 MONTHS
SEXUAL MATURITY/MALES: 4–5 YEARS
SEXUAL MATURITY/FEMALES: 3–4 YEARS (USUALLY DO NOT BREED FOR AT LEAST ANOTHER YEAR)
LONGEVITY: 26 YEARS

OKAPI

GESTATION: 421–457 DAYS
NUMBER OF YOUNG: 1
HEIGHT AT BIRTH: 2.2–2.7 FT (72–83 CM) AT SHOULDER
WEIGHT AT BIRTH: 35 LB (16 KG)
WEANED: 8–10 MONTHS
SEXUAL MATURITY/MALES: 4 YEARS
SEXUAL MATURITY/FEMALES: 3 YEARS
LONGEVITY IN WILD: NOT KNOWN (33 YEARS IN CAPTIVITY)

GOAT ANTELOPES

The 26 species of caprines live in a range of habitats—from the Asian jungle and the sunbaked Ethiopian highlands to the Arctic tundra. Mating strategies and individual appearance are conditioned by the surroundings, but on a more basic level, the subfamily shares a number of fundamental similarities in reproduction and life cycle.

The range of habitats, although diverse, is almost completely inhospitable or remote. This can affect the number of offspring and the life span. Litter size is usually small, a response to territories that are either productive yet strictly delineated or looser and potentially unsupportive. Three offspring is usually the maximum, but most litters have only one or two newborn; these are always well developed and precocious.

Population growth, or stability, is achieved not through endless waves of litters but through small annual increases. This is especially true where climatic conditions are extreme. It is not surprising that two species with life spans of 20 years—the musk ox and American bighorn—are natives of the Arctic tundra and rugged mountains respectively.

SOCIAL CUSTOMS

The major mating differences among goat antelope are dictated by social structure. Among the more primitive resource defenders, such as the two species of serows, the sexes look very similar; both, too, observe scent-marking behaviors. The mating season is in October and November and mating itself is preceded by an elaborate courtship. The male licks at the female's mouth, strikes between her hind legs with his forelegs, and rubs his horns against her genitalia.

The sexes differ more greatly in appearance among the more social goat antelope. Social hierarchies, often linked to horn length, dictate mating strategy. Ritual combat between high-ranking males involves head butting and prolonged clashes of horns. Dominant males in some species, such as the saiga, can even acquire harems.

in SIGHT

SMELLY BILLIES

Scent marking and scent recognition play an important role in the behavior of many caprine species. This is usually the domain of the bucks, which need to establish and enforce territorial limits or to be warned of approaching rivals. The source of the distinctive scent is usually a secretion from a gland such as the preorbital gland in the skull.

Billy goats (male goats) often adopt a simpler—yet equally effective—way of advertising their presence. They simply spray themselves with urine and let the resulting body odor speak for itself.

SCENT FRENZY
During the rut, adult males use the scent glands at the base of their horns to mark more or less everything in sight — including each other (above).

EARLY LEARNER
The juvenile mountain goat rapidly develops in skill and confidence, and before long it is surefooted on the rocky slopes, just like its parents (left).

Stephen Message/Wildlife Art Agency

John Daniels/Ardea

The American bighorn displays many of the "typical" behaviors of long-horned, social goat antelope. It is a native of alpine and desertlike habitats of western North America. The massive spiral horns of older males reach spectacular lengths—up to 3.75 feet (1.15 m).

During the mating season, high-ranking males of similar horn size have dramatic battles, rushing at each other and crashing their horns together fiercely. Such encounters are often protracted, and may continue for hours. Occasionally one of the animals is killed, but certain adaptations reduce the possibility of fatal wounds. A double layer of bone covers the brain, and skull bones are particularly hard. The neck bones, too, are tough, and form an especially strong joint with the skull. Fractured horns, however, are a common occurrence.

Like so many young ungulates, the mountain goat kid is soon mobile and keeping up with its mother (left).

Although these high-ranking feuds are fierce, lower-ranking—and therefore smaller-horned—males are not excluded from the herd. Instead, they are treated as females by the dominant males, an instinctive strategy that sustains herd sizes and provides extra defense while grazing. Correspondingly, younger males are tacitly encouraged to stay with the herd in order to acquire knowledge from the older males about the best grazing areas and escape routes. These well-stocked sites are widely scattered in extensive forested regions.

The bighorn ewe produces one or two lambs in June after about a six-month gestation. The offspring are well developed and within days are able to accompany her to graze on high mountain pastures. Nevertheless, the mother maintains close links with her young, and they are fully weaned only by the time they are six months old.

By winter, ibex bucks have stopped fighting for superiority, and high-ranking males are accorded deference by those who remember the outcomes of the summer battles. The rut has two stages. In the first or common rut, all the bucks court the does by repeating a series of foreplay gestures: These include stretching out the body, pulling the head back, raising the tail, flipping the tongue, rotating the head, and swinging a foreleg forward. Lesser-ranking bucks recede in the second (individual) rut, in which the highest-ranking male courts, and mates with, most of the does. ■

GROWING UP

The life of an American mountain goat

QUICK START

The kid scrambles to its feet almost at once after its birth. It sticks close by its mother's side (above), bleating piteously to attract her attention in times of danger.

KIDS AT PLAY

At two weeks old, the kids are indulging in lively games, butting and leaping in mimicry of the adults (left).

FROM BIRTH TO DEATH

BIGHORN SHEEP

GESTATION: 175 DAYS
LITTER SIZE: 1
BREEDING: OCTOBER–DECEMBER
WEIGHT AT BIRTH: 8.8 LB (4 KG)
EYES OPEN: AT BIRTH
WEANING: 4–6 MONTHS
GRAZING: 3–6 DAYS
LONGEVITY: AVERAGE 9 YEARS IN WILD; 24 YEARS IN CAPTIVITY

MOUNTAIN GOAT

GESTATION: 186 DAYS
LITTER SIZE: 1, RARELY 2 OR 3
BREEDING: NOVEMBER–JANUARY
WEIGHT AT BIRTH: 7 LB (3.2 KG)
EYES OPEN: AT BIRTH
WEANING: 3 MONTHS
GRAZING: 1 WEEK
SEXUAL MATURITY: 30 MONTHS
LONGEVITY: MALE 14 YEARS, FEMALE 18 YEARS

MUSK OX

GESTATION: 8.5 MONTHS
LITTER SIZE: 1
BREEDING: JULY–SEPTEMBER
WEIGHT AT BIRTH: 18–33 LB (8–15 KG)
EYES OPEN: AT BIRTH
WEANING: 10–18 MONTHS
BROWSING: 1 WEEK
SEXUAL MATURITY: 3–4 YEARS
LONGEVITY: 20–24 YEARS

SAIGA

GESTATION: 139 DAYS
LITTER SIZE: FIRST YEAR 1, THEN 2
BREEDING: DECEMBER
WEIGHT AT BIRTH: 7.5 LB (3.4 KG)
EYES OPEN: AT BIRTH
WEANING: 3–4 MONTHS
GRAZING: 8–10 DAYS
SEXUAL MATURITY: FEMALE 8 MONTHS, MALE 20 MONTHS
LONGEVITY: 6–10 YEARS

GORILLAS

There are no clearly defined seasons in the warm, humid equatorial forests, and gorillas may breed in any month of the year. Mating will be more or less restricted to the dominant silverback, depending on his age, tolerance level, and powers of vigilance.

The females in the group breed every three to four years or so. They come into estrus for one to three days in every 27–30 days, but since there are no visible signs of her receptivity, she presents her rump flirtatiously to the male. It takes a while to attract his attention, since he usually responds with a show of utter boredom; eventually, however, he takes the hint. Gorillas mate in a variety of ways. In one of the favorite positions, the male sits down and lifts the female into his lap. Alternatively, she backs into him and he crouches behind her hips. Very rarely, gorillas mate face-to-face. The coupling, which may last from 15 seconds to 20 minutes, is a vocal affair in which both sexes whimper and hoot.

Meanwhile, the atmosphere in the group may become highly charged, and excited subadult males mount nonreceptive females. Adult males may also try to mate with receptive females, and the dominant silverback often—but not always—interjects such activity. Lone silverbacks are even drawn to the group by the commotion; their presence may occasionally incur the leader's wrath, although he generally tolerates such intrusions.

Gestation lasts for about eight and a half months, after which the female gives birth lying down, and usually at night, to a single infant. Sometimes two are born, but very rarely do both survive. The mother is highly attentive to the infant, holding it to her single pair of breasts to suckle.

For the next six months she barely releases her grasp on the tiny baby. For its part, the infant can only cling to its mother's hairy belly at first, but it develops rapidly. Within a couple of months it is a lively toddler, and three or four months later it can ride on its mother's back and has the confidence to wander off and play with other infants. When the youngsters run out of games to play among themselves, they do not hesitate to clamber over adults and juveniles to pull their hair and try their patience otherwise. The adults simply put up with it all.

The young gorilla spends two and a half to three years suckling, during which time it gradually interacts more and more with other group members—regardless of their age or sex. By the time it is three or four years old, its mother may well be pregnant again; at this point the pair usually part company. If the youngster is female, she will remain in the group for a few years more. But eventually she, too, will leave for a solo male or another, smaller group where she can gain rank more rapidly and breed herself. Because of the high infant mortality, she may raise only two or three young to adulthood during her entire life. ■

MOTHER LOVE

The infant is regularly groomed by its mother, who carefully picks off particles of fecal matter, parasites, and loose skin (below).

John Cancalosi/Bruce Coleman Ltd.

Baby gorillas can walk when less than a year old; like us, however, they are helpless at birth (left).

FROM BIRTH TO DEATH

GORILLA

GESTATION: 8.5 MONTHS	**SEXUAL MATURITY/MALE:** 8–9 YEARS
NO. OF YOUNG: 1, RARELY 2	**SEXUAL MATURITY/FEMALE:** 7–8 YEARS
WEIGHT AT BIRTH: 4.4 LB (2 KG)	**LONGEVITY:** 37 YEARS IN THE WILD; MAY LIVE MORE THAN 50 YEARS IN CAPTIVITY
FIRST CRAWLING: 9 WEEKS	
FIRST WALKING: 35–40 WEEKS	
WEANED: 2.5–3 YEARS	
INDEPENDENT: UP TO 4.5 YEARS	

MATING

When receptive, the female incites the male to mate by thrusting her rump toward him. But gorillas are not by nature oversexed creatures, and it may take a while to break down his typically cool reserve (left).

INFANTICIDE

This phenomenon is not unusual among primates and has been observed in gorillas. When a new dominant male joins a widowed group, this new male will sometimes seek to kill young infants. When infants die for any reason, their mothers come into estrus right away and become pregnant by the resident male. A new male will instinctively prefer to invest his protective efforts in his own offspring. Naturally, the females will try to counteract infanticidal behavior and often succeed.

Barry Croucher/Wildlife Art Agency

GROWING UP

The life of a young gorilla

APE CHILD

The newborn weighs about 4.4 lb (2 kg) and has sparse hair on its pinkish gray skin. It also looks eerily human — far more so than any adult ape (right).

PATERNAL PRIDE

The silverback is touchingly protective toward his tiny offspring, even taking time out to play with it (left).

GRAY WHALES

During the summer feeding frenzy, gray whales are usually too busy to indulge in courtship or sexual behavior, but as they migrate south, their intentions turn to reproduction. Males and females swim close and may caress each other with their flukes or flippers. As they approach the winter areas, groups of males and females loll about, but there are no strong pair bonds: Males leave and join other groups at random, and females mate several times with several males in the group.

The males are not aggressive with each other, as in some whale species, and there is no fighting or overt competition. Males seem to rely on sperm competition—producing enough sperm to displace any that the female may already have received. The male gray whale has large testicles and a penis over 3.3 ft (1 m) long to achieve this.

Assisted Mating

Mating has been observed at all times of the year, but it becomes more common toward the end of the autumn migration. The peak time for conception for California gray whales is during early December. Only females who gave birth the previous year, and whose calves are now growing up, are usually receptive to males; those about to give birth or with newborn calves are usually not.

Mating may involve two, three, or as many as five animals; the extras may help the mating pair to stay afloat. Actual copulation lasts 30–100 seconds; the pair involved may lie on their sides at the surface for up to an hour and copulate several times, waving their topside flippers in the air. Another one or two males may position themselves on the far side of the female, often in the vertical spy-hop position, to support her during this time.

Birth Days

Most of the gray whale calves are born in Baja California's Laguna Ojo de Liebre, Laguna San Ignacio, Laguna Guerro Negro, and Estero Soledad. The majority arrive within one month of each other, with the peak in mid-January. The actual birth is in water only 33 ft (10 m) deep, and the calf emerges tail first, as in many other whales.

The new calf often has difficulty swimming and coordinating its movements to surface and breathe or to suckle its mother's milk from the teats on her rear underside. The mother is attentive and highly protective, however, and helps by holding it at the surface with her back or flipper. In the shallow lagoons, mother and calf stay close and touch often. The youngster has barely any blubber at this stage, but the water is warm and insulation is hardly necessary.

By the time that the northward migration looms, the calf is about

MOTHER'S HELP
The newborn calf needs encouragement to take its first breath, so its mother gently nudges it to the surface (below).

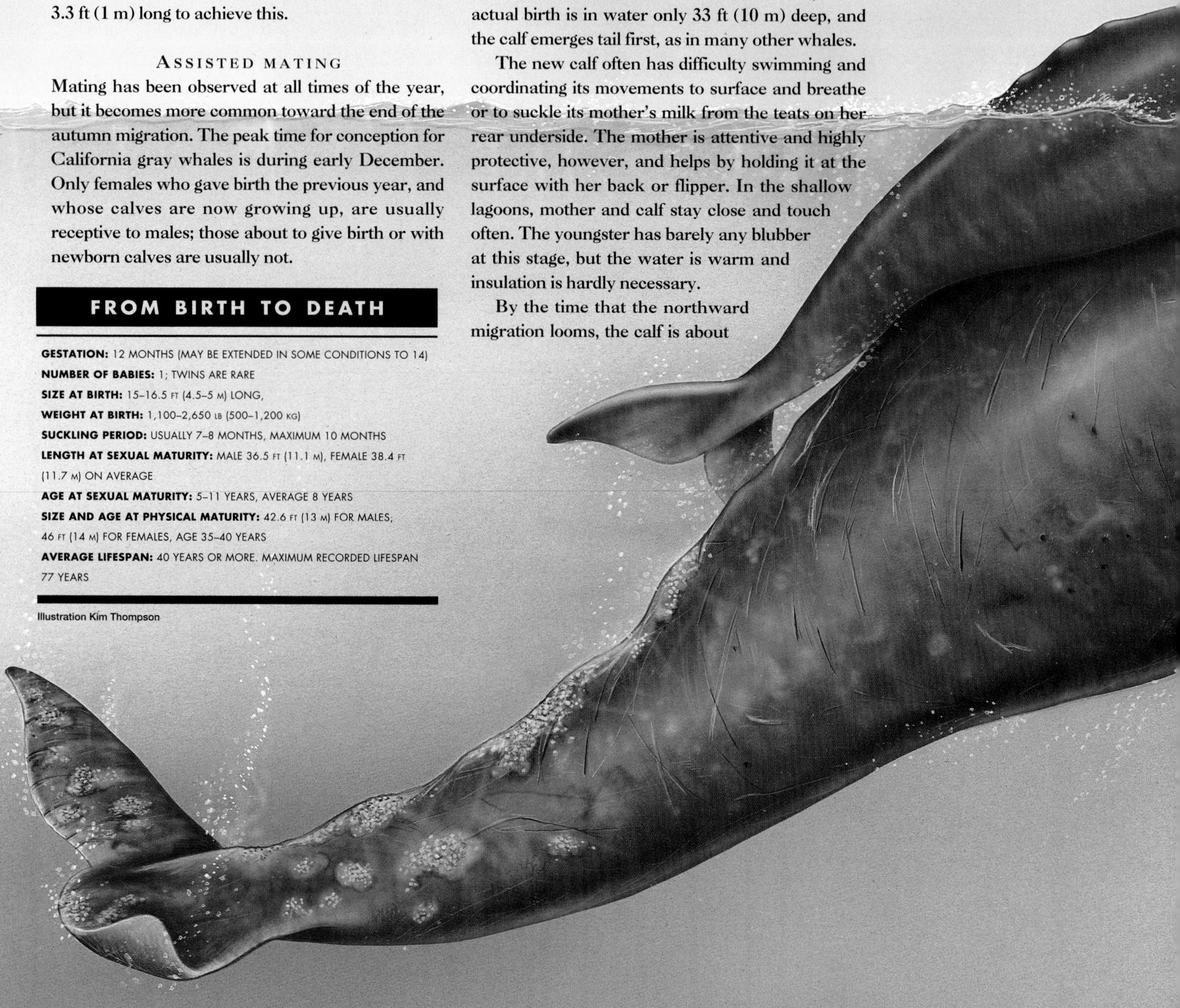

FROM BIRTH TO DEATH

GESTATION: 12 MONTHS (MAY BE EXTENDED IN SOME CONDITIONS TO 14)
NUMBER OF BABIES: 1; TWINS ARE RARE
SIZE AT BIRTH: 15–16.5 FT (4.5–5 M) LONG,
WEIGHT AT BIRTH: 1,100–2,650 LB (500–1,200 KG)
SUCKLING PERIOD: USUALLY 7–8 MONTHS, MAXIMUM 10 MONTHS
LENGTH AT SEXUAL MATURITY: MALE 36.5 FT (11.1 M), FEMALE 38.4 FT (11.7 M) ON AVERAGE
AGE AT SEXUAL MATURITY: 5–11 YEARS, AVERAGE 8 YEARS
SIZE AND AGE AT PHYSICAL MATURITY: 42.6 FT (13 M) FOR MALES; 46 FT (14 M) FOR FEMALES, AGE 35–40 YEARS
AVERAGE LIFESPAN: 40 YEARS OR MORE. MAXIMUM RECORDED LIFESPAN 77 YEARS

Illustration Kim Thompson

PESTS AND DISEASES

Gray whales succumb to killer whales, and rarely to large sharks. Otherwise, they have no natural predators. However, like other baleen whales, they may suffer from a variety of diseases such as cancer, stomach ulcers, heart disease, pneumonia, jaundice, and osteoarthritis. They also have internal parasites such as worms, which may take more of a toll as the whale gets older. The gray whale also has the most external pests of any whale: These include whale lice, which are about the size of a large coin.

two months old. When it reaches the Arctic it will have built up a thick underlayer of blubber, made from the nutrients in the milk of the mother. The calf is also bolder and leaps and breaches some distance from its mother. She has not eaten for perhaps eight months, so she feeds hungrily to restore her body fat and keep up the milk supplies. At the end of the summer, the calf is usually weaned, but the mother still protects it on the way, until they reach the warm lagoons again.

THE REPRODUCTIVE CYCLE

The average gray whale female gives birth every other year. Her usual cycle is a gestation period of twelve to thirteen months, followed by seven or eight months of lactation, and then three or four months of rest and recuperation. There are, however, occasional sightings of a possibly pregnant female with a calf still feeding on her milk.

The gray calf grows at an incredible rate, putting on over 2 lb (1 kg) every hour through the summer. Most young reach sexual maturity at about eight years old, when the male is 36.5 ft (11.1 m) long and the female 38.4 ft (11.7 m). The female usually remains slightly larger than the male throughout life, and full physical maturity is not attained until after thirty years.

Much of this information about the whales' age comes from the waxy earplugs that fill the outer ear canals of baleen whales. These plugs usually add on a layer each year, much like the growth rings in a tree trunk, so zoologists can analyze the plugs to check a whale's age. In a large adult gray whale, the earplug can be over 16 in (40 cm) long. ■

François Gohier/Ardea

Adult grays pass their warm, balmy days down south, frolicking and mating (right).

GROUND-LIVING SQUIRRELS

For ground-living squirrels, every aspect of breeding is connected with the sense of smell. Odors—probably gland-based scents called pheromones—influence all elements of reproduction, from first attraction to the departure of young from the family home.

Most squirrels can breed at one year old. The gestation period in squirrels is quite short: only three to six weeks. All infant squirrels are born without teeth and with their eyes closed, but by the time they are six weeks old, they are furred and are capable enough to leave the burrow. Usually the female alone is responsible for parental care of the young, while the father often leaves the home altogether after mating. In some ground-living rodents, such as prairie dogs and marmots, however, both sexes nurture their offspring, especially while the pups are playing or exploring outside the burrow. The young seem to respond to this parental care by staying in the burrow through the next hibernation and the next summer.

Marmots can breed from one year old, although they mature fully at two. They usually mate within

PRAIRIE DOG COTERIES INTERMINGLE DURING BREEDING SEASON, DIMINISHING THE CHANCE OF MATING WITH CLOSE RELATIVES

A golden-mantled ground squirrel (below) sleeps through the winter in a nest of dried grasses.

Jeff Foott/Bruce Coleman Ltd.

GROWING UP

The life of a young prairie dog

THE MOTHER *raises the young, unaided by other members of the coterie. However, the young pups do suckle from any lactating females in the group and they are gently groomed by any male in the coterie. The pups' eyes open after about thirty-three days, and this is when they first start to venture out of the burrow.*

THE FEMALE GIVES BIRTH *to a litter of usually four pups in March, April, or May. The young are born with their eyes closed. The mother suckles the young pups until they are weaned, which is normally within about seven weeks.*

THE COTERIE
is the prairie dog's basic family unit. In a breeding coterie, there is usually one adult male for every four adult females, with a few young or juveniles. A female mates with a male from the coterie or from a nearby group, and if she becomes pregnant she will produce one litter in the year.

THE NEST IS BUILT
in one of the burrows using material carried in from the outside. Pregnant and lactating females nest alone and are hostile to any approaches from the other members of the unit. Gestation takes about five weeks.

All illustrations Simon Turvey/Wildlife Art Agency

a few days of leaving their winter home. Gestation takes five weeks, and the pregnant female seals off her nesting area with grass and hay a few days before the birth to secure a little privacy.

Prairie dog pups can take up to about 15 months to grow to adult size, breeding only when they reach about two years old. Unusual for rodents, mature females bear only one litter a year.

The breeding habits of the various species of African rock squirrel differ, but they are basically typical of squirrels. Some breed all year, while others have a defined breeding season. Their litters may vary from two to six pups, and the young are sexually mature at about one year old. The long-clawed ground squirrel of central Asia mates during February and March and gives birth to between three and six young in April or May.

For gophers, the mating season is about the only time when the animals socialize. Female western pocket gophers have one litter each year; they mate during April or early May in Canada, and in July and August in colder mountain areas. After a gestation period of 18–19 days, usually three or four young are born. The young stay in the burrow for about two months before moving on to new areas. They reach adult weight at about five months and become sexually mature within a year.

Female eastern pocket gophers may have more than one litter each year, especially in the warmer states. In these cases the litter size is usually smaller. The newborn weigh about 0.2 oz (5 g). Their eyes open at 22–23 days; they are weaned at 28–35 days and leave their mother at about seven weeks (49 days). ■

FROM BIRTH TO DEATH

BLACK-TAILED PRAIRIE DOG

GESTATION: 34–37 DAYS
LITTER SIZE: USUALLY 4
EYES OPEN: 5 WEEKS
WEANED: AFTER 7 WEEKS
INDEPENDENCE: 15 MONTHS
SEXUAL MATURITY: 18–24 MONTHS
LIFE SPAN IN WILD: NOT WELL KNOWN IN WILD, BUT UP TO 8.5 YEARS IN CAPTIVITY

BELDING'S GROUND SQUIRREL

GESTATION: 23–31 DAYS
LITTER SIZE: 1–15, USUALLY 5
EYES OPEN: NOT KNOWN
WEANED: 4–6 WEEKS
INDEPENDENCE: 5–7 WEEKS
SEXUAL MATURITY: 11–15 MONTHS
LIFE SPAN IN WILD: TYPICALLY 2–3 YEARS FOR MALES, 3–4 YEARS FOR FEMALES; SOME LIVE 6–10 YEARS

HAMSTERS

Hamsters start looking for a mate after emerging from their winter sleep. The mating season lasts from early April until well into August. The male hamsters first have to find the burrow of a female. On finding the female's territory, a male hamster marks the area near the burrow entrance with scent secretions produced from its flank glands. This will warn other males that he is in the area. The male may try to mate with the female by force, but more usually the two hamsters will watch each other nervously, chattering or grinding their teeth. The female may jump around, trying to bite the male, but if she is receptive, she will allow the male to enter her burrow. Once mating is over, the female drives the male out, and reverts to her solitary way of life.

Although the female is capable of producing a litter just about every month, in the wild she usually has just two litters a year. After about 18 to 20 days, the female gives birth to a litter of between

IF A PREDATOR SEIZES A DORMOUSE BY ITS TAIL, THE TIP BREAKS OFF, LEAVING THE ATTACKER WITH A MOUTHFUL OF FUR

four and twelve young. They are born naked and blind and are very tiny. The young may nibble at grass after about a week, although they are not weaned until they are three weeks old. By the time they are two weeks old, they have a thick coat of fur and have opened their eyes.

As soon as the young are weaned, they leave their mother and have to fend for themselves. Although they are only with their mother for a short space of time, she is extremely caring. If there is any danger, she will move her young quickly to safety by gathering them into her mouth. She will put them into her cheek pouches or carry them in the space between her incisors and the cheek teeth.

Young female hamsters are sexually mature after about sixty days. Because of this high rate of reproductivity, hamsters are in little danger of extinction, even though they have many natural predators, such as polecats, wolves, bears, wildcats, kestrels, and falcons, and, of course, humans.

DORMICE

Like hamsters, dormice awake at the start of spring and start looking for a mate. Some are quite vocal in their search. Male edible dormice may emit high-pitched squeaks as they pursue the females; and

One of the ten species of African dormouse (right), which is found throughout the forest and savanna zones of Africa.

THE DORMOUSE'S DEEP SLEEP

Hibernation is a particularly dangerous time for small mammals. They must store enough fat on their bodies to last the whole winter—even if spring is later than usual. The first winter hibernation is usually the most perilous. Some 40 percent of small mammals fail to wake up after this deep sleep. Hibernating mammals are unable to defend themselves. They rely on their ability to hide and hope that predators will not find them.

Peter Ward/Bruce Coleman Ltd.

Owen Newman/Oxford Scientific Films

A litter of week-old common dormice (above) in their nest.

female garden dormice whistle to attract males. Male dormice compete ferociously for the right to mate with a female.

After mating, males and females part company, and the males do not take any further part in the rearing of the young. They then spend the rest of the spring searching for other females to mate with. The females build a nest that they line with moss, leaves, hair, and feathers. Usually this nest is built in a hollow tree, fairly near to the ground, and it is bigger than her usual sleeping nest. Sometimes several nests are built close together, and if suitable nesting sites are few and far between, two, and occasionally three, females will share a nest, each rearing its own offspring.

After a gestation period of about 19–30 days, the female gives birth to between two and ten young. The young are born naked and blind and are wholly dependent on their mother. She leaves the young in the nest at night while she goes out to feed, but returns periodically to suckle them.

The young get their first fur after about seven days. This is usually gray in color, and molts at about two weeks to give a lighter version of the adult's coloring. Young dormice open their eyes at between 10 and 18 days. They are fully weaned after about one month, but will remain with their mother until they are about two months old. At this point they leave the

The adult garden dormouse (below) is slightly smaller than the fat dormouse.

Francisco Marquez/Bruce Coleman Ltd.

nest to begin searching for their own accommodation. They remain within a short radius of the maternal nest for the first year. The young are sexually mature after their first hibernation. If the weather is good, the adult female may produce two litters of young each year.

Dormice are quite long lived compared with other small mammals. Some species, such as the garden dormouse, may live for about five years in the wild. In captivity they have been known to live for almost twice this length of time. While fattening up for winter, dormice also reduce their protein intake, which automatically makes them much sleepier than usual. They then find a snug place to nest, usually in the hollow of a tree, fairly close to the ground. After adding a few nuts and seeds, the dormice settle down to their long winter sleep. All dormice sleep curled up, with their tails wrapped around them for extra warmth. They sleep so soundly that hibernating dormice have been known to fall to the ground without even stirring.

MATING
When the male and female meet for the first time, they sniff each other, first on the nose, then the flank gland, and lastly in the anal region.

FORAGING
The young are now ready to begin foraging for food without their mother's help.

At risk

All hibernators are at risk if the outside temperature drops too low. At temperatures below 32°F (0°C) there is the risk of ice crystals forming in the sleeping animal's blood. This would be fatal. Like other hibernating mammals, dormice usually allow their body temperature to fluctuate with that of their surroundings. But if the temperature drops to within a fraction of a degree of freezing point, the animal's bodily functions "cut in," either making the animal wake up and move around, or keeping its temperature ticking over at just above freezing.

Dormice, like other hibernating mammals, must raise their body temperature to about 86°F (30°C) in order to wake up fully. They have special tissues in the shoulder region called brown fat. The sole

Jane Burton/Bruce Coleman Ltd.

Young golden hamsters (Mesocricetus auratus) leave home by thirty to forty days old (right).

GROWING UP

The life of a young hamster

NEST BUILDING

The common hamster builds its nest from grasses, wool, and feathers in the burrow. Burrows vary in size and number of chambers.

FROM BIRTH TO DEATH

COMMON HAMSTER

GESTATION: 18–20 DAYS
LITTER SIZE: 4–12
WEIGHT AT BIRTH: 0.2 OZ (5.7 G)
EYES OPEN: 12–14 DAYS
WEANING: 21 DAYS
INDEPENDENCE: 21–27 DAYS
SEXUAL MATURITY: 45–60 DAYS
LONGEVITY IN WILD: 2 YEARS

GOLDEN HAMSTER

GESTATION: ABOUT 16 DAYS
LITTER SIZE: 5–7
WEIGHT AT BIRTH: 0.07 OZ (2 G)
EYES OPEN: 12–14 DAYS
WEANING: 21–27 DAYS
SEXUAL MATURITY: 45–60 DAYS
LONGEVITY: 2–2.5 YEARS

COMMON DORMOUSE

GESTATION: 22–24 DAYS
LITTER SIZE: 2–7
EYES OPEN: 14–18 DAYS
WEANING: 21 DAYS
INDEPENDENCE: 40 DAYS
SEXUAL MATURITY: ABOUT ONE YEAR
LONGEVITY IN WILD: 4 YEARS (6 YEARS IN CAPTIVITY)

FAT DORMOUSE

GESTATION: 19–30 DAYS
LITTER SIZE: 2–10
EYES OPEN: 12–14 DAYS
WEANING: 28 DAYS
INDEPENDENCE: 25–28 DAYS
SEXUAL MATURITY: AFTER FIRST HIBERNATION
LONGEVITY IN WILD: UP TO 5 YEARS (UP TO 9 YEARS IN CAPTIVITY)

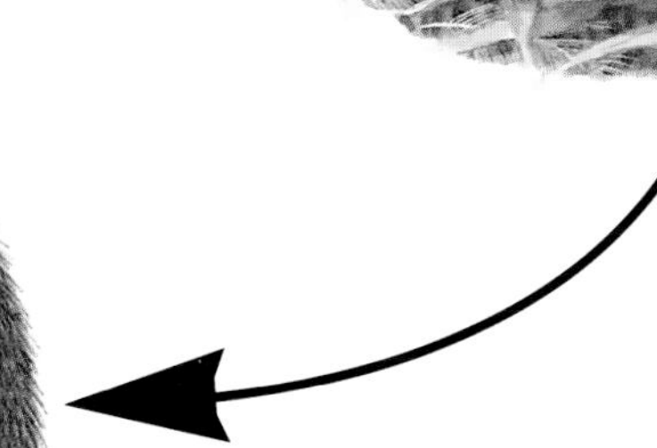

BABIES

Between four and twelve young hamsters are born, hairless and blind.

Wayne Ford/Wildlife Art Agency

MATURITY

The young leave home by thirty to forty days and are ready to mate by the following spring.

purpose of brown fat is to generate warmth when required. Exactly what triggers this is not known, but it is widely believed that when the outside temperature rises to a certain level, the brown fat begins to generate heat. When sufficient heat is generated, the sleeping dormouse's muscles start to shiver, generating even more heat. It may take about half an hour for a hibernating dormouse to wake up.

When the outside temperature rises, dormice wake from their hibernation. If this is just a warm patch in the winter, the dormouse may feed on the stored nuts before resuming its sleep. But this is a particularly perilous time for dormice. If they are awake for too long, they will use up their reserves of fat and may not have enough stored food to keep them going, and will starve to death. ■

HARES

Despite the wide range of climate and terrain encompassed by the various species of hare, breeding patterns point to some underlying consistency. As a rule, females in most species produce about ten young each year. However, the strategies used to achieve this total differ greatly—usually in relation to latitude. Northern species tend to have one large litter annually, with up to eight young being born. At the other extreme are the species living nearer the equator, where females have up to eight litters of only one or two young during the year.

This level of consistency contrasts with the pattern of many rabbit species. Cottontails in a selected area, for example, produce anywhere between ten and thirty-five young in a year. Snowshoe hares are the nearest equivalent to rabbits in this respect, with reproductive output varying between areas and years from about six to eighteen annually.

MATING
(above) reaches its peak in March and results in a glut of infants in early summer, although some hares in southerly climates may breed throughout the year.

YOUNG HARES
(left) leave the natal area soon after weaning; many are lost to foxes or diseases.

Pikas also exhibit different breeding strategies, but these differences tend to reflect variations in habitat. Rock inhabitants usually have two litters—each with fewer than five offspring—annually. Few of the second litter survive. Den-dwelling pikas give birth to more offspring in the course of the year, and females reach sexual maturity early, so that some born in spring will reproduce in the summer of the same year. The difference is explained by the shorter summers at higher altitudes, which reduces the time available to raise young, as well as the shortage of food compared with the fertile prairies. Significantly, however, the talus-dwellers have longer life spans—up to seven years—and their populations remain stable over time.

Dieter & Mary Plage/Survival Anglia

Pikas (right) are born blind and helpless but grow rapidly on their mother's rich milk.

GROWING UP

The life of a young brown hare

THE LEVERETS *(above) crouch low in the grass, and the mother periodically removes their feces to reduce the risk of detection by predators.*

SUCKLING *lasts only a month or so; the mother sits up to offer her teats to the tiny young (above). The leverets are utterly helpless and clueless at this stage; they have been known to follow birds about in the hope of a feed.*

The March breeding antics of most hares leads to a "baby boom" in May and June. Females give birth to a litter of up to four leverets (young hares); there might be as many as three more litters in the same year. Desert-dwelling species, such as the antelope jackrabbit of the southwest, tend to have smaller litters, and litter size depends on rainfall.

The actual birth and development of the young provides a major difference with rabbits. The leverets are born in the open, they are well furred at birth, their eyes are open, and they can move about soon after birth.

Each leveret soon makes its own form, but joins others to be visited by their mother for twilight nursing. This is one of the few times that hares use vocal contact: The mother warns the leverets of her approach with a low call; their responses help her locate them. Nursing itself lasts only ten minutes. Such a brief time is possible because hare's milk, with its high fat and protein content, is much richer than that of goats or cows.

During this four-week nursing period the leverets grow from a birth weight of about 4.6 oz (130 g) to about 2.2 lb (1 kg). For about a week before weaning they will have been supplementing the milk diet with plant material. The leverets must fend for themselves after being weaned, although it takes about another five to six months before they attain full adult weight. As a rule young hares do not breed in their first year—the late-born leverets would stand little chance of surviving the winter.

Efficient mothers

Pikas are born in litters ranging in size from one to thirteen. Newborn pikas are blind and totally helpless, but they grow quickly on a diet of the mother's rich milk, doubling their 0.2 oz (6 g) birth weight within about five days. Maternal care among pikas is very limited. The Gansu pika, a burrowing species native to central China, is a typical example: Mothers sometimes spend as little as ten minutes nursing their young. Males play no part at all in the care of these young. Young pikas continue suckling until they are about three weeks old; they must disperse several days later.

Representatives of some pika species, such as the American pika, have territories that have been held by a male or female for many generations. The likelihood of a juvenile—of either sex—reaching adulthood depends on its ability to find a vacant territory. The problem is made more acute by the inhospitable terrain that adjoins most talus areas: juveniles crossing these exposed zones are easily dispatched by predators. The result, in many talus-dwelling pika communities, is a type of genetic stagnation, and periodic inbreeding is common. ■

FROM BIRTH TO DEATH

STEPPE PIKA

GESTATION: 20–24 DAYS
LITTER SIZE: 7–13
BREEDING: TWICE YEARLY (SPRING AND SUMMER)
WEIGHT AT BIRTH: 0.2 OZ (6–7 G)
EYES OPEN: 8–9 DAYS
WEANING: 3 WEEKS
FORAGING: 30 DAYS
SEXUAL MATURITY: 25–30 DAYS IN THE FEMALE; PROBABLY 6–8 WEEKS IN THE MALE
LONGEVITY: 4 YEARS

BROWN HARE

GESTATION: 42–44 DAYS
LITTER SIZE: 2–4
BREEDING: FEBRUARY–OCTOBER
WEIGHT AT BIRTH: 4.6 OZ (130 G)
EYES OPEN: AT BIRTH
WEANING: 30 DAYS
FORAGING: 3 WEEKS
SEXUAL MATURITY: 1 YEAR
LONGEVITY: USUALLY 4 YEARS IN WILD (A MAXIMUM 12.5 YEARS RECORDED)

Illustrations Carol Roberts

HEDGEHOGS

In Europe hedgehogs breed from about April to September, with the main period of activity in May and June when the nights are warm. Second litters may be born, but most arrive too late to survive the oncoming winter. Tenrecs usually wait for the wet season, when invertebrate numbers are greatest, but most tropical hedgehogs can breed for much of the year, because there is always food available. For the desert-dwelling long-eared and desert hedgehogs, there is only enough food to raise a single family between July and September.

RAISING A FAMILY PUTS A GREAT STRAIN ON A FEMALE HEDGEHOG'S RESOURCES, SO THE BREEDING SEASON MUST COINCIDE WITH A TIME WHEN FOOD IS PLENTIFUL

During the breeding season, a male European hedgehog will court any female he meets by circling around her. She will usually rebuff him by turning

NEWBORN *young are tiny, blind, and helpless. Their pink skin soon begins to shrink and their soft, white spines eventually start to poke through.*

BY FLATTENING HER SPINES *and stretching her body out flat, the female makes mating easier for the male who mounts her from behind.*

AMAZING FACTS

Mark Pidgeon/Oxford Scientific Films

BABY BOOM

The common tenrec can have up to 32 young at a time, which is the largest family produced by any mammal. Females have up to 29 teats with which to suckle a litter.

With so many young to support, the mother and her offspring often need to carry on foraging for food through the night and well into the daytime.

Because it is so dangerous for young tenrecs to be moving about in daylight, they are camouflaged with a striped coat of spines that they lose with later molts.

GROWING UP

The life of a young European hedgehog

TWO DAYS OLD
After a couple of days, the typical brown spines of the adults begin to appear here and there among the white spines.

FROM BIRTH TO DEATH

EUROPEAN HEDGEHOG

GESTATION: ABOUT 34 DAYS
LITTER SIZE: 2–7; USUALLY 4 OR 5
BREEDING: SEASONAL; BETWEEN APRIL AND SEPTEMBER
WEIGHT AT BIRTH: 1 OZ (28 G)
EYES OPEN: 14 DAYS
MOBILITY: 3 WEEKS
WEANING: 4–6 WEEKS
SEXUAL MATURITY: 1 YEAR
INDEPENDENCE: 4–6 WEEKS
LONGEVITY: 3–5 YEARS; MAXIMUM ABOUT 10 YEARS

to keep her flank toward him, all the while puffing and snorting, so that the couple repeatedly shuffle around and around in circles.

If the female allows the male to mate her, he will do so from behind. The female's spines are very slippery, so the male holds on to the spines on her shoulder with his teeth. There is no pair bond between the male and female, and the male takes no part in rearing the young.

ONE-FIFTH OF ALL HEDGEHOGS DIE IN THEIR FIRST MONTH BECAUSE THE MOTHER CANNOT PRODUCE ENOUGH MILK

BABY HEDGEHOGS
When they are about eleven days old, the babies start to experiment with rolling up into a ball. Their eyes open after fourteen days.

The female builds a nest using dry leaves or grasses in a sheltered spot and, after about thirty-four days, four or five blind, pink, and helpless babies arrive. They are fed on milk from the mother's five pairs of nipples. When they are about three weeks old, the mother leads her family out of the nest each night to look for food. The young become independent of their mother at about four to six weeks of age. The family then disperses to lead solitary lives.

DIFFICULT TIMES

Over half the hedgehogs born never see their first birthday. During the autumn, they must increase their weight eighteen times from birth to survive hibernation. Animals smaller than this do not have enough fat to get through to the following season.

Hedgehogs that do survive their first hibernation stand a fair chance of living another two or three years. However, every winter is a fresh hazard and only about 30 percent of adult hedgehogs survive from one year to the next. For the hedgehog "old age" is about five years and the maximum age is likely to be about ten years. ■

IN SINGLE FILE, *youngsters follow their mother on a nighttime foraging expedition, keeping close together.*

Illustrations Toni Hargreaves

HIPPOPOTAMUSES

For the hippo, breeding begins in the dry season so that births occur during the wet season, when food will be abundant for lactating mothers.

If an adult bull does not already have control of a receptive female, he must go out and select one—and in his quest for a mate, he exhibits a rare submissiveness. He approaches a herd of females to seek out a sexually receptive mate, but if any female rises to her feet, he hastily cowers to the ground and defecates as a gesture of submission. Once she has settled down again, he works his way quietly through the crowd, dropping to his haunches at the smallest sign of female irritability.

When he finally finds a female in estrus, it is his turn to assert authority again. Chasing her into the shallows, he subdues and mounts her, punctuating his efforts with loud wheeze-honks. When his mate raises her head from the water to breathe or tries to break away from his hold, he responds by snapping his jaws at her until, the coupling accomplished, he releases her from his immense weight.

At 32–37 weeks, gestation is short for such a massive mammal. As a female nears her birthing time, her aggression mounts. She leaves her group shortly before giving birth, seeking the seclusion of reed beds some distance away. She gives birth either in shallow water or on dry land.

Slipping hind-first into the world, the calf is far from helpless. Within a few minutes it can walk and also suckle underwater; however, it can hold its breath for little more than 30 seconds at this stage.

Precocious it may be, but the newborn is still highly vulnerable, measuring only 3 ft (91 cm) long and weighing a paltry 60 lb (27 kg). Adult males are no less a threat than lions or hyenas, and the female guards her young determinedly. The pair stays away from the herd for up to two weeks, during which period the calf suckles regularly. After this, it takes its place in a female-led nursery, where it receives a greater level of protection. Here it enjoys the company of other young hippos, with whom it wrestles and jaws in play.

Although its mother lactates for a year or so, the youngster first receives grass at around a month old, and, within five months of birth, is visiting the pastures to graze. The first year of life is the most dangerous: Some 45 percent of youngsters do not survive it. If a bull hippo makes it to sexual maturity, at 3–4 years of age, his search for a mate may drive him into deadly conflict with other, more senior bulls.

Nestling against its mother in the water (right), a young calf has her complete protection. When feeding underwater, it breaks away regularly to gasp for air.

MATING
Hippos mate either in water or on land. The cow lowers her body to encourage the bull, who then holds her down with his body weight.

BONDING
The calf soon learns to recognize its mother and never strays far from her side. It frequently rides piggyback when she enters deeper waters. The mother and young rejoin the rest of the group after a week or two.

Illustrations Evi Antoniou

L. Lee Rue/FLPA

BRINGING UP BABY

The female hippo must bring up her calf without the help of her jealous mate, who may try to drive away and even kill the youngster. For its first few weeks, the calf looks upon its mother as a source of milk, protection, and education.

The newborn calf, however, has no idea who its mother is. Given the chance, it is just as likely to trot toward any other large moving object, such as a buffalo or even a human. So it must imprint upon, or learn to recognize, its mother. The pair's virtual isolation from the group helps in this respect, and within a couple of weeks each recognizes the other.

GROWING UP

The life of a young hippo

BIRTH
When the calf is born in water, its mother supports it so it can breathe. Sometimes birth takes place on land or in shallow water.

SUCKLING
The calf suckles a few times each day, holding the nipple with the surface of its tongue. It can even suckle underwater.

Cows reach sexual maturity at 3–4 years old; they too must learn to stand their ground in a life that is seldom free from aggression or outright violence.

Pygmy hippos

Pygmy hippos may breed at any time in their rain forest home, but mating probably peaks in the dry season. A bull tracks down a cow in estros probably by sniffing out her dung piles. As a rule, cows give birth to a single calf every other year.

Gestation lasts 25–30 weeks. The pygmy hippo cow does not give birth in water, but she makes sure that the calf's sensitive skin is kept moist to prevent inflammation. She sets up her newborn in concealing vegetation by a forest stream, returning to nurse and suckle it about three times each day.

The calf suckles for several months, putting on about a pound (0.5 kg) each day, and at about three months old is ready to take solid food. It stays with its mother for about three years. When sexually mature, the young hippo must make its own way in life, in a new part of the forest. ■

FROM BIRTH TO DEATH

HIPPOPOTAMUS	PYGMY HIPPOPOTAMUS
GESTATION: 32–37 WEEKS	**GESTATION:** 25–30 WEEKS
NO. OF YOUNG: 1, VERY RARELY 2	**NO. OF YOUNG:** 1
WEIGHT AT BIRTH: 75–120 LB (35–55 KG)	**WEIGHT AT BIRTH:** 10-15 LB (4.5–7 KG)
FIRST WALKING: WITHIN MINUTES	**FIRST WALKING:** WITHIN MINUTES
WEANING: 6–8 MONTHS	**WEANING:** 6–8 MONTHS
SEXUAL MATURITY/BULL: 3–4 YEARS	**SEXUAL MATURITY/BULL:** 3–5 YEARS
SEXUAL MATURITY/FEMALE: 3–4 YEARS (BUT 4–5 YEARS IN CAPTIVITY)	**SEXUAL MATURITY/FEMALE:** 3–5 YEARS
LIFE SPAN: 40–50 YEARS	**LIFE SPAN:** UP TO 42 YEARS

HORSES

GROWING UP

The life of a young horse

AS MARES
come into estrus, fights break out between stallions for mating rights; these can be very violent.

YOUNG MARES
generally leave the herd when they become sexually mature, often lured or stolen away by young stallions. Young stallions also leave when sexually mature, forming bachelor groups until they establish harems of their own.

Equids can breed all year round, but in the wild they will all give birth when grazing conditions are at their best. In the feral mustangs of America, for example, births tend to peak from April to June. Przhevalski's horses normally produce their foals at this time of year, too. The African wild ass usually gives birth during the wet season in its native habitat, while the Asiatic wild ass usually produces its foals from late April to October. For the kiang, mating takes place in mid-September, with birth occurring the following July or August. Courtship and mating rituals among these animals depend slightly on their herd arrangement.

The dominant stallion in a herd has access to the mares in his group, although he may have to fend off many rivals. As the mares come into estrus, the stallion repeatedly checks their urine. If he judges a mare ready, mating will follow. Gestation varies: In Przhevalski's horse, it is about 335 days; domestic horses gestate for 315-387 days according to the breed, and asses for 330-360 days.

DOMINANT MALE ASSES ARE BESET BY RIVALS, WHO COMPETE FOR THE RIGHT TO MATE WITH THE RECEPTIVE FEMALES

Most equid mares leave the herd to give birth (kiang mares sometimes go off in small groups at this time), seeking a sheltered spot among rocks, trees, or tall grasses. The mare generally lies down to give birth, then stays with the foal, letting it take its first drink of her rich milk.

THE NEWBORN FOAL

In all species, the foal can stand within minutes of birth; it can walk and run soon afterward; its ears and eyes are open; it can urinate and defecate by itself; and it is able to regulate its own body temperature. This is typical of herd animals whose main form of defense is to run from predators. However, the foal is born toothless. Its incisors start to appear at about ten days old, and it has a full set of milk teeth at about six months old. Like humans, it gradually loses these, growing all its adult teeth by the time it is five or six years old.

Fritz Prenzel/Tony Stone Worldwide

This Arabian foal (right) is already displaying the elegant proportions of its breed as it canters alongside its mother.

BIRTHS
occur in a sheltered spot, usually a little way away from the remainder of the grazing herd. The foal is born with all its senses operating and can stand and follow its mother within a short time of birth.

THE MARE
and foal rejoin the herd shortly after birth. Foals quickly interact with other youngsters in the group, gamboling while mares graze peacefully nearby.

Illustration Robin Budden/Wildlife Art Agency

WHEN MOVING,
a foal stays by its mother's side. If there is danger around, the other herd members will close around the youngsters, giving them extra protection.

FROM BIRTH TO DEATH

PRZHEVALSKI'S HORSE

GESTATION: AVERAGE 335 DAYS	**SEXUAL MATURITY:** MALES 4–5 YEARS, FEMALES 3–4 YEARS
NUMBER OF YOUNG: 1	**LONGEVITY:** MAXIMUM RECORDED 34 YEARS
BREEDING: MATING AND BIRTHS OCCUR FROM APRIL TO JUNE	

AFRICAN WILD ASS

GESTATION: USUALLY 1 YEAR	**SEXUAL MATURITY:** MALES 2–3 YEARS, FEMALES 1–2 YEARS
NUMBER OF YOUNG: 1	**LONGEVITY:** MAXIMUM RECORDED IN DOMESTICATED STATE 47 YEARS
BREEDING: THROUGHOUT YEAR, BUT BIRTH GENERALLY COINCIDES WITH RAINY SEASON	

ASIATIC WILD ASS

GESTATION: AVERAGE 330 DAYS	**SEXUAL MATURITY:** MALES 2–3 YEARS, FEMALES 1–2 YEARS
NUMBER OF YOUNG: 1	**LONGEVITY:** MAXIMUM RECORDED IN DOMESTICATED STATE 35 YEARS
BREEDING: MATING OCCURS FROM MARCH TO SEPTEMBER	

Mares and their newborn foals rejoin the herd as soon as possible to benefit from the protection of numbers. Equine mares are protective, calling their young to them when alarmed and aggressively repelling intruders. Foals run alongside their mothers when the herd is on the move, but at other times they often stray a little way away, prancing and leaping with the other youngsters of the herd.

TO PROTECT HER FOAL, A MARE WILL CHARGE AT UNWELCOME VISITORS, BITING AND KICKING THEM TO DRIVE THEM AWAY

Foals start to graze at about six weeks old. Most continue to suckle for up to a year, although in domestic situations many will be weaned before this. Both sexes usually leave the herd upon reaching sexual maturity; females are usually lured away to a harem, while young males bond together until they are mature enough to form herds of their own.

BREEDING CAPABILITIES

Sexual maturity is reached at different ages according to species. African and Asiatic wild mares seem able to breed in their second year, males a year later. The kiang probably breeds a little later. Przewalski's mares become mature at three to four years old, and males a year later. Mares of domestic breeds can produce young when they are two, and stallions are sexually mature at one, but breeding is generally delayed for a while. In theory all species could produce young each year, since they come into estrus a few days after they give birth; in practice most births occur every other year. All species usually give birth to a single young; when twins are conceived, they often do not develop to term. ■

GROWTH OF A FOAL

Newborn foals have disproportionately long legs to help them run with the herd to escape danger. At one year old, they still appear leggy and slender; the muscling process takes at least another two years.

The long leg bones are not fully formed and strengthened until the animal is about two years old. Until this time, a horse cannot do long, hard work; if forced to do so, there is a high risk of damage or even deformation to the legs.

HYENAS

Youth can be a traumatic experience for a hyena. Spotted hyenas in particular have a very strange start to life. Squeezed into the world through their mother's penislike birth canal, they emerge fully furred, with their eyes open, a set of sharp teeth, and an instinctive ferocity that is unique among mammals. A new born spotted hyena will fall upon its brother or sister, grab it by the neck, and shake it, exactly as its mother will shake a gazelle fawn to kill it. The intention is equally murderous, and a quarter of all cubs starve to death because siblings bully them out of their share of milk.

The result is that only the strongest survive. But they need to be strong, for their mothers may leave

WEANING

After a few days without milk, the yearling cubs start to follow the adults as they forage and to learn how to find food for themselves.

Clem Haagner/Ardea

in SIGHT

GENETIC INTEREST

All the females in a spotted hyena clan breed if they can. In clans of brown hyenas, only one female breeds and all the adults in the clan help take care of the cubs, bringing food back to the den for them. The helping adults are usually older siblings or other close relatives, making the cubs a good "genetic investment."

GROWING UP

The life of a young hyena

COURTSHIP
Courtship can be a hazardous process for a male spotted hyena, for the female is often aggressive. Even if she accepts his advances, she may change her mind if a bigger, stronger male appears.

Illustration John Morris/Wildlife Art Agency

MATING
A successful courtship culminates in mating — a complicated process in which the male has to probe right underneath the female to penetrate her fully retracted sexual organs.

SUCKLING
Spotted hyenas raise their cubs communally in a clan den, but each mother suckles her own cubs. The cubs may feed for over an hour at a time.

FROM BIRTH TO DEATH

SPOTTED HYENA
GESTATION: 110 DAYS
LITTER SIZE: 1–2
BREEDING: NONSEASONAL
WEIGHT AT BIRTH: 3.5 LB (1.5 KG)
EYES OPEN: AT BIRTH
WEANING: 12–16 MONTHS
HUNTING: 18 MONTHS
SEXUAL MATURITY: 2 YEARS FOR MALES, 3 YEARS FOR FEMALES
LONGEVITY: 25 YEARS IN WILD, 41 YEARS IN CAPTIVITY

BROWN HYENA
GESTATION: 90 DAYS
LITTER SIZE: 2–5
BREEDING: NONSEASONAL
WEIGHT AT BIRTH: 1.5 LB (770 G)
EYES OPEN: 8 DAYS
WEANING: 6 MONTHS
FORAGING: 14 MONTHS
SEXUAL MATURITY: 2–3 YEARS
LONGEVITY: 24 YEARS IN CAPTIVITY

them for days at a time to go hunting. When the females return they call the cubs out of the den—an abandoned aardvark burrow or similar tunnel system—and suckle them, often for an hour or more at a time. Spotted hyena adults never bring solid food to their young, so the cubs are fed entirely on milk for at least nine months.

Eventually the milk supply dries up, to the displeasure of the young hyenas, who throw tantrums and may even bite at their mothers. Eventually they accept the situation and start tagging along on the hunt, but they can only hunt effectively on their own at the age of about eighteen months. Meanwhile they learn scent marking and social skills through play, and at puberty the young males leave the clan to try their luck elsewhere.

Young females usually stay within the clan and solicit the attentions of roving males. Being smaller and less aggressive, a male has to work hard at courtship, and he will often grovel before a female to appease her. After some days of this she may accept him, but she may switch her attention to another male of higher rank. Such status is closely associated with strength and aggression, and she instinctively looks for these qualities in the animal that will sire her cubs. ■

JACKALS

Jackals form pair bonds that may last for life. A pair may split up after their pups disperse, or at least forage apart, but the bond is normally renewed for the next breeding season. Such fidelity is normal in wild canids, and the random promiscuity of many domestic dogs is quite untypical of dogs in general.

Jackal fidelity is not quite what it seems, though. Each animal is careful to repel any rivals that might abduct its partner, for there is no system of canine ethics that prevents promiscuity. Simien jackal females in particular are always ready to accept the advances of other males, and they may even mate with a brother of their regular partner. Of the matings recorded among wild Simien jackals, only about a third were between true pairs; the others were all in some sense illicit. This is a problem for the male, since he invests a lot of time and energy rearing his mate's pups. From a genetic point of view, if he is not actually their father or uncle his time is wasted. So he does all he can to stop his partner consorting with other males, especially unrelated males, while she is in heat.

A female jackal can afford to be more relaxed about her partner's activities, since she never invests time and energy in a family that is not her own. On the other hand she may get very repressive about the behavior of the other young adults in a family group, because if they raise families of their own she will lose their vital services as den "helpers." Among black-backed jackals in particular, the survival chances of the pups seem to be directly linked to the number of adults in the group, who bring them food, play with them, groom them, and defend them from predators.

in SIGHT

MOB TACTICS

Young jackal pups are very vulnerable. Their most powerful enemy is the leopard—which also preys on adult jackals—but most of the pups that die violently are probably carried off by birds of prey, such as the mighty martial eagle. In Africa spotted hyenas are also a serious threat.

A single jackal is no match for a leopard or a hyena, but a powerful instinct to defend the pups encourages jackals to gang up and harass any intruders. If a hyena comes too close an adult jackal may bark a warning to the pups so they dive for cover, and then start biting at the hyena's hind legs, dodging nimbly to avoid its bone-crunching jaws. This bold defense encourages other jackals to join in the skirmish, and by taking turns to nip at the hyena they force it to turn back and forth until it gives up and beats a retreat.

GROWING UP

The life of a black-backed jackal

COURTSHIP
involves a lot of licking and nuzzling (below). Many jackals stay with the same mate year after year, as the close bond improves their success rate when hunting.

THE PUPS
greet a returning adult with a lively begging routine (below); an adult is often surrounded by pups, all wagging their tails and leaping up to lick its face.

Breeding is timed so that whelping takes place when there is enough food to sustain the pregnant mother; she will need to produce milk and, later, food for the pups without foraging too far afield. A den may be a rock crevice, an old aardvark run, or a cavity dug into a termite mound. The same den is often used for several years, but at the slightest disturbance the family will move on.

HELPLESS PUPS

The pups—usually two to six per litter—are born blind and helpless in the den after a gestation of about two months, and their mother stays with them for 90 percent of the time for the first three weeks. Golden jackal pups begin exploring outside the den after about two weeks, and at about a month old they start taking solid food regurgitated by adults. By this time their mother will have begun leaving the den area for part of the day to forage, and if there are no adult helpers the pups may be left alone for up to 30 percent of the time, increasing their vulnerability to predators. Black-backed pups may be left for up to 60 percent of the time, which may explain why adult "child-minders" are so important to their survival.

Clem Haagner/Ardea

Singing for their supper; a trio of pups show their impatience as they await the next meal (above).

MATING
(above) is timed so that births occur in times of plenty, particularly in regions where there are seasonal shortages of food.

SUCKLING
continues for about four months. In the early stages of the cubs' development, the female rarely leaves their side (below).

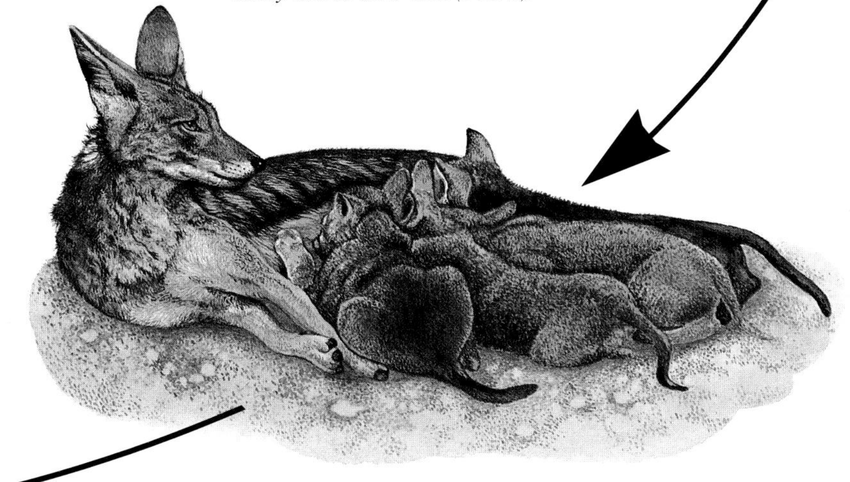

In time, the pups begin foraging for insects near the den site, venturing farther each week. By the time they are fully weaned at about four months old they can follow their parents on foraging trips and often sleep in the open. Their play routines develop a serious edge as they compete for dominance and learn how to hunt, and by about six months a pup can often catch its own prey. It still has a lot to learn, though—about where and how to find food, how to deal with large prey, and how to react to other jackals—and it may be another two months before a young jackal is truly self-sufficient. ■

FROM BIRTH TO DEATH

GOLDEN JACKAL

BREEDING: TIMED SO THAT BIRTHS OCCUR WHEN FOOD IS ABUNDANT
GESTATION: 63 DAYS
LITTER SIZE: 1–9, AVERAGE 2–4
EYES OPEN: 10 DAYS
FIRST LEAVE DEN: 2 WEEKS
FIRST SOLID FOOD: 1–2 MONTHS
WEANING COMPLETE: 4 MONTHS
SEXUAL MATURITY: 11 MONTHS
LONGEVITY: 10 YEARS OR MORE

Illustrations Joanne Cowne

JAGUARS

Like many animals of the humid tropics, the jaguar does not tie its breeding behavior to a particular season. Female jaguars are physically capable of breeding in any month, and because their fertile habitat offers adequate food and shelter all year round, the cats can raise their young at any time of the year. Nevertheless, there is evidence that births reach a peak during certain periods, at least toward the geographical extremes of the jaguar's range. Mating seems to be most prevalent in Paraguay from August to September, when the sound of jaguars calling is heard much more frequently. Since gestation lasts about three months, the subsequent births peak in November and December. In Mexico, most mating takes place in spring, with the highest number of births recorded from July to September.

When a female jaguar is approaching readiness to mate, her scent marks, her vocalizations, and, sometimes, her wandering habits may attract several males from the vicinity. As they pursue her, perhaps for a period of several days, rivalry for the female's attention leads to bickering, threats, and sometimes fighting between the males. Usually, though, weaker males quickly give way to stronger individuals, and before long one male succeeds in driving off the others. However, it might still take a few more days before the female is ready and willing to mate with him.

After mating, the male jaguar seldom takes any further part in the proceedings and soon returns to his patch. The female locates a suitable refuge for her den—perhaps in a cave or canyon, under a riverbank or uprooted tree, in a dense thicket, or even in an abandoned building. There she gives birth to a litter of up to four cubs, though twins are the norm.

Despite their salt-and-pepper appearance (right), these cubs are in fact twins. In cases where one of the parents is melanistic, it is common for one cub to be black and the other spotted.

WHEN A FEMALE *is ready to mate, she allows a pursuing male to mount (right). According to some reports, noisy calls are common during mating and the two partners may even exchange a few blows.*

AT 18 MONTHS *or so, a young jaguar has adult coloring and is fast approaching adult size (below). It will continue to hunt in its mother's home range for several months more before striking out on its own.*

AT A MONTH OLD, *jaguar cubs can see and are growing fast, but it will still be a few weeks before they start to explore the surroundings of the den (right).*

Rod Williams/Bruce Coleman Ltd.

The young, which are blind at birth and about 16 in (40 cm) long, have long buff-colored fur dotted with large, indistinct spots.

At first, the mother stays permanently in the den, guarding her vulnerable offspring. Any disturbance may lead her to abandon the den, carrying the offspring in her teeth to a new shelter. But after a few days she starts going out to feed. Some cubs open their eyes as early as the third day, but most take several days more. After about six weeks or so, the cubs begin to venture outside the den and may accompany their mother while she hunts, although while she is stalking they hide in dense cover. By the time they start to eat solid food provided by their parent—at about ten weeks—they have increased in weight about five fold since birth.

OVER THEIR FIRST TWO YEARS, JAGUAR CUBS LEARN ALL THEY NEED TO KNOW FROM THEIR MOTHER

GROWING UP

The life of a young jaguar

THE NORMAL *jaguar litter is two cubs, although as many as four may be born. Small and sightless at birth, they can do little but take in milk from their mother for the first few days (above).*

LOOK AND LEARN

Suckling of the young does not fully end until about five or six months, but soon after this the young take on the body coloration of the adults. They learn the rudiments of hunting from trial and error and from observation of the adult on the prowl. This includes not just what is good to eat, but also how to stalk, overpower, and kill prey.

A mother jaguar allows the young to stay with her for about two years, by which time they have grown considerably and are fully able to fend for themselves. Within another year, most offspring have reached adult size and are ready to breed, although young males may have to wait a while before they can successfully compete with other males for mating partners. Female jaguars appear to be physically capable of breeding in successive years, but in the wild breeding is more likely to take place every other year. ■

FROM BIRTH TO DEATH

THE JAGUAR

BREEDING: NONSEASONAL IN THE TROPICS, ALTHOUGH DISTINCT BIRTH PEAKS OCCUR IN SOME AREAS
GESTATION: 90–105 DAYS
LITTER SIZE: 1–4
WEIGHT AT BIRTH: 1.5–2 LB (700–900 G)
EYES OPEN: 3–13 DAYS
FIRST SOLID FOOD: AT ABOUT 70 DAYS
WEANING: 5–6 MONTHS
ADULT COLORATION: 7 MONTHS
SEXUAL MATURITY: 2–4 YEARS
LONGEVITY: UP TO 22 YEARS IN CAPTIVITY; NOT KNOWN IN WILD

Color illustrations Nick Pike/Wildlife Art Agency

KANGAROOS

The basis of the kangaroo social group is the close relationship between the female and her young. They stay together in small groups, long after the young have been weaned from their mothers, and form the core of the mob. Kangaroos do not usually form permanent breeding pairs.

BEFORE A FIGHT, *males stand upright and approach each other with a stiff-legged walk. They also engage in a grooming display.*

PUNCH-UPS

The bucks or male kangaroos of the mob have a hierarchy that is based on strength, and therefore on size. From time to time bucks will confront each other in trials of strength to establish their position, usually in competition for females, and a boxing match will ensue. Standing on their hind legs, they hit out at each other with their forearms. They will also kick out with their hind legs, aiming at their opponent's belly while resting on their tail.

THE LARGEST MALE IS USUALLY THE MOST SUCCESSFUL FIGHTER AND SO FATHERS THE MOST OFFSPRING

Having fought off the competition, the dominant male courts each receptive female for anything from a few hours to two to three days, following her around and sniffing her. Mating eventually takes place and may be brief or, in the case of some gray kangaroos, may take over an hour.

After conception, the red kangaroo's developing

AMAZING FACTS

LETHAL WEAPON

The massive hind legs and feet of the kangaroo, with their sharp claws on the fourth and fifth toes, make impressive weapons for kicking. In fact, the kangaroo's kick is so powerful that it can disembowel a man or a dog with one blow.

In practice, however, kangaroos have few enemies in the wild and, as a result, are relatively docile animals. Kicking is mainly restricted to adult males, who compete with one another in trials of strength for dominance of the females. Powerful kicks are aimed at the opponent's belly, but no real injury is caused; this is because the skin on the buck's stomach is especially tough and does not tear.

Ford Kristo/Planet Earth Pictures

LOCKING FOREARMS, *the males attempt to knock their opponents over backward, pushing with their forepaws and kicking out with their hind feet.*

Illustrations John Morris/Wildlife Art Agency

FROM BIRTH TO DEATH

RED KANGAROO	GRAY KANGAROO
GESTATION: 33 DAYS	**GESTATION:** 37 DAYS
LITTER SIZE: USUALLY 1	**LITTER SIZE:** 1
BREEDING: MATING OCCURS AT ANY TIME OF YEAR	**BREEDING:** SEASONAL; BETWEEN SPRING AND EARLY SUMMER
WEIGHT AT BIRTH: LESS THAN 0.03 OZ (1 G)	**WEIGHT AT BIRTH:** LESS THAN 0.03 OZ (1 G)
MOBILITY: 190 DAYS	**MOBILITY:** 190 DAYS
LEAVES POUCH: 235 DAYS	**LEAVES POUCH:** 300 DAYS
WEANING: 1 YEAR	**WEANING:** 18 MONTHS
SEXUAL MATURITY: BETWEEN 15 MONTHS AND 2 YEARS	**SEXUAL MATURITY:** BETWEEN 15 MONTHS AND 2 YEARS
LONGEVITY: 12–18 YEARS IN THE WILD; UP TO 28 IN CAPTIVITY	**LONGEVITY:** UP TO 18 YEARS IN THE WILD

young stays in the womb for just 33 days. The gestation period is 37 days for the gray kangaroo, 30 days for the red-necked wallaby, and only 27 days for the quokka. At the end of this period, the pregnant female cleans her pouch by licking the inside. She then sits in the birth position, stretching her tail and hind legs forward, until the tiny pink baby, or joey, appears from the birth opening.

THE INCREDIBLE JOURNEY

The way in which marsupial young are born and how they manage to find their way to their mother's pouch makes an amazing story. The aborigines and early explorers thought that the baby was actually born inside the pouch but then, in 1830, Alexander Collie first described the birth of the baby and its incredible journey to the pouch unaided.

Not everyone believed him, and various alternative theories were put forward, including the theory that the mother lifted the baby to the pouch using her forepaws or lips. It was not until 1923 that

UNTIL RECENTLY, THE BIRTH AND DEVELOPMENT OF MARSUPIAL YOUNG HAD LONG BEEN A MYSTERY TO MAN

Collie's description was finally accepted, and in 1959-1960 the birth of a kangaroo was actually filmed at Adelaide University, setting the controversy to rest once and for all.

Yet, even now, the experts are not certain how the tiny baby knows how to find its way to the teat in its mother's pouch. Possibly it has some perception of gravity that tells it which way to climb and, once it reaches the pouch, perhaps it can locate the teat by smell. The journey is quite remarkable, and all the more so because the baby receives no help from its mother.

The newborn red kangaroo is only 0.75 inch

(2 centimeters) long and weighs less than 0.03 ounce (under 1 gram). In some of the smaller wallabies, the newborn weighs only a third as much. Blind, hairless, and only partially formed, the baby somehow climbs up the mother's fur, pulling itself with its forefeet, which, at this stage, are larger than the hind legs. Within three minutes it has reached the pouch and its mouth is firmly attached

ABOUT THE SIZE OF A BEAN, THE NEWBORN KANGAROO OR JOEY STRUGGLES TO ITS MOTHER'S POUCH UNAIDED

to one of the four teats inside. The teat swells in its mouth, acting as an anchor as well as a source of food. Here the young joey will remain until it has grown large enough to leave the pouch.

Sometimes twins are born, but usually one of the two does not survive, probably because there is not enough room in the pouch when they grow.

CONTINUOUS CYCLE

In some species, the females are able to mate again immediately after giving birth. The fertilized egg develops into a bundle of cells called a blastocyst (BLAS-toh-sist), which lies dormant in the womb for a period that is known as diapause. A few weeks before the joey is due to leave the pouch, the blastocyst begins to develop into an embryo, which will be born as soon as the pouch is vacated.

The cycle thus repeats itself so that the female is in a state of continuous breeding. At any time she

AMAZING FACTS

DOUBLE TROUBLE

At any one time, a female kangaroo may be suckling two young—an older joey at her feet, and a younger one in the pouch. Two of her four teats are always in use, and each provides a different kind of milk for the different needs of the youngsters.

The teat that feeds the young in the pouch provides milk that is high in carbohydrates and low in fats, but its composition changes as the joey develops, increasing in fat and protein and decreasing in sugars. The teat from which the older joey feeds is elongated, to allow it to suckle from outside the pouch. It supplies milk that is very rich in fats, which the youngster needs because it is burning up much more energy moving around.

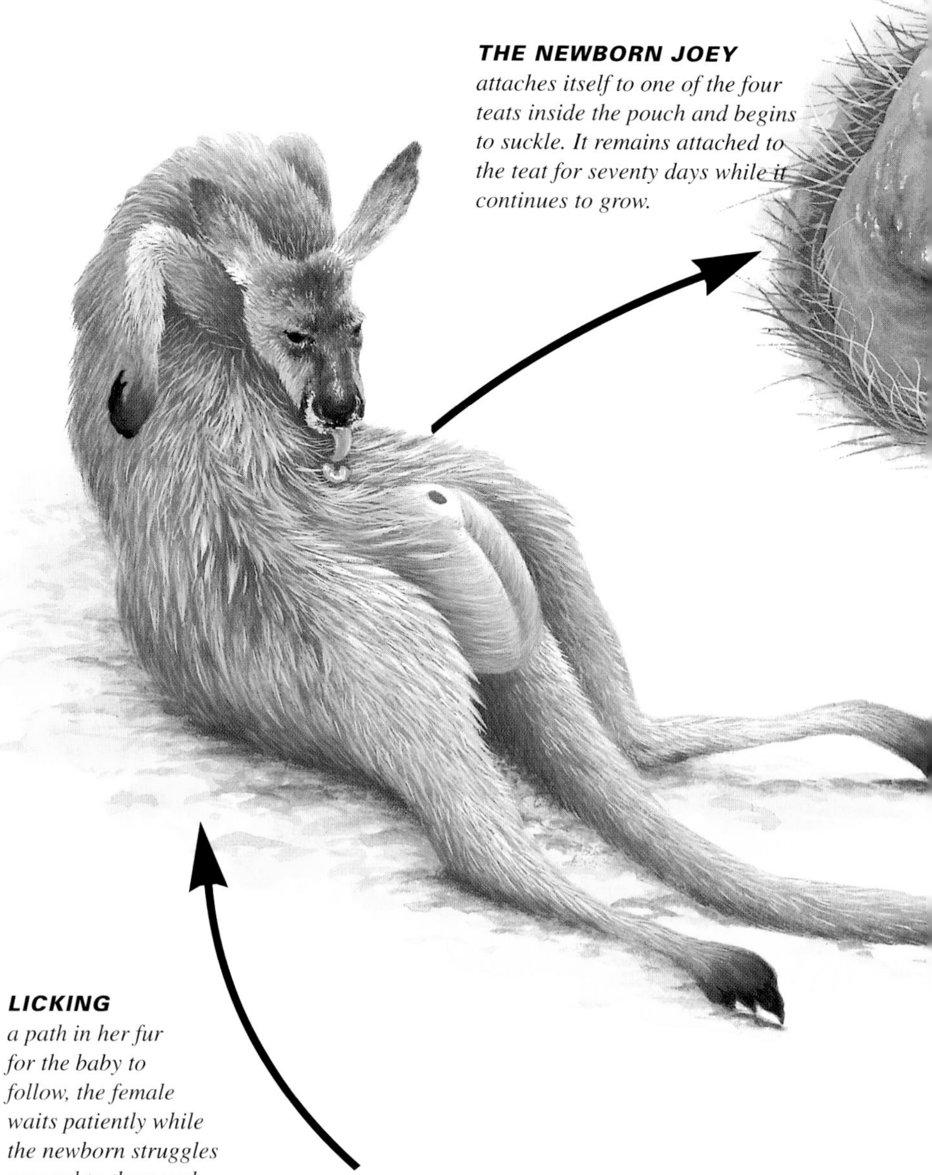

THE NEWBORN JOEY *attaches itself to one of the four teats inside the pouch and begins to suckle. It remains attached to the teat for seventy days while it continues to grow.*

LICKING *a path in her fur for the baby to follow, the female waits patiently while the newborn struggles upward to the pouch.*

Illustrations John Morris/ Wildlife Art Agency

GROWING UP

The life of a young red kangaroo

IN THE POUCH
the joey continues to suckle its mother's milk. During this time, the female licks the inside of the pouch and the joey clean several times a day. At about six months old, the joey starts to leave the pouch for a few minutes at a time.

may have a joey in her pouch, an older joey outside the pouch that may still be taking milk, and a fertilized egg in her womb waiting to develop.

Some species, such as the red kangaroo, are able to mate and give birth at any time of year. They are known as opportunistic breeders. The western gray kangaroo is a seasonal breeder because it only mates to give birth in the summer. Diapause does not feature in its breeding; the female only mates a few weeks before the joey is due to leave the pouch, so the fertilized egg develops in time to be born when the pouch is empty.

YOUNG ADULTS

The young stay with their mothers until they are sexually mature—less than a year for the smaller species, but fifteen months to two years for the larger kangaroos. During this time they begin to find their own food and learn about social relationships in the mob. Eventually the young males form their own groups, while the young females remain with their mothers. Although males and females are the same size when they leave the pouch, the males rapidly outgrow the females and at two years old male red kangaroos are twice as big as the females.

During their lifetime, kangaroos must face the threat of starvation during drought and predation by their enemies—the dingo, the red fox, and the wedge-tailed eagle. Many are killed by culling and by collisions with motor vehicles. If they survive these threats, red kangaroos may live for 12 to 18 years in the wild: One kangaroo lived for 28 years in captivity. Smaller species have shorter life spans. ■

AT ONE YEAR OLD,
the young joey leaves its mother's pouch for good when the female prevents it from jumping back in. About this time the joey is weaned, but it stays close to its mother for a considerable time afterward.

JOEY ACROBATICS

A joey climbing back into the pouch is aided by its mother. Making gentle clucking sounds, she bends her body near the ground as low as she can and spreads her forelegs. If the joey is young and inexperienced, she bends her body lower by leaning backward on her hind legs. The joey jumps back in headfirst, reaching up with its forepaws and then diving in. Once inside, it turns a full somersault, bringing its body around so that its head pokes from the pouch opening.

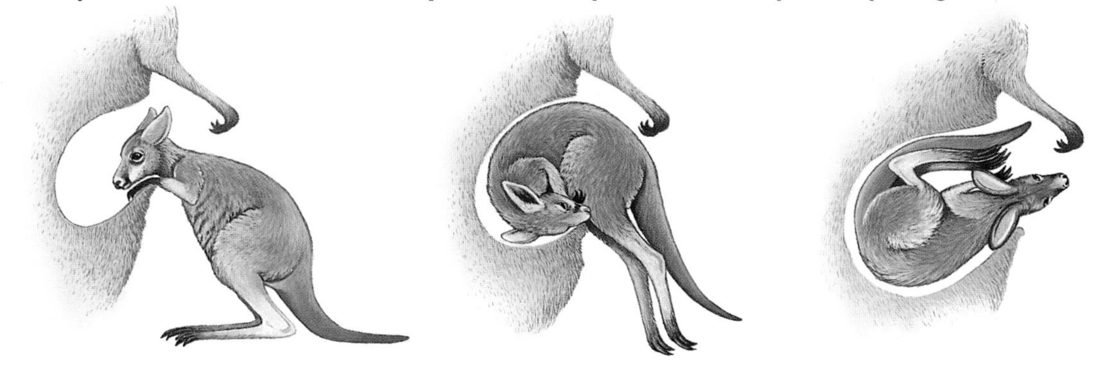

Illustrations Kim Thompson

KOALAS

Mating is a cursory, sometimes violent affair for a koala, usually taking less than two minutes. Pregnancy lasts a mere thirty-five days, partly because the fetus within the uterus is not "plugged in" to its mother's system in the same way as an unborn placental mammal. A koala fetus—unlike that of many marsupials—does have a connection with the uterine wall that permits some nutrients and waste products to pass to and fro, but the system does not permit extended development within the uterus, for one very good reason.

Any young mammal is a mixture of genetic material derived from two unrelated individuals: its mother and father. This means that the unborn young contains material that is alien to the mother's system. Under normal circumstances such foreign matter would be rejected by her body—just as a transplanted kidney is rejected unless special drugs are used—but placental mammals have evolved a way of suppressing this reaction. The marsupials have not, and as a result the hapless infant is expelled into the world at a very tender age indeed.

Scrap of Life

Tiny, semitransparent, and glistening wet, weighing a fraction of an ounce, a newborn koala is little more than an embryo set adrift in a hostile environment. Driven by what is probably the only instinct programmed into its barely formed brain, this scrap of life crawls through its mother's fur toward the nipple within her marsupial pouch. Luckily for the koala the pouch opens to the rear, so the journey is not as long and arduous as that of a newborn kangaroo, but it is a monumental achievement. Once within the pouch it locates one of two nipples and sucks it into its mouth; the end of the nipple then enlarges to lock the tiny creature to its life support system, and its ordeal is over. In effect it has returned to the womb, but instead of receiving its nutrients through an umbilical cord, it sucks them into its stomach through its mother's nipple.

For some weeks the infant koala—or "joey"—is literally inseparable from its mother, but eventually its jaw muscles develop to the point where it can

MATING
If the female is remotely willing, the male mounts her without ceremony, clinging to the scruff of her neck with his teeth.

PIGGYBACK
At about eight months, the young koala leaves the pouch completely, riding instead on its mother's back.

PAP FEEDING
In preparation for its solid diet, the young koala feeds on pap expelled from its mother's anus. This semidigested liquid provides the youngster with the digestive bacteria it will need when it starts to feed itself.

Jean-Paul Ferrero/Ardea

At about six months old the young koala will make occasional forays from its mother's pouch (left).

GROWING UP

The life of a young koala

GIVING BIRTH
The female usually gives birth between December and April, depending on the region. The tiny newborn makes its way through its mother's fur toward her nipple or pouch.

POUCH FEEDER
The tiny baby remains firmly attached to its mother's nipple for thirteen weeks. Even when it releases its hold, it will continue feeding on milk for three more months.

FROM BIRTH TO DEATH

KOALA	TREE KANGAROO
GESTATION: 35 DAYS	**GESTATION:** 32 DAYS
LITTER SIZE: 1, OCCASIONALLY 2	**LITTER SIZE:** 1, OCCASIONALLY 2
BREEDING: MIDSUMMER	**BREEDING:** NONSEASONAL
WEIGHT AT BIRTH: 0.013 OZ–0.018 OZ (0.37 G–0.51 G)	**WEIGHT AT BIRTH:** ABOUT 0.018 OZ (0.51 G)
LEAVES POUCH: 7–8 MONTHS	**LEAVES POUCH:** 10 MONTHS
WEANING: 11–12 MONTHS	**WEANING:** 14–15 MONTHS
SEXUAL MATURITY: 2 YEARS (FEMALE)	**SEXUAL MATURITY:** ABOUT 2 YEARS
LONGEVITY: ABOUT 10 YEARS	**LONGEVITY:** UNKNOWN IN WILD; UP TO 20 YEARS IN CAPTIVITY

open its mouth and release the nipple. Even so, it remains in the pouch for at least five months, feeding exclusively upon milk. At six months it is fully furred, alert, and making occasional excursions into the branches alongside its mother—but it rarely stays out for long. Gradually it becomes bolder, only returning to the pouch to sleep, and at seven to eight months it abandons the pouch entirely in favor of its mother's back.

It is during this phase of its life that the joey begins to take solid food—not from the trees it lives upon, but from its mother. For some six weeks its milk diet is supplemented by a semidigested pap of eucalypt foliage expelled from its mother's anus. The apparent health risk this might involve is obviously nullified by some mechanism within the mother's digestive system, and her baby gets the benefit of her digestive bacteria, still working away at the pap when the joey eats it. The bacteria are carried to the young koala's cecum where they establish a new colony, enabling their host to digest raw eucalypt foliage when it starts browsing for itself at nine months or so.

THE YOUNG KOALA STAYS CLOSE TO ITS MOTHER FOR A FEW MONTHS AFTER BECOMING INDEPENDENT

INDEPENDENT AND MATURE

Once it starts feeding on leaves, the joey puts on weight rapidly, and at eleven to twelve months it is fully weaned and technically independent.

Female koalas are sexually mature at two years and may start breeding almost immediately, producing a single baby each year in midsummer (December to April). Males mature later and rarely mate before they are four years old, when they are big enough to compete with other males for access to females. Meanwhile they live alone, taking care to avoid the big males and awaiting their opportunity to claim territories of their own. ■

Illustrations Andie Peck/Wildlife Art Agency

LEMURS

Male lemurs tend to be most active just before the breeding season starts. This is when male ring-tailed lemurs swap troops, lured perhaps by the prospect of mating with the females from "next door." Some Verreaux's sifaka males transfer between groups, apparently according to their social status within the group. Even solitary lemurs, such as aye-ayes, are often seen in companionable couples during this period.

Courtship takes place in the buildup to the breeding period and involves the male and female lemurs, in this case ruffed lemurs, grooming each other.

PLAY TIME

Indris mark the arrival of the breeding season in January with bouts of friendly playing. Stretching their arms out in a formal invitation, they wrestle, gently twisting their bodies around each other for periods of up to fifteen minutes at a time. While mouse lemurs give birth to two litters of up to four babies each during their breeding season from September to March, indris reproduce much more slowly. Indris do not become sexually mature until they are three years old, and females give birth only

BABY LEMURS

Indris and sifakas are caring parents, both males and females sharing the task of raising the family. Infants are passed from one family member to another to be groomed and played with. In other lemur families, it is usually the females that raise the young. Most of the "typical lemur" mothers allow other female members of their troop to touch a newborn, but they are reluctant to allow males the same access.

Konrad Withe/Bruce Coleman Ltd.

Ruffed lemur females often leave their young with nonbreeding females and males while foraging, while in other lemur species mothers only allow females access to their babies.

GROWING UP

The life of a young lemur

Lemur mating seasons vary according to the species. For sporting lemurs, the mating season is from May to August, and for ring-tailed lemurs, from about April to June.

Ruffed lemurs usually give birth to twins. During the postnatal period, the mother parks them on a branch or in a nest while she forages.

All pictures John Cox/Wildlife Art Agency

once every two to three years.

The period of gestation is long compared to that of nonprimate mammals of a similar size, ranging from 162 days in the indri down to 63 days for the mouse lemur. Female Verreaux's sifakas give birth in June and July after a 160-day gestation period, while the gestation period for ring-tailed lemurs is 136 days. Twins are sometimes born, although one baby is normal. Mouse lemurs and dwarf lemurs

FROM BIRTH TO DEATH

RUFFED LEMUR
GESTATION: 102 DAYS
INDEPENDENCE: 5–6 MONTHS
FULLY GROWN: 1 YEAR
SEXUAL MATURITY: FEMALES, 20 MONTHS; MALES, UP TO 3 YEARS
LONGEVITY: 19 YEARS IN CAPTIVITY

SPORTIVE LEMUR
GESTATION: 135 DAYS
INDEPENDENCE: ABOUT 5 MONTHS
FULLY GROWN: 10–12 MONTHS
SEXUAL MATURITY: 18 MONTHS
LONGEVITY: 15 YEARS IN CAPTIVITY

INDRI
GESTATION: 162 DAYS
INDEPENDENCE: 8–12 MONTHS
FULLY GROWN: 2 YEARS
SEXUAL MATURITY: 3 YEARS
LONGEVITY: OVER 20 YEARS IN WILD, IF PROTECTED FROM HUNTERS

RING-TAILED LEMUR
GESTATION: 136 DAYS
INDEPENDENCE: 5 MONTHS
FULLY GROWN: 12 MONTHS
SEXUAL MATURITY: 24–30 MONTHS
LONGEVITY: 15–18 YEARS IN CAPTIVITY, BUT PROBABLY MUCH LESS IN THE WILD

average two or three infants, and the variegated lemur gives birth to up to five.

Lemurs tend to give birth around the same time, often synchronized to within 10 days of one another so that they can wean their young just as the first buds of spring burst into leaf. This gives the youngsters a chance to grow before the onset of winter.

Dwarf and mouse lemur babies are born inside a hollow tree or in a nest made of leaves. They are born naked and undeveloped and are the only lemurs whose eyes are not open at birth. Most of them do not cling to their mother's fur, but are carried around in

BABY-SWAPPING SESSIONS ARE COMMON AMONG RING-TAILED LEMURS. FEMALES SEEM INDIFFERENT TO WHICH BABY THEY ARE SUCKLING

her mouth—although they can climb and grip branches within a few hours of birth. Most infants cling to the mother's belly for the first few weeks of life, then switch to riding on her back. It may be several months before they can follow the troop independently, and baby indris may continue to be carried for up to five months. The mouse lemur has the fastest development of any primate. It is independent of its mother after four months, and fully mature at seven to eight months. Even so, this is a longer period of maternal care than in any nonprimate mammal of a comparable size.

Although young lemurs often taste leaves and fruit at a young age, they continue to suckle for as long as they are carried. Sifaka infants are often carried up to the age of six or seven months, when their weight prevents the mother from leaping safely across broad gaps in the forest canopy. ■

LEOPARDS

Toni Angermayer/Photo Researchers/OSF

Hidden from predators in a secluded den in a cave, hollow tree, or thicket is a litter of blind, helpless, newborn leopard cubs. Their long, matted fur is densely covered with spots. The size of a litter ranges from one to six, though it is usually between two and four—but only half of these are likely to survive the first few dangerous months of life.

Cubs take their first steps at about thirteen days and at four weeks can walk quickly and even climb, but they will be six to eight weeks old before they venture out of the safety of their den—and then only under the strict supervision of their mother.

BORN IN A SECLUDED DEN, THE BLIND AND HELPLESS LEOPARD CUBS HAVE A POOR CHANCE OF SURVIVAL

ALMOST GROWN UP, *this cub has left its mother and is practically old enough to mate.*

Young cubs are very playful, stalking and pouncing on grasshoppers or chasing each others' tails. Their mother will give a gentle call that sounds like *aaoui* if she approves of their behavior, but if she's annoyed she will hiss or thump her tail.

At three months the cubs are weaned and start to eat meat caught by their mother, practicing the killing bite common to all cats; and after a few more months they start to catch their own food. Soon they will begin to spend some time on their own.

Clouded leopard cubs (below) are quite active by the time they are five weeks old. Male cubs seem to develop faster than females.

Tom Brakefield

PLAYING IN THE TREES. *After they reach the age of eleven months, cubs will spend less time socializing and will usually rest and sleep alone.*

Even after the young leopards have left home and established their own home ranges—when they are about two years old—they will often stay in contact with their mothers for a short period of time, licking each other's faces and rubbing their bodies together when they meet.

A DANGEROUS TIME

This early stage of independence is dangerous: The cubs may starve to death because their hunting skills aren't yet fully developed. They are also at risk of being killed by other animals or by man.

Maturity comes at two and a half or three years. When a female is in heat (or estrus), she will advertise the fact by scent marking. A male soon notices

GROWING UP

The life of a young leopard

THREE-DAY-OLD *cubs make a humming sound when nursing. They are gaining about 1.2 ounces (34 grams) a day in weight.*

FROM BIRTH TO DEATH

LEOPARD
GESTATION: 90–112 DAYS
LITTER SIZE: 1–6
WEIGHT AT BIRTH: 15–20 oz (430–570 g)
EYES OPEN: 6–10 DAYS
FIRST WALKING: 13 DAYS
INDEPENDENCE: 18–24 MONTHS
SEXUAL MATURITY: 30–36 MONTHS
LONGEVITY IN WILD: 12 YEARS (20 IN CAPTIVITY)

SNOW LEOPARD
GESTATION: 93–110 DAYS
LITTER SIZE: 1–4
WEIGHT AT BIRTH: 10.5–25 oz (280–700 g)
EYES OPEN: 7–9 DAYS
FIRST WALKING: NOT KNOWN
INDEPENDENCE: ABOUT 1 YEAR
SEXUAL MATURITY: 32 MONTHS
LONGEVITY IN WILD: NOT KNOWN (17 YEARS IN CAPTIVITY)

CLOUDED LEOPARD
GESTATION: 86–92 DAYS
LITTER SIZE: 1–5
WEIGHT AT BIRTH: 5 oz (140–150 g)
EYES OPEN: 2–11 DAYS
FIRST WALKING: 19–20 DAYS
INDEPENDENCE: ABOUT 9 MONTHS
SEXUAL MATURITY: 25–30 MONTHS
LONGEVITY IN WILD: NOT KNOWN (15 YEARS IN CAPTIVITY)

Illustrations Priscilla Barrett/Wildlife Art Agency

HELD FIRMLY *by the scruff of its neck, this cub is being moved to a new shelter by its mother. This happens frequently in the first few weeks of a leopard's life.*

STICKING CLOSE *to mother. For six to eight weeks, the cubs are kept well hidden from the outside world in a den or other secluded place.*

her smell and lets out throaty calls. The female will appear, then hiss and strike at him with her paws, then rub cheeks with him as his scent marks a tree.

MATING

They are then ready to mate, which they will do several times over the next few days. When mating, the male growls and grasps the skin on the back of the female's neck, and when they are finished she turns and swats him with her paw. The female will mate again when the cubs she has conceived leave home, and the cycle starts again.

Although lifespans of 20 years have been recorded for a captive leopard, the longest a leopard has been known to live in the wild is 12 years. ■

OUT OF ACTION

COMMON DISEASES

Like all other living things, leopards can suffer from various diseases.

- **Anthrax, which causes fever and a swelling of the throat, can be fatal.**
- **Cases of rabies, which leads to convulsions and paralysis, have been reported.**
- **Leopards often play host to various internal parasites such as tapeworm, hookworm, or roundworm.**
- **Viral infections can also make leopards sick.**

LIONS

Lions usually become sexually mature between three and four years of age, although they may not finish growing until they are six years old.

Females come into heat more than once a year at irregular intervals, for three to five days (or more) each time. In some areas, however, most or all of the females in a pride tend to give birth at about the same time—which often coincides with the time when their prey are rearing young.

Males approach receptive females after detecting a distinctive scent in their urine. While he is courting her, a male will remain close to a female for several days on end. She may tease the male, rolling over on her back and slapping at him playfully with one of her great paws, then running off, returning to rub noses, and bounding away again.

Mating itself lasts about a minute and takes place frequently. A pair may mate every twenty minutes or so, day and night, for as long as five days. During the time she is in heat, a female may mate with several of the pride males. The male of the mating pair licks the female frequently on the shoulder, neck, or back and gently bites her neck, to which she responds by grunting gently.

MATING
There is little real aggression during mating. Snarling, roaring, or growling seem to be part of the ritual.

YOUNG BLOOD
While learning hunting skills, older cubs may be lucky and catch themselves a young gazelle or smaller prey.

LIFE BEGINS

After an average gestation period of 110 days, the cubs are born, weighing a mere 2–4 lb (1–2 kg) each. When their eyes open, within two weeks, they are blue-gray; they do not change to the distinctive amber color until the cubs are two to three months old.

At birth, they have soft, woolly, grayish yellow fur, covered in pale spots. Their coats become sleeker and lose their spots after three to five months, though the cubs may not lose the spots on their sides and legs until they are fully grown.

The cubs' first teeth appear when they are about three weeks old. At this age, they can walk reasonably well, but before then, their mother may need to move them from one hiding place to another if she is suspicious or disturbed. She will gently pick up each cub in her great mouth by the scruff of its neck and carry it, the cub hanging limply with its legs drawn up to its chin. Small cubs are highly vulnerable to predators, such as jackals, leopards, and hyenas—and strange male lions. When their mother leaves to hunt, they spend most of their time hiding silently among rocks or concealed in vegetation. The lioness

Tony Stone Worldwide

A young cub (right) chews on bark, which helps keep its teeth and gums strong and healthy.

Illustrations Robin Budden/Wildlife Art Agency

GROWING UP

The life of a young lion

NEWBORN CUBS
The tiny cubs, born with their eyes closed, are helpless and barely able to crawl.

EATING OUT
Cubs can feed even if their own mother's milk has dried up or if she is temporarily absent, because other suckling lionesses share feeding duties.

PLAY FIGHTING
helps older cubs develop muscles and learn skills that will be essential later in life, when they will have to tackle large prey to the ground or fight intruders or rivals.

may spend twenty-four hours or more away from her cubs.

When they are about two months old, the cubs begin to follow their mother on her expeditions, and if they have been reared mainly alone, they must learn to socialize with the rest of the pride. Other lionesses may allow cubs to suckle from them. This unusual behavior makes sense because, no matter who the cubs' mother is, she will be a relative of the other lionesses, and her offspring will carry some of the same genes.

Weaning is a gradual process. By the time they are about two and a half to three months old, the cubs are given their first taste of meat. They are taken to a kill, where they are allowed small scraps of flesh. They eat increasing amounts of meat, but continue to suckle until they are about six months old. They do not participate in kills until they are at least a year old. By 14 to 15 months, they have lost all their milk teeth and start to grow the large canines they will need to capture and kill prey. The youngsters remain entirely dependent on the adults for food until they are 16 months old. About two months later, their mother stops leading them to kills and caring for them in other ways, letting them stand on their own within the pride. Soon, she will give birth to more young. On average, females produce a litter of cubs every two years, and may continue to do so until they are fifteen years old. ■

FROM BIRTH TO DEATH

THE LION

GESTATION: 100–119 DAYS (TYPICALLY 105–110 DAYS)
LITTER SIZE: 1–5 (USUALLY 3–4); UP TO 6 IN CAPTIVITY
BREEDING: ANY TIME OF YEAR, THOUGH IN SOME AREAS MORE CUBS MAY BE BORN IN SOME SEASONS THAN IN OTHERS
WEIGHT AT BIRTH: 2–4 LB (1–2 KG)
EYES OPEN: 3–15 DAYS
FIRST WALKING: 3 WEEKS
WEANING: ABOUT 6 MONTHS
SEXUAL MATURITY: 3–4 YEARS
LONGEVITY: UP TO 17 YEARS IN THE WILD; UP TO 24 YEARS IN CAPTIVITY

MANATEES

Manatees are at best semisocial animals, with most groupings occurring only at warm-water refuges during the winter. When a female is sexually receptive, however, she becomes the focus of attention for a group of a dozen or more males, who follow her around for up to a month, jostling agitatedly for position and the chance to be the first to mate with her. The female seems an unwilling participant; she does her utmost to avoid her suitors by twisting, turning, and tail-slapping. She may even swim into dangerously shallow water in her efforts to escape. Eventually, however, she succumbs—and usually to more than one male. After mating, the males disperse to look for other receptive females. They play no further part in the life of the mother or her calf.

A FAMILY FEED

The calf forms a close bond with its mother. She nurses it for up to eighteen months, although it starts to graze solid food by the age of three months (below).

Birth of a Manatee

Although breeding occurs all year round, it is often timed so that the calf is born when food supplies are at their peak. Gestation lasts 12–13 months and generally produces one calf, which is almost always born tail first, although breech births do occasionally occur; a few cases of twins have been reported. The calf of the West Indian and West African manatee is about 47 in (119 cm) long and weighs 65 lb (30 kg). Amazonian manatee calves are somewhat smaller. Although the fetuses are covered in hair, the newborn animal is completely hairless. Observers often report that the mother assists her newborn calf to the surface to take its first breath. However, scientists now believe that the calf is able to swim to the surface by itself and that the female is just exhibiting attentive maternal behavior.

The female's mammary glands are located in an axillary (armpit) position, not too far from the pectoral (chest) position in humans. This has given rise to some imaginary tales of the mother cradling her calf in her "arms" while it suckles, but this is wholly untrue: The calf lies beside its mother, just below her flipper. It begins to nurse a few hours after birth and usually suckles for up to three minutes at a time, taking in milk, which is rich in proteins, fats, and salt. Although the calf will begin to eat vegetation within a few weeks of the birth, it will not be completely weaned for 12–18 months, during which time it will learn from its mother about migration routes, food, and feeding areas.

Douglas Faulkner/Oxford Scientific Films

Sirenians have a low reproductive rate, and a twin birth is an extremely rare occurrence (left).

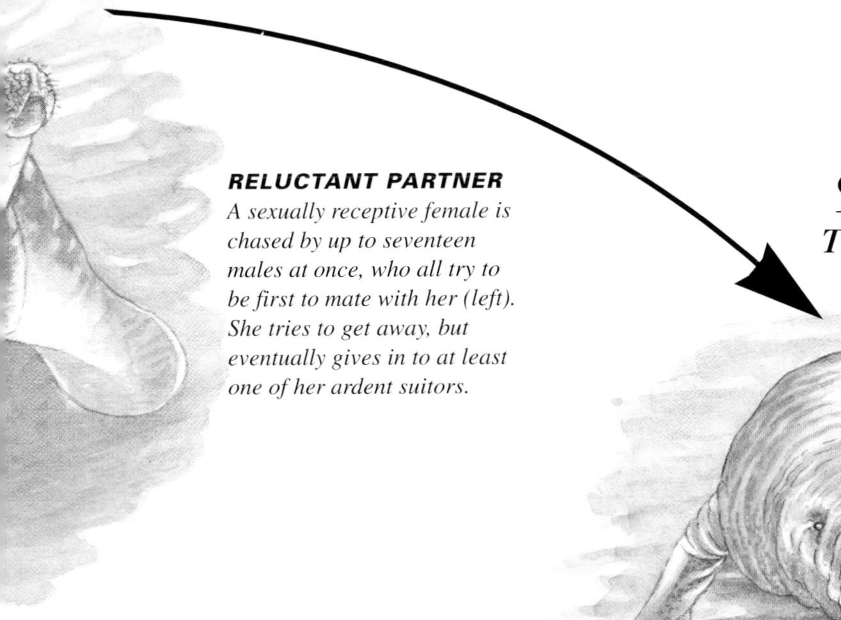

GROWING UP

The life of a West Indian manatee

RELUCTANT PARTNER

A sexually receptive female is chased by up to seventeen males at once, who all try to be first to mate with her (left). She tries to get away, but eventually gives in to at least one of her ardent suitors.

SECRET BIRTH

The expectant female seeks out a sheltered backwater in which to give birth. The instant the calf is born (right), she nuzzles it to the surface to take its first gulp of air.

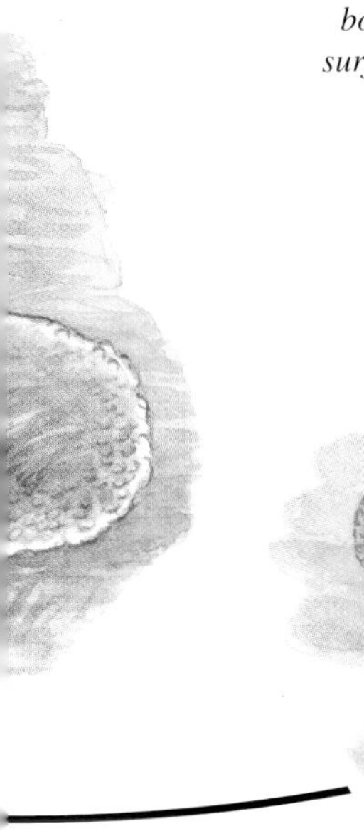

TAKING MILK

The mother's teats are located in the armpits, so her calf swims slowly alongside to suckle from her (right).

Manatees breed slowly, which is one of the reasons they are so rare. They do not reach sexual maturity before the age of six years, and a female will usually give birth only once every two years.

Dugongs

The mating behavior of the dugong is similar to that of the manatees, but it differs in one significant respect. As with the manatees, a receptive dugong female is hotly pursued by a group of mature males, but in this case the males are far more aggressive. They claim territories, which they staunchly defend, engaging in violent combat with rivals in attempts to win breeding rights. This is the only time when the otherwise docile dugong shows any kind of aggression, but many males bear the scars that confirm that this is no mere display of bravado.

The dugong calf stays with its mother for up to two years, often riding on her back to feed. Adults reach sexual maturity fairly late in life, sometimes not until the age of 18 years, and this, coupled with the fact that a female is unlikely to produce more than five or six calves during her long life, is a key reason why the dugong is threatened. ■

FROM BIRTH TO DEATH

WEST INDIAN MANATEE

GESTATION: 13 MONTHS
NO OF YOUNG: 1
LENGTH AT BIRTH: 47 IN (119 CM)
WEIGHT AT BIRTH: 65 LB (30 KG)
SEXUAL MATURITY: BOTH SEXES 6–8 YEARS
LONGEVITY: 50 YEARS

AMAZONIAN MANATEE

GESTATION: 13 MONTHS
NO OF YOUNG: 1
LENGTH AT BIRTH: 33–41 IN (85–105 CM)
SEXUAL MATURITY: BOTH SEXES 6–8 YEARS
LONGEVITY: 50 YEARS

DUGONG

GESTATION: 13 MONTHS
NO OF YOUNG: 1
LENGTH AT BIRTH: 39–47 IN (100–120 CM)
SEXUAL MATURITY: MALE 9–10 YEARS, FEMALE 9–18 YEARS
LONGEVITY: 50 YEARS

WEST AFRICAN MANATEE

GESTATION: 13 MONTHS
NO OF YOUNG: 1
LENGTH AT BIRTH: 47 IN (119 CM)
WEIGHT AT BIRTH: 65 LB (30 KG)
SEXUAL MATURITY: BOTH SEXES 6–8 YEARS
LONGEVITY: 50 YEARS

Illustrations Carol Roberts

MARMOSET MONKEYS

Marmosets, unlike many of the higher primates, have a courtship ritual. They may mate at almost any time of year, probably because the seasons vary so little in the Tropics. The male walks with his body arched, smacking his lips and flicking his tongue. He and the female groom each other, licking and using their incisors as combs. When the female is in season, the male busily scent marks objects with glands on his scrotum.

Only the dominant adult female in the group breeds during a season, although she may mate with more than one male. She keeps other females

ONCE PREGNANT, A FEMALE REMAINS FAITHFUL TO HER MATE: SHE WILL NEED HIS HELP IN REARING HER OFFSPRING

from breeding by secreting special chemicals (pheromones) from her scent glands. Gestation lasts about 20 weeks. Twin births are common with marmosets—for two-thirds of cases in the common marmoset and nine-tenths in the pygmy marmoset. Triple births are not unusual.

Most tamarins, too, seem to be nonseasonal breeders. Their courtship, however, is brief. The young are born after a gestation period of 20–21 weeks; in 80–90 percent of cases these are twins. They are close replicas of their parents, but with shorter hair and less pronounced manes. Young lion tamarins are born fully furred and with their eyes open and weigh around 2 oz (60 g). All newborn

FROM BIRTH TO DEATH

COMMON MARMOSET

GESTATION: 140–150 DAYS
LITTER SIZE: 1–4, USUALLY 2
BREEDING: NO SPECIFIC TIME
WEIGHT AT BIRTH: NOT KNOWN
EYES OPEN: NOT KNOWN
FIRST WALKING: 21 DAYS
WEANING: 4–7 WEEKS
INDEPENDENCE: 9 WEEKS
SEXUAL MATURITY: 12–18 MONTHS
LONGEVITY: NOT KNOWN (UP TO 10 YEARS IN CAPTIVITY)

GOLDEN LION TAMARIN

GESTATION: 126–133 DAYS
LITTER SIZE: 1–3, USUALLY TWINS
BREEDING: NO SPECIFIC TIME
WEIGHT AT BIRTH: 2 oz (60 g)
EYES OPEN: AT BIRTH
FIRST WALKING: 21 DAYS
WEANING 4–7 WEEKS
INDEPENDENCE: 10–20 MONTHS
SEXUAL MATURITY: 15 MONTHS
LONGEVITY: NOT KNOWN (10–15 YEARS IN CAPTIVITY)

AT 2-3 WEEKS *the youngster is starting to investigate its surroundings, but its father is never far from its side.*

THE YOUNG SUCKLE *from their mother. They start taking soft food from about four weeks.*

Illustrations Robin Budden/Wildlife Art Agency

GROWING UP

The life of a young marmoset

THE FEMALE
is receptive every two and a half weeks. She mates with one or more of the males.

THE YOUNG
are carried (below) until six or seven weeks old.

THE MALES
do their share of the parental duties, carrying the young when they are not being suckled.

A CARING FATHER

After the birth of twins it is normally the father who plays with them, and carries them on his back for their first month or two. This helps relieve the load on the mother. When they are very small, the father sometimes carries them around his neck like a scarf. The mother may carry them too, but as a rule she tends to them only when they need to feed from her.

This caused a tragedy the first time marmosets were bred in captivity. The keepers decided to take away the male to "be on the safe side," and they removed the animal that was not carrying the young. This turned out to be the female, and it led to the young marmosets starving to death.

animals cling tightly to the mother or father. If the male is caring for the young, then every two to three hours he transfers one to the mother, passing it into her arms. She suckles the offspring for 15–30 minutes and then hands it back to the father.

When they are about three weeks old, the young start exploring their surroundings, but rush back to their parents if even slightly alarmed. At four weeks old they start taking soft food, although they

WHILE A BREEDING PAIR TENDS TO ITS YOUNG, THE REST OF THE FAMILY GROUP KEEPS A SHARP LOOKOUT FOR PREDATORS

are not yet weaned. They can survive independently at the age of two to five months, but prefer to stay with their parents, running to them if alarmed, and often begging food from them.

Marmoset litters are heavy, at 19–25 percent of the mother's weight. Helpless at birth, the newborns are carried for their first two weeks by other group members. By two months they can travel alone, catch insects or rob them from others, and spend long periods in play, chasing and tussling with one another and other group members. (This is a little earlier than young tamarins, which take about two and a half months to reach independence.) They reach puberty at 12–18 months and adult size at two years of age. The tamarins, lion tamarin, and Goeldi's monkey give birth to smaller young; in these species the male does not take charge of offspring until they reach 7–10 days old. ■

MEERKATS

For their size, mongooses are slow to mature and reproduce. They live for about ten years and breed from the age of two. This applies to the dwarf mongoose as well, whose smaller size might suggest a shorter life span.

Courtship

When the female is ready to mate, she sometimes engages in mock fights with the male, jumping and snapping at him. The dwarf and Egyptian mongooses are much more gentle, mutually grooming each other and making soft noises as a prelude to mating. In most species the female will crouch and then run away, with her tail in the air, encouraging the male to follow her. This may occur a number of times before she allows the male to mate.

Birth

Some species, such as the dwarf mongoose and the meerkat, have several litters a year. Their deliveries coincide with the rainy season, when there is plenty of food. There are more litters born in areas where there is an abundant supply of food. Banded mongooses that are living in a warm climate where there is plenty to eat may have four litters in a year, but the same species in a less productive area will only breed in the rainy season. Egyptian mongooses only have one litter a year, but may have a second if their first brood is lost.

A litter can consist of between one and six young, but most commonly there are three or four babies, born after a gestation of sixty days. Gestation does vary, though, between thirty-five days in the dwarf mongoose and eighty days in the slender mongoose. Most young are hardly able to move when they are born and they are blind and deaf with very little fur. Their adult markings are

COURTSHIP
When the female is ready to mate she jumps up and down in front of the male in mock battle.

PLAY LEARNING
When they leave the den at about five weeks of age, the day is spent playing and learning how to defend themselves. By the time they are two they will be ready to mate.

in SIGHT

ALPHA MALES AND FEMALES

Dwarf mongooses have a breeding hierarchy not found among meerkats. The oldest male and female are the only breeding pair, and all other members of the pack help to feed and look after their babies. The "alpha" female usually remains dominant for several years, and then another female takes over.

Other females do mate within the pack, but they tend to abort or lose their young. This may be because the alpha female kills all infants so that their mothers can suckle her babies. The dominant female will allow the other males to mate with her only after the alpha male has lost interest.

Clem Haagner/Ardea

GROWING UP

The life of a young meerkat

OUTSIDE THE DEN

One to four young are born in a nursery den. At about five weeks of age they take their first look at the world outside.

WEANING

The young will continue to suckle from the mother until they are about nine weeks of age.

THE NEXT LITTER

The mother will be ready to mate again the following year in September or October. Her next litter will be born in November or December.

Illustrations Mike Donnolly/Wildlife Art Agency

barely recognizable. The narrow-striped mongoose, however, is an exception to this rule, as the young have visible stripes at birth and their eyes are open.

The babies are born in a nest in the mother's den, which may be hidden away in a rock crevice, a termite mound, or a hollow tree. Mongooses feed their newborn infants in a sitting position, curled forward. As the babies grow, the female will lie on her back or her side to suckle. To get rid of waste the mother stimulates the babies to defecate by licking them and consuming their feces. Mongooses frequently move from one den to another and the babies are then transported by the mother or a baby-sitter, who carries each one by the nape of the neck. Baby dwarf mongooses are sometimes brought outside when they are only a day old, and the baby-sitter will groom and lick them in the sunshine.

When the babies are two to four weeks old their eyes open, and they leave the nest soon afterward. They begin to eat food other than milk at about the age of three weeks or even less, and are fully weaned by nine weeks, earlier in some species.

To maintain her supply of milk the mother must leave the den to find food. Other mongooses baby-sit while she is away, males as well as females, and as the babies grow these surrogate parents bring insects and other food for them to eat. They also play with the babies.

Adolescent young have a difficult role to play. While still at the stage of begging for food from the adults for themselves they are obliged to pass it on to the new babies, doing so with obvious reluctance. As the young develop, the mother teaches them to forage by holding prey in her mouth and encouraging them to chase her and snap at it while she runs about.

As they grow older and emerge from the den each baby meerkat is assigned a "tutor" who has the responsibility of teaching it to hunt. This mongoose, usually an adult male, will bring the young live prey to deal with, and the babies fight to keep other young away from "their" teacher. In this way they learn to deal with such prey as scorpions and ants, both of which are dangerous or painful if handled wrongly. It is some time before they learn to tackle large prey such as the cobra, and occasionally they end up the loser. ■

FROM BIRTH TO DEATH

DWARF MONGOOSE
GESTATION: 5 WEEKS
LITTER SIZE: 1–6
WEIGHT AT BIRTH: UNKOWN
FIRST EMERGE: 3 WEEKS
INDEPENDENCE: 6–7 WEEKS
SEXUAL MATURITY: 2 YEARS
LONGEVITY: UP TO 10 YEARS

MEERKAT
GESTATION: 11 WEEKS
LITTER SIZE: 1–4
WEIGHT AT BIRTH: 1.2 OZ (33 G)
EYES OPEN: 2 WEEKS
EMERGE FROM DEN: 4 WEEKS
INDEPENDENCE: 6–9 WEEKS
SEXUAL MATURITY: 1-2 YEARS
LONGEVITY: UP TO 10 YEARS

RING-TAILED MONGOOSE
GESTATION: 79–92 DAYS
LITTER SIZE: 1
WEIGHT AT BIRTH: 1.8 OZ (50 G)
SEXUAL MATURITY: 2 YEARS
LONGEVITY IN WILD: NOT KNOWN (13 IN CAPTIVITY)

YELLOW MONGOOSE
GESTATION: 45–57 DAYS
LITTER SIZE: 2–4
WEANING OCCURS: 6 WEEKS
LONGEVITY IN WILD: NOT KNOWN (15 IN CAPTIVITY)

MOLES

In the Northern Hemisphere, most moles give birth during the spring, when food is most abundant and females can produce plenty of milk. The onset of breeding is, rather surprisingly, triggered by the increasing light levels. Moles are subject to light more often than is commonly supposed, for example when they surface to collect nesting materials and push up spoil heaps.

Female moles can breed in their first year. The ovaries are unique among mammals, being made up of two parts. At the start of the breeding season, the part of the ovary that produces eggs enlarges and follicles begin to develop. Other changes at this time include perforation of the vagina and enlargement of the uterus. The female comes into estrus probably for only 24–36 hours, and then produces eggs.

SUBTERRANEAN SEARCH

During February and March, male moles start to venture outside their home ranges, usually digging long, straight tunnels until they reach the burrows of a female. Sometimes these excursions occur above ground. The daily pattern of activity changes at this time, with males becoming increasingly restless. Instead of returning to the nest to sleep after bouts of feeding, males just "catnap" in their tunnels and dig until exhausted, in a bid to find as many females as possible. The animals usually mate within the burrows; copulation has only occasionally been seen to occur above ground. In spite of the tremendous efforts of the male to seek out his partner, the pair spend only an hour or so together. Having mated with the female, the mole proceeds to seek out further mates.

Gestation lasts for about four weeks. The number of young varies from two to eight in the European mole and several of the North American species, with a litter size of four being typical. Young moles grow and develop rapidly; they increase their weight almost twenty times within the first three weeks of life—typically from 0.12 oz (3.4 g) at birth to 2 oz (56.7 g) at three weeks old.

Even within the nest chamber, these youngsters are at risk from predators; foxes may dig out nests and destroy the entire litter. Predation of young is not confined to the European mole; the American

TUNNEL OF LOVE

Once the male has dug through to a female's domain, he may need to chase her for some distance before she consents to mate (above).

OVER THE TOP

Juveniles face great peril as they disperse to find new territories; above ground, they are helplessly exposed to enemies (below).

David Thompson/Oxford Scientific Films

Moles are born deep down in a snug chamber, where they are confined for more than a month (left).

GROWING UP

The life of a European mole

NEWBORN MOLES *are blind, naked, and bright red, but soon fade to a healthy pink, and within 9 or 10 days take on a bluish cast when the fur begins to form.*

AT 14 DAYS OLD *the coat sprouts from the skin, and within 17 days is complete (above), but the eyes do not open until about the 22nd day.*

coast mole frequently loses young to a snake known as the rubber boa. Probably more importantly, any food shortage at this critical time may cause whole litters to starve to death.

Having spent about a month in the nest, the young moles are ready to venture out for the first time, but they generally stay within the home territory until ten weeks old. Local populations of moles may triple during May and June, when the young at first emerge from the nest, and dispersion quickly follows. They usually move above ground to seek new territories, and will even swim open stretches of water, paddling gamely for as long as fifty minutes at a stretch. But during these migrations, the young moles are vulnerable to buzzards, barn and tawny owls, and stoats, and many are killed crossing roads.

By the autumn, some young moles will have survived to establish territories of their own. Having done so, a mole will live out its days there, with only minor boundary alterations resulting from changes in food or soil conditions or the disappearance or arrival of neighbors.

DESMANS AND GOLDEN MOLES

Pyrenean desmans mate in March or April, and as they usually form a solid pair bond there is sometimes intense rivalry for mates between existing territory holders and solitary males. At this time of year, males become far more vigorous in the protection of their territories, swimming up and down the river, particularly at the fringes of their domain. Females, meanwhile, seek out a suitable nest site and start to gather nesting material.

After a four-week gestation period, three or four young are born. They do not venture into the open until they are about seven weeks old, remaining within the parents' territory until they are about ten or eleven weeks old. During the time they are in the nest, the female goes out foraging for food while the male defends the territory.

Russian desmans can give birth twice a year, and generally there are between three and five young in each litter. Desmans advertise the boundaries of their territory by scent marking, the strong, musky odor being produced from a gland at the base of the tail. The young remain with the parents over the summer period before dispersing, usually overland, during early autumn. The female builds a nest of her own away from the young soon after they are born, and visits her offspring only to suckle them. The male, on the other hand, takes a more active interest in the young, often sharing the nesting chamber and helping to keep them warm.

The breeding cycle of golden moles is little studied. It is known that one of the most studied species, the Cape golden mole, mates during the rainy season from April to July, and that the two offspring are suckled in a circular nest made of leaves. ■

FROM BIRTH TO DEATH

EUROPEAN MOLE	PYRENEAN DESMAN
GESTATION: 35–42 DAYS	**GESTATION:** 3–4 WEEKS
LITTER SIZE: 2–9	**LITTER SIZE:** 1–5
WEIGHT AT BIRTH: 0.1 OZ (3.8 G)	**WEIGHT AT BIRTH:** UNKNOWN
WEANING: 2 MONTHS	**WEANING:** UNKNOWN
SEXUAL MATURITY: 10–12 MONTHS	**SEXUAL MATURITY:** 12 MONTHS
LONGEVITY IN WILD: 3–4 YEARS	**LONGEVITY IN WILD:** 4 YEARS

Color illustrations Wayne Ford/Wildlife Art Agency

NEW WORLD RATS & MICE

Nearly every species of the hesperomid subfamily is an example of r selection. This ecological term describes a pattern of breeding and survival in a potentially unstable environment. Animals using successful r selection breed early and often, producing large litters to ensure that at least some of the offspring survive. Within this pattern there are some variations and one or two exceptions, but it serves as a safe generalization about the subfamily as a whole.

The usual hesperomid pattern is for short gestation periods, large litters, early sexual maturity, and short life span. The pygmy mouse is the foremost example of hesperomid r selection. Females can become pregnant when they are only four weeks old, giving birth three weeks later. Climbing rats and cotton rats occupy the other extreme, giving birth to relatively more developed young after a longer gestation period (see Insight below).

Grasshopper mice can breed at any time of year, although they usually do so in late spring and summer. The female is sexually receptive for up to a week at a time, and gestation varies from 26 to 47 days. These mice are spectacularly fecund; the females of one species can produce as many as 12 litters during one breeding season. The youngsters themselves are sexually active within six weeks.

The generalist species conform to the standard pattern, with variations usually ascribed to local climate differences. Those living in environments with extreme climatic fluctuations, such as deer mice in their northern range, produce the greatest numbers of young. Related species living in more stable climates produce fewer—and smaller—litters. Likewise, they live longer and have a larger brain capacity.

Reproduction in Deer Mice

As in so many areas of hesperomid study, deer mice are the ideal candidates for adding statistical evidence to such broad generalizations. Deer mice in the northern range have a defined breeding period, normally March to October. For those deer mice in milder climates, breeding may also occur throughout the year. Females have a sexually receptive period of between five and seven days; this can sometimes occur immediately after giving birth.

Gestation lasts about twenty-four days (up to forty days in lactating mothers), leading to litters of up to nine, but usually averaging three or four. The newborn deer mice are tiny, weighing just over 0.07 oz (2 g). Their ears unfurl after about three days, but their eyes remain shut for two weeks. Young deer mice remain totally dependent on their mother for another six weeks, although they are usually weaned after about three or four weeks of nursing.

They continue to grow until they are about six months old, but both sexes reach sexual maturity well before that time, and breeding will have begun. This rapid succession of reproductive milestones is necessary for deer mice, which rarely live to two years old in the wild.

Deer mice have proven to be tolerant of other individuals within their territory. Males and females form pairs, but severe weather conditions will often

MATING *takes place above ground, within the security of ground cover (right).*

THE YOUNG *are weaned within a month, but they may not venture from the nest for three or four more weeks. By this time, they are fully furred miniature mice (right).*

MOUSE FACTORIES

The deer mouse and pygmy mouse display a reproductive pattern that typifies that of most New World rats and mice—a short gestation period and a litter of small, hardly developed young.

But there are departures from this norm. The big-eared climbing rat has a gestation period of about fifty days—nearly twice as long as the average—and the newborn rats are fully haired. Their eyes open after about six days—about twice as early as most species. Cotton rats are a mixture of these two patterns, combining a short gestation with well-developed young.

Nick Bergkessel/Oxford Scientific Films

GROWING UP

The life of a young deer mouse

BIRTH
occurs deep underground in a snug nesting chamber lined with dry grass, moss, and feathers. The newborn young are sightless, deaf, and practically naked (above right).

lead to enforced congregations of up to thirteen individuals. In normal conditions, however, most males will define a territory and concentrate on the paired family unit. Confrontations are marked by thin squeaks and sharp buzzings.

Deer mice also drum their forefeet rapidly when excited. This behavior is sometimes related to breeding and territory definition, but most zoologists believe that it is confined to defensive responses to predators. In the same way, some nesting females will warn other females off their territory. ■

FROM BIRTH TO DEATH

	DEER MOUSE	PYGMY MOUSE
GESTATION:	21–40 DAYS	20–25 DAYS
LITTER SIZE:	1–9, AVERAGE 3–4	1–5, AVERAGE 2–3
BREEDING:	MARCH–OCTOBER IN NORTHERN EDGE OF RANGE; NONSEASONAL ELSEWHERE	NONSEASONAL IN MOST AREAS
WEIGHT AT BIRTH:	0.08 OZ (2.3 G)	0.04 OZ (1.2 G)
EYES OPEN:	13 DAYS	10–12 DAYS
WEANING:	3–4 WEEKS	14–20 DAYS
FIRST FORAGING:	7–8 WEEKS	18–22 DAYS
SEXUAL MATURITY:	7 WEEKS	28 DAYS IN FEMALE; 70–80 DAYS IN MALE
LONGEVITY:	UP TO 2 YEARS IN THE WILD; UP TO 8 IN CAPTIVITY	UP TO 3 YEARS IN CAPTIVITY; NOT KNOWN IN WILD

Illustration Joanne Cowne

THE YOUNG
are capable of little more than gripping a teat and suckling (above). Even if the mother moves around in the nest, they will still hang on to their milk supply, trailing along behind her.

OPOSSUMS

Opossums live only for about two years, so they must take bold steps to propagate the species—and as their 65-million-year history shows, their success rate is high. Most opossums have some sort of pouch for the young, but even the pouchless species give birth to tiny, helpless offspring. Most development takes place during lactation, when all nourishment comes from the mother's milk.

Breeding is timed so that the young will leave the pouch when food resources are most plentiful. Most tropical species, as a result, can breed at any time, while those in temperate or montane habitats have specific seasons. Opossums in the seasonal tropics breed so that the young will emerge at the start of the rainy season. Virginia opossums usually breed twice a year, in January or February and then again about 110 days later. In their warmer southern range they might have a third litter, while in the north there is sometimes just one.

There are no elaborate courtship rituals or long-term bonds. If a male meets a female during the breeding season, the initial aggressive displays of hissing and teeth-baring quickly give way to courtship. The male initiates proceedings by approaching the female while making distinctive, metallic vocal clicks. If the female is in estrus, she will allow the male to mount her. Copulation may last as long as six hours.

Gestation is remarkably short—only twelve to thirteen days. The female gives birth in her nest to as many as twenty-five offspring, which are born in a space of about five minutes. These tiny pink babies look more like worms than mammals. They do, however, have claws on their forefeet to help them climb the 3 in (8 cm) from the birth canal to the pouch. The claws then drop off.

More than half of these young might die on the way to the pouch, and the number of nipples inside defines the upper limit of litter size. Virginia opossums have thirteen nipples arranged in a circle with one central nipple, but there are usually about seven young in a litter. Most other species have smaller litters, averaging about four.

The young are in effect "feeding machines" at this stage. They cannot yet regulate their body heat, but the mother's pouch keeps them warm. Another feature enables them to feed almost continuously. The passage from the nasal chamber to the larynx is so separated from the esophagus that the young can breathe and feed simultaneously. The aquatic female yapok has a pouch that shuts tightly while she swims, trapping sufficient oxygen for the young prior to submersion.

COURTSHIP

The male approaches the female (above) while making clicking noises. If she is not in estrus, she remains aggressive, and the male will eventually give up and go away. If she is in estrus, copulation will follow.

CARE OF THE YOUNG

Seen from a human perspective, opossums display a curious mixture of ruthlessness and generosity in their care of the young. A litter containing only one offspring will fail because the single mouth is not enough to stimulate the mammary glands. And a Virginia opossum mother will not respond to distress calls of detached infants until they have left the pouch for good.

But Virginia opossums have been known to carry other females' young, and female pale-bellied mouse opossums will retrieve the distressed young of another female. Less is known about the possible parental-care function of the male's pouch in some species, such as the yapok.

Kenneth W. Fink/Ardea

GROWING UP

The life of a Virginia opossum

TINY YOUNG

After a gestation of twelve to thirteen days, several young are born in rapid succession. They use their foreclaws to crawl to the pouch.

LIFELINE

Once the young reach the pouch, they seize a nipple and hang on for fifty days. If there are more babies than available nipples, the surplus of the litter will simply starve.

EASY RIDERS

After about seventy days in the pouch, the young are finally ready to leave it. They soon get the hang of riding on the mother's back. The young will themselves breed within a year.

The young begin to release their grip on the nipples at about fifty days and first leave the pouch briefly about three weeks later. At first they crawl around on the mother or stay in the nest while she forages. The pouch soon becomes too small for the young, although they have not yet been weaned. During that interim they follow the mother while she forages, sometimes riding on her back.

Pouchless opossums develop in similar fashion. When the mother moves, the young are kept in a "bundle" between her hind legs or on her back.

Opossums are fully independent at three to four months old, and sexually mature two to three months later. They soon breed, because they have only about two years of reproductive activity. ■

Life can be very trying for the female Virginia opossum, especially once her pouch is no longer large enough to house her litter of dependent young (left).

OUT IN A FLASH

The southern opossum has the shortest gestation period of any mammal. Normally 12 to 13 days, it can sometimes be as short as 8 days. The longest gestation record is held by the Asiatic elephant, whose 608-day average gestation is about 50 times longer than that of the opossum.

FROM BIRTH TO DEATH

VIRGINIA OPOSSUM

GESTATION: 12–13 DAYS
LITTER SIZE: 5–25
BREEDING: FEBRUARY AND JUNE
WEIGHT AT BIRTH: 0.007 oz (0.2 g)
EYES OPEN: 3–4 WEEKS
WEANING: 12 WEEKS
FORAGING: 3–4 MONTHS
SEXUAL MATURITY: 6–10 MONTHS
LONGEVITY: 2–3 YEARS (UP TO 8 IN CAPTIVITY)

SHORT-TAILED OPOSSUM

GESTATION: ABOUT 2 WEEKS
LITTER SIZE: 5–12
BREEDING: AT ANY TIME (UP TO 4 BROODS ANNUALLY)
WEIGHT AT BIRTH: 0.004 oz (0.1 g)
EYES OPEN: 10–15 DAYS
WEANING: 7 WEEKS
FORAGING: 7–8 WEEKS
SEXUAL MATURITY: 4–5 MONTHS
LONGEVITY: 2–3 YEARS

Illustrations Simon Turvey/Wildlife Art Agency

ORANGUTANS

Baby orangutans are born in their mother's sleeping nest high up in the trees. The mother bites through the umbilical cord and, like many animals, eats the placenta and membrane surrounding the baby for nourishment. Orangutans are slow-breeding animals. Gestation lasts for eight to nine months and a female normally gives birth to only one baby every four to five years. Rarely, a mother gives birth to twins. Some babies die of natural causes, which means that a female may rear as few as three young in her lifetime.

A MALE ORANGUTAN, LIVING IN PHILADELPHIA ZOO, WAS ESTIMATED TO BE 57 YEARS OLD WHEN HE DIED IN 1977

At birth, a baby orangutan weighs about 3 lb (1.5 kg). In common with many baby animals, it has an extremely appealing appearance, with spiky hair on its head and a moonlike face. This, together with its small size and jerky movements, is designed to send out a message to other orangutans that here is a baby needing to be cared for.

All mammals feed their young on milk and show some form of parental care toward them. This care lasts for the longest time among the primates,

OUT OF ACTION

COMMON DISEASES

Like the other great apes, orangutans can carry several diseases also found in human beings. These include:

- **Malaria, transmitted by mosquito bites, which causes high fever and can be fatal.**
- **Other infections of the blood, which cause sickness and fever.**
- **Viral infections, such as those that cause the common cold.**
- **Infections caused by parasites, such as tapeworm and ringworm.**

However, injury is the main risk to animals in the wild. Fights between rival males that may result in cut faces and necks, broken, bitten-off fingers, or, in some cases, death.

NEWBORN
The baby can cling to its mother's fur as soon as it is born, although she tends to hold it cradled in her arms at first.

ESSENTIAL SKILLS
The young orangutan is taught essential social skills, such as which foods to eat, how to build nests, and how to avoid predators.

Illustrations Kim Thompson

GROWING UP

The life of a young orangutan

PLAYTIME

Young orangutans wrestle and chase each other through the trees. This sociability declines as they get older.

AGGRESSION

Male orangutans develop the characteristic throat and cheek pouches.

FROM BIRTH TO DEATH

ORANGUTAN

BREEDING: NONSEASONAL
GESTATION: 8–9 MONTHS
USUAL NUMBER OF YOUNG: 1
NUMBER OF YOUNG IN LIFETIME: 3–6
WEIGHT AT BIRTH: 3 LB (1.5 KG)
FIRST SOLID FOOD: 3 MONTHS
WEANING: 2 YEARS
INDEPENDENCE: ABOUT 7–10 YEARS
SEXUAL MATURITY: 6–8 YEARS
FULLY GROWN: ABOUT 6–7 YEARS FOR FEMALES 10–14 YEARS FOR MALES
LONGEVITY IN WILD: 30–40 YEARS
LONGEVITY IN CAPTIVITY: OVER 50 YEARS

especially among the great apes. A baby orangutan is dependent on its mother for the first three years of its life. She provides it with food, transport, and protection. It takes its first solid food at about three months and is weaned at about two years. However, it stays with its mother for several more years until it is about seven to ten years old. Both males and females reach sexual maturity between the ages of six to eight. Females are fully grown by the age of seven; males by fourteen. By the time a young orangutan reaches the age of three, its mother is probably pregnant again, and the first baby soon has a younger brother or sister to play with.

SURVIVAL SKILLS

The time spent with its mother is put to good use by the young orangutan. During this time, it learns all the skills it needs to survive on its own. These include practicing nest building using small twigs and leaves, learning to forage for food, and recognizing and avoiding would-be predators. It learns the best travel routes through the forest and the times at which the trees comes into fruit.

As male orangutans mature, they gradually develop the characteristic throat and cheek pouches of adulthood. They also grow longer hair than the females—it can reach over a yard in length on parts of the coat. Adolescence is the time for both males and females to set off on their own separate ways and to fend for themselves in the forest. In the wild, orangutans usually have a life span of some thirty to forty years.

Male and female orangutans reach sexual maturity at about six to eight years old. Mating can take place at any time of the year and is the only occasion on which adult orangutans actively seek each other's company. When the female has weaned her youngest baby and is fertile again, she seeks out a male to mate with. First, however, the two engage in a period of peaceful courtship lasting for several days or even weeks. Mating itself takes place high up in the trees. Then the two separate and return to their individual lives. ■

OTTERS

Illustrations John Morris/Wildlife Art Agency

When a female Eurasian otter is ready to mate, she gives off signals to the male by scent marking the spraint heaps in her home range. Several males may show interest, in which case they will fight for her favors.

The winner will usually participate in vigorous and noisy courtship-swimming with the female, when the animals twist and dive around each other in the water. This may look like play but, in fact, it may serve the purpose of stimulating ovulation (egg production) in the female. Some otter pairs spend several days together, sleeping and eating as a couple, before they mate.

The courting couple

Mating usually takes place in the water but is also recorded on land, and normally takes between 10 and 30 minutes for the Eurasian otter. It will occur several times during the next few days, probably to make sure fertilization occurs. Mating in otters, and in other mustelids, is very vigorous; it is thought that this activity insures that the female ovulates.

Soon after mating, the two part company, but the male will occasionally return to the female after she has given birth, occupying a nearby den or accompanying the family for a few days. The giant otter male, on the other hand, is a "good father," often staying with the female until one of them dies. When this happens, the survivor becomes distressed and completely nonaggressive.

> MALE OTTERS COURT THEIR CHOSEN FEMALE VIGOROUSLY, THEN WILL OFTEN VISIT HER AFTER MATING

Gestation is usually about nine weeks, but in some otter species such as the sea otter and American river otter it can last as much as a year. This long period can be explained by a process known as delayed implantation: After mating, the fertilized egg develops slightly, then, instead of implanting itself into the uterus wall immediately, it floats around in the uterus and only implants itself and develops after a certain period of time. For otters, this allows the birth to occur in the spring, when climate and availability of prey are at their best.

Blind and helpless

Except for the sea otter, birth always occurs on land, in a safe, undisturbed den. (Sea otters give birth in the water or, occasionally, on the beach.) The blind and toothless young are completely helpless, and their development is quite slow, even though the fat content of their mother's milk may be six times that of cow's milk. They make peeping sounds like young chicks.

Young Eurasian otters take their first wobbly steps at about seven weeks, and at the same time have their first taste of solid food. They can be seen playing outside the den from about the age of ten weeks, and in another fortnight they will have acquired their first waterproof coat and are ready to take to the water. They will not be fully weaned until they are about fourteen weeks old. After about four months they are able to catch their own food and will accompany their mother as she moves throughout her home range.

Out and about

Young otters are independent at seven to twelve months, when they will search for their own home range. They are sexually mature after two years.

In the wild otters are likely to die before they are mature, and few will survive beyond their eighth birthday. In captivity, however, where there is plenty of food and no dangers to face, otters tend to live much longer. ■

COURTSHIP *Male and female swim together under the water.*

INDEPENDENCE *comes at about a year old, when the youngster leaves its mother's territory to establish one of its own.*

Nick Gordon/Survival Anglia

Young giant otter cubs in Guyana, South America, wait eagerly for their mother's return and the promise of food (left).

GROWING UP

The life of a young otter

TINY NEWBORNS

For the first four or five weeks of life, the feeble young suckle from their mother every few hours.

ROUGH AND TUMBLE

At two months old, the young otters are more adventurous. They spend most of their time playing games on the riverbank.

TESTING THE WATER

Young otters are first brought to the water's edge at about two months, but will not be able to swim for another month.

FROM BIRTH TO DEATH

EURASIAN OTTER

GESTATION: 62–63 DAYS
LITTER SIZE: USUALLY 2
BREEDING: NONSEASONAL
WEIGHT AT BIRTH: 2 OZ (60 G)
EYES OPEN: 28–35 DAYS
WEANING: 7 WEEKS (FULL WEANING 14 WEEKS)
FIRST SWIMMING: 3 MONTHS
INDEPENDENCE: UP TO 1 YEAR; REACH ADULT SIZE AT 2 YEARS
SEXUAL MATURITY: 2 YEARS
LONGEVITY: UP TO 8 YEARS IN THE WILD; UP TO 12 IN CAPTIVITY

SEA OTTER

GESTATION: 4–12 MONTHS
LITTER SIZE: 1
BREEDING: VARIABLE, MAY BE ONLY 4–5 MONTHS
WEIGHT AT BIRTH: 3.3–4 LB (1.5–1.8 KG)
EYES OPEN: AT BIRTH
WEANING: 1 YEAR
FIRST SWIMMING: ALMOST IMMEDIATELY AFTER BIRTH
INDEPENDENCE: AT LEAST 1 YEAR
SEXUAL MATURITY: THOUGHT TO BE 3 YEARS FOR FEMALES, 5–6 FOR MALES
LONGEVITY: NOT KNOWN

in SIGHT

A BREEDING DEN

Most otters bear their young in underground dens. The female will choose a secluded site near a good supply of food. She will then line the den with a variety of things, including grass, reeds, moss, and twigs. These twigs, though not particularly comfortable to lie on, insure a good flow of air through the nesting material and help to keep it dry.

Eurasian otters prefer sites under the roots of bankside trees, while coastal otters will use caves and piles of boulders if tree sites are unavailable. Dens are also used by both male and female otters as safe places to rest in. Though ordinary dens are often marked with feces, breeding dens are not, as mothers are careful not to give away the location of their young.

Illustration Graham Allen/Linden Artists

PLATYPUSES

Platypuses mate in the water. First, the female slowly approaches the male. Then there is an elaborate courtship. The male chases the female, grasps her tail, and the two swim in circles before mating. Some days later the female goes off to start digging the long breeding burrow where she lays her eggs.

About two to four weeks after mating, usually between July and October (midwinter in Australasia), the female platypus lays two eggs in a nest at the end of her breeding tunnel, out of sight of any predators. The burrow is dug in a riverbank and is usually about 40–50 ft (12–15 m) long, with many branches to it. There may be more than one leaf-lined nesting chamber, and the female barricades herself in with piles of dirt and moist plant matter, which helps to keep the eggs from drying out during the incubation period.

The female probably lies on her back, curling her tail up to form a cup near the base of her belly, into which she rolls her two eggs. The leathery eggs are soft shelled, between 0.6–0.7 in (15–18 mm) in diameter, and are very sticky and probably cling to the mother's fur, as well as to each other, to keep them from rolling out. As there is no brood pouch, the female broods and incubates the eggs by curling around them to keep them warm, holding them between her tail and abdomen for usually seven to ten days.

AFTER GIVING BIRTH, THE FEMALE PLATYPUS MAY STAY IN THE BURROW FOR UP TO FOURTEEN DAYS WITHOUT FEEDING UNTIL HER EGGS HAVE HATCHED

The baby platypuses, just about 0.5 in (12.7 mm) long on hatching, have another feature unique to monotreme mammals, but common in birds and reptiles. This is a temporary egg tooth with which to cut their exit from the egg. When the young are born they have hardly any bill, but they instead have lips. A few days after the young hatch, the mother begins to secrete milk from her mammary glands. The female platypus has no teats or nipples, and the milk is actually delivered from the mammary glands through the equivalent of sweat glands. These ducts from the mammary glands open into two long folds from which the young lick up the milk. The young also lick milk from the fur on the mother's abdomen.

The young have relatively large forelimbs for clinging to the fur, and they are very immature

MATERNAL CARE
The young platypus remains with its mother until it is a year old.

SUCKLING
The tiny youngsters suckle milk that is produced by the mother's mammary glands. Since she has no nipples, the milk oozes out onto her skin and fur and the infants suck it up from there.

All illustrations Simon Turvey

GROWING UP

The life of a young platypus

THE EGGS

The female platypus normally lays two eggs in a nest in her long burrow. She broods them for seven to ten days, between her abdomen and tail. The infant platypus breaks out of its egg using its special egg tooth.

PARENTAL CARE

In mammals, the sex involved most often in parental care is the female, since she is the one that can provide nourishment. The involvement of the male is rare, and in all monotremes parental care seems to be given by the female.

The females feed their young on milk after they hatch. The young echidna remains in the pouch until it becomes so large that it has to stay in a nest. The mothers return to the nest at intervals to suckle their offspring. Neither the young platypus nor the echidna is allowed to leave the nest until it is self-sufficient and able to protect itself to some extent.

when they are born. They continue to suckle milk for a long time, not being weaned until they are four to six months old. They are then about 12–13.5 in (30–34 cm) long and able to take their first swim—they emerge from the nest and burrow in late summer (January to early March in New South Wales). They stay with their mothers until they are one year old. The fathers do not seem to be involved in caring for the young platypuses.

Females start to breed at two years of age but they do not breed every year. They take good care of the few young that they produce, and this seems to mean that they have a high survival rate, in spite of their low reproductive rate.

THE PLATYPUS BURROW

A mother platypus digs an extralong breeding burrow, sometimes up to 65 ft (20 m) long. The platypus uses its burrow to help it regulate its temperature in the extremes of the Australian climate. But, as mammals, they are able to regulate their body temperature to a reasonable extent. The female platypus makes a nest of leaves and grass for her eggs. When she goes into the burrow, she piles up dirt to block the entrance. Each time she enters or exits the burrow, she rebuilds her blockade. The mother does not leave the nest until the eggs are hatched. The male is excluded from the nursery burrow.

POLAR BEARS

Female polar bears breed only every three years, so competition between males is fierce. Often, two or more males come across the same female at the same time and bitter fighting may ensue. The bears grapple on the ice, lunging at each other with open jaws. The victor will stay with the female for a week or more, keeping other males away, while the pair mate many times over this period.

THE ARCTIC CLIMATE IS SO HARSH THAT FEMALE POLAR BEARS MUST SHELTER WITH THEIR CUBS IN A DEN DUG OUT IN THE SNOW UNTIL SPRING ARRIVES

Although the bears mate in late April and May, the fertilized egg only begins to grow sometime in October. This process, known as delayed implantation, ensures that the development of the egg starts to take place only when the females have migrated back up north either to winter in last year's dens or to build new ones.

SAFE AND WARM

Pregnant females dig dens in snowdrifts around the end of October and remain inside until the cubs are born between late December and early January. About 75 percent of mothers give birth to twins, 20 percent to single cubs, and only 5 percent to triplets. The helpless newborn cubs are blind and deaf, with thin, white fur. To keep them warm, their mother cradles them into her body and, every so often, she lies on her back to allow them to suckle from one of the four nipples on her chest.

The mother suckles her young for up to two years and the cubs grow at a remarkable rate—polar bear milk is the richest of all terrestrial

AMAZING FACTS

SPECKS OF LIFE

All bear cubs are tiny at birth, but those of the polar bear are particularly minute. Little bigger than a rat and weighing about only 1 to 1.5 pounds (500 to 700 grams), they are the smallest newborn young relative to their mother's body size of any mammal besides marsupials. If newborn human babies were the same relative size, they would be only the size of your thumb!

YOUNGSTERS
closely follow their mother's tracks when they travel long distances across the ice and snow. They become independent at about two years old.

RIDING HIGH
When traveling across deep snow or crossing a bay, a cub will often climb onto its mother's back and cling on with its sharp claws.

GROWING UP
The cubs stay close to their mother during their first few months. They will continue to suckle until they are two years old.

Illustrations Barry Croucher/Wildlife Art Agency

GROWING UP

The life of a young polar bear

NURSING CUBS
The mother suckles the tiny cubs at regular intervals. They will grow rapidly while being fed on her rich milk.

IN SPRING, *the female breaks out of the den and the three-month-old cubs begin to explore their new surroundings.*

mammals, containing on average 33 percent fat.

At about a month old, the cubs can see and hear. By the time they are two months old, when they weigh some 12 to 15 pounds (5 to 7 kilograms), they start to explore the dark interior of the den, often digging out their own tunnels and small chambers.

Between late February and late April, the female breaks out of the den and the cubs emerge. Intensely curious about their surroundings, they frolic in the snow, chasing each other and sliding down slopes. However, the family often continues to shelter in the den for a week or two so that the cubs can become acclimatized to the bitter cold.

After having fasted for several months, the mother is ravenous, and as soon as possible she leads her offspring to the frozen sea and its abundance of seals. The nearest sea ice is usually 5 to 10 miles (8 to 16 kilometers) away, and the female regularly stops to allow her weary cubs a rest and a feed. Usually the cubs follow in their mother's tracks, but occasionally they ride on her back, clinging to her with their sharp claws.

When they reach the sea, the cubs watch the mother hunt and try to imitate her actions. Their early attempts at hunting are usually unsuccessful, because they are too impatient and the prey escapes.

in SIGHT

Illustration Douglas Ingram

BREEDING DENS

Dens are dug in snowdrifts in the lee of hillocks, rocks, or cliffs where the wind will blow a layer of fresh snow over the top as a covering. The bear may plug the entrance of the den with a mound of snow to keep out the wind, and the warmth of its body will keep the interior snug. Dens may be as much as 40°F (20°C) or more warmer than the air outside.

Dens vary in shape and size, but their basic design is the same. An entry tunnel leads into a living chamber—typically about 5 to 7 feet (1.5 to 2 meters) across and 3 feet (1 meter) high—in which the cubs will be born, though females may enlarge their dens as winter progresses.

ON THEIR OWN

At two years old, the cubs are able to hunt but they remain with their mother until she allows them to leave or until they are frightened off by a male who wants to mate with her.

Few polar bears live beyond 18 years of age in the wild, but some reach their twenties, and two have been found that were 32 years old. In zoos, polar bears have lived longer: One old male in London Zoo survived to the ripe old age of 41. ■

PORCUPINES

The autumn mating season is one of the few times of the year when the solitary North American porcupine seeks company. Its acute sense of smell probably helps it locate a female in estrus.

Courtship between North American porcupines can be rowdy. Grunting and wailing, the male dances about energetically, then finally stands up on his hind legs and soaks the female in a shower of urine. Mating generally follows shortly after this; when the female is sufficiently aroused she relaxes her quills and raises her tail over her back, presenting herself to her mate.

Gestation is remarkably long for such a small animal—nearly seven months—at the end of which a single young is born, usually between April and June. A gestation period of this length ensures that the newborn is well developed; it weighs up to 22.5 oz (638 g), its eyes are open, and it is able to walk almost immediately. Covered in long, black hair, it already possesses short, soft quills. To avoid injury to the mother, the young is born headfirst in an amniotic sac. Within half an hour, the quills have hardened.

Precocious porcupines

The newborn porcupine seems to have an instinctive knowledge of its defense reaction. Before even witnessing a parental demonstration, within fifteen minutes of its birth it will whirl around and wave its tail in the direction of any unusual noise or movement. In just a few days, it starts to climb trees—not without a few false starts, particularly when the youngster tries to descend headfirst! Generally it

THE SOCIAL SCALE

Most porcupines are loners, even though the crested porcupines of the Old World may share the same burrow and even forage together. The most overt exceptions are the brush-tailed porcupines of Africa and Asia. These small animals seem to live in family colonies—six to eight individuals sharing a burrow and feeding together. The colony comprises a mated pair with young from a few litters. They occupy a small territory in the forest, which they mark with deposits of dung.

MATING
is one of the few times that the solitary porcupines come together. Courtship can be dramatic and noisy but, needless to say, mating itself is a more cautious affair.

INDEPENDENCE
is reached by the time the porcupine is two months old. The time has come for it to leave the parent and begin establishing its own feeding areas and dens.

In sole charge of its upbringing, a female North American porcupine nuzzles her offspring (below).

Dr. Robert Franz/Planet Earth Pictures

GROWING UP

The life of a young North American porcupine

AFTER MATING,
the female drives away the male. He has no further involvement with the rearing of his offspring.

AT TWO WEEKS
of age, the young porcupine has started to nibble at vegetation and puts on weight rapidly. It continues to suckle, however, for a few more weeks.

Illustrations Joanne Cowne

takes a few tumbles before it discovers that the way to descend is by leading with the rear end.

Within two weeks of birth, the young porcupine is nibbling away at soft vegetation and puts on weight at a rate of 1 lb (454 g) a day. It generally continues suckling for up to about seven weeks; it becomes fully independent shortly after this. Females can begin breeding from the time they are about eighteen months old; although males can also mate from this time, they generally do not do so for another year.

Other New World species also give birth to well-developed young after a relatively long gestation period. The prehensile-tailed species produce a single offspring weighing some 14 oz (397 g), which is able to climb right away. It becomes totally independent by the time it is ten weeks old, and at eleven months is fully grown. The newborn young of the South American tree porcupines are also well developed, although the soft quills that cover them at birth take longer to harden than those of the North American porcupine's young—usually about one week.

BORN IN THE BURROW

The Old World's crested porcupines produce their young after a gestation period that is only about half that of their New World counterparts—usually 100–112 days. There may be up to four in a litter, although there are usually only one or two. The young are well developed at birth, although they weigh only 3.5–10.5 oz (100–300 g). Birth takes place in a grass-lined chamber within the burrow, and the young porcupines are able to move around in the warren in just a few hours. They are born with soft spines that harden and resemble those of the adult by the time the young are ten days old. They suckle for at least three months and become fully grown at one year. At this time, they are also sexually mature, although they are unlikely to breed for at least another six months. Some species, such as the brush-tailed porcupines, produce two or even three litters a year. ■

FROM BIRTH TO DEATH

NORTH AMERICAN PORCUPINE

MATING SEASON: SEPTEMBER TO NOVEMBER
GESTATION: 205–217 DAYS
LITTER SIZE: 1
FIRST SOLID FOOD: 14 DAYS
WEANED: 50 DAYS
LONGEVITY: 18 YEARS IN THE WILD

CRESTED PORCUPINE

MATING SEASON: ALL YEAR
GESTATION: 93–112 DAYS
LITTER SIZE: 1–4, USUALLY 1–2
WEIGHT AT BIRTH: 12 OZ (340 G)
WEANED: 90–100 DAYS
SEXUAL MATURITY: 8–18 MONTHS
LONGEVITY: AT LEAST 15 YEARS IN THE WILD

PRONGHORNS

At the start of the rut (mating season) in September, the territorial bucks move off, each with a chosen female. Young bachelor bucks pursue females but are usually rejected. The older, territorial bucks lead their mates into secluded sites such as ravines. Here they mate, hidden from all rivals. The most dominant bucks have the most mating hideouts. Courtship is ceremonious; the buck circles the doe with exaggerated steps and shows her the black patches on his cheeks. Only after this do they mate.

MALES
take their mate to a private site away from the herd to court and copulate. Sometimes they manage to round up a number of females.

A FEMALE WITH TWIN CALVES HIDES THEM IN SEPARATE SITES, TO REDUCE THE RISK OF A PREDATOR FINDING THEM BOTH

After the rut the bucks shed their horns. They are, at this stage, so exhausted that they would be easy prey for predators, but without their horns they are virtually indistinguishable from females, whose tiny, but lethal, horns are worth avoiding.

Calves are born in May after a gestation period of 230–240 days. A doe usually has one calf in her first season and thereafter twins or, rarely, triplets. At birth a pronghorn calf weighs 4–6.6 lb (1.8–3 kg). It suckles its mother's rich milk, and at four days it can outrun a human. At three weeks it is already grazing, and its coat bears adult coloration. It is weaned at about four to five months. Does become sexually mature at fifteen to sixteen months, while bucks probably do not mate until over two years old. Both sexes seem to breed throughout life.

The water chevrotain mates at any time of year. The only form of courtship is a cry; this brings the

YOUNG MALES
do not achieve territories easily; they are often driven away by older, dominant males.

EMBRYONIC COMPETITION

Unborn pronghorn calves fight to the death inside their mother's womb. Although usually only two fetuses reach full term, four to six are actually implanted in the wall of the uterus at the start of pregnancy. Research has shown that long projections grow out of the embryonic membranes: Some of these projections puncture the membranes of other embryos, killing them. In the end all but two, occasionally three, of the embryos are reabsorbed into the mother's body.

A newborn pronghorn struggles to its feet for the first time in Yellowstone National Park (below).

Stan Osolinski/Oxford Scientific Films

GROWING UP

The life of a young pronghorn

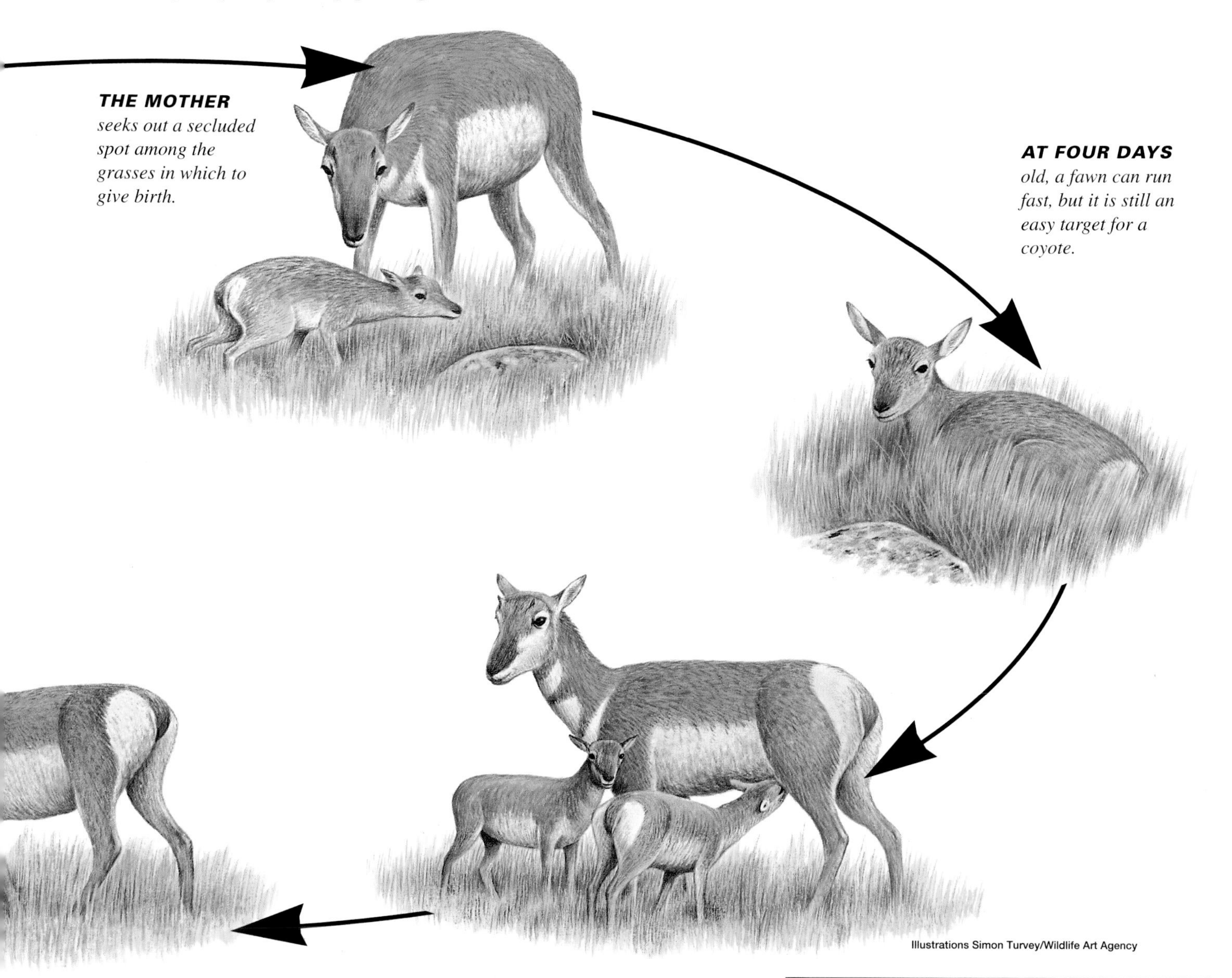

Illustrations Simon Turvey/Wildlife Art Agency

female to a halt, ready for copulation, which may last only a couple of minutes. Gestation takes six to nine months, and only one offspring is born. Most calves are born at the end of the rainy season, when there is plenty of lush vegetation available. Weaning takes place at about three months and the young reach sexual maturity at ten months.

The greater Malay chevrotain mates at any time of year, while the other two Asian species mate in June and July. Gestation in all three species lasts about five months. The lesser Malay chevrotain produces a single calf that is weaned at three months and reaches sexual maturity at four to five months. The greater Malay chevrotain and the Indian spotted chevrotain may produce two offspring, and the adults mate again just two days after the birth of their young. ■

FAWNS
spend twenty to twenty-five minutes each day with their mother. She nurses them for four to five months.

FROM BIRTH TO DEATH

PRONGHORN

GESTATION: 230–240 DAYS
LITTER SIZE: 1–3
WEIGHT AT BIRTH: 4–6.6 LB (1.8–3 KG)
EYES OPEN: AT BIRTH
FIRST WALKING: WITHIN HOURS OF BIRTH
WEANING: 4–5 MONTHS, SOMETIMES SHORTER FOR MALES
SEXUAL MATURITY: DOE AT 15–16 MONTHS, BUCK AT 2 YEARS
LONGEVITY IN WILD: USUALLY 7–10 YEARS

WATER CHEVROTAIN

GESTATION: 180–270 DAYS
LITTER SIZE: 1
WEIGHT AT BIRTH: NOT KNOWN
EYES OPEN: AT BIRTH
FIRST WALKING: WITHIN HOURS OF BIRTH
WEANING: 3 MONTHS
SEXUAL MATURITY: 10 MONTHS
LONGEVITY IN WILD: NOT KNOWN

PUMAS

The mating season is the only time of the year that most New World cats stay in each other's company for any length of time. Although males of most species will be able to tell by their urine markings if the females in their territory are sexually receptive, it is quite often the females that seek out males, making loud mating calls to attract them.

Across much of its range, the puma has no set mating season, and it is the act of mating itself that stimulates the female to ovulate. In the northern part of its range, females generally give birth in late winter and early spring, when the weather is better and more prey is available. Having come together, a male and female will stay in each other's company for a couple of weeks, hunting and sleeping side by side.

As the gestation period of 90 to 95 days comes to an end, the female will find a cozy, protected den for herself, usually in a cave or between rocks. She lines the ground with foliage to make it warm and comfortable, and here she gives birth to up to six cubs—three or four being the common number.

All cats are born blind and helpless, but they are generally fully furred. Initially, the female puma does not stray too far from the den; she spends a lot of time suckling the young. If the cubs survive, the female will not come back into estrus for about two

AT BIRTH *the coat of the 12-in- (30-cm-) long puma cubs is spotted and the tail is ringed. These markings fade when the cubs are six months old or so. The eyes open at ten days old and gradually change from blue to amber.*

YOUNG ADULTS *establish their independence at two years old, but males will not mate for another year. Females are sexually mature at two-and-a-half years old.*

LESSONS *The cubs' mother teaches them all her hunting skills, including tactics for killing deer, before they leave her territory.*

FROM BIRTH TO DEATH

PUMA
GESTATION: 90–95 DAYS
LITTER SIZE: 1–6
WEIGHT AT BIRTH: 8–16 OZ (227–454 G)
EYES OPEN: 6–10 DAYS
WEANED: ABOUT 3 MONTHS
INDEPENDENCE: 1–2 YEARS
SEXUAL MATURITY: MALES, 3 YEARS; FEMALES, 2.5 YEARS
LONGEVITY: UNKNOWN IN THE WILD; OVER 20 YEARS IN CAPTIVITY

JAGUARUNDI
GESTATION: 72–75 DAYS
LITTER SIZE: USUALLY 2, OCCASIONALLY 3.
TAKE SOLID FOOD: 6 WEEKS

LYNX
GESTATION: 63–70 DAYS
LITTER SIZE: 1–5, USUALLY 2–3
WEIGHT AT BIRTH: 7–7.5 OZ (198–213 G)
WEANED: 5 MONTHS, BUT TAKE SOLID FOOD AT 1 MONTH
INDEPENDENCE: 9–10 MONTHS
SEXUAL MATURITY: MALES, 33 MONTHS; FEMALES, 21 MONTHS
LONGEVITY: UNKNOWN IN THE WILD; OVER 26 YEARS IN CAPTIVITY.

BOBCAT
GESTATION: 60–63 DAYS
LITTER SIZE: 1–6, USUALLY 3
WEIGHT AT BIRTH: 10–13 OZ (283–369 G)

GROWING UP

The life of a young puma

HIDDEN IN *the undergrowth, a cub waits for its mother to return from hunting. It will eat meat at six weeks old, but suckles for about six weeks more.*

WITHIN WEEKS *baby pumas have developed into strong, playful kittens, ready to try most things. When they learn to climb trees, they are merely following an inborn instinct.*

All illustrations Kim Thompson

THE BOBCAT'S YOUNG

The bobcat mother commonly gives birth to two or three young in a cozy, sheltered nest during the spring. They open their eyes when they are nine days old and suckle for about two months. At three to five months old, they will go on hunting forays with the mother. By their first winter, they become totally independent and leave the mother, and she is ready to mate again.

ZEFA

years. Females begin breeding soon after they are two years old; males usually do not mate until they are at least three years old.

North America's bobcat generally mates in the late winter. Birth occurs after a 60- to 70-day gestation period in late April to early May. It seems, however, that some females—probably younger ones or those that have lost a litter for some reason—may sometimes give birth later on in the year, toward the end of the summer or in early autumn. A male bobcat may mate with several females, chasing off any intruding males at this time. It is also at this time that the bobcat is at its most vocal—loudly yowling to attract mates.

The lynx's breeding habits are similar to the bobcat's, although these cats tend to mate and give birth a little later in the year.

Although there seems to be no fixed breeding season, the majority of jaguarundi births occur in the spring and summer. The common litter size is two, born in a sheltered den after a gestation of 72–75 days. Like the puma, the cubs are born spotted, although these marks quickly fade. Cubs are often found with different colors within one litter.

Little is known about the breeding habits of South America's small cats, but in the Tropics there is probably no particular breeding season. ■

RACCOONS

The mating season for the common raccoon is at its height in February and March, although activity may occur beyond this time. Raccoons in southern climes have been known to begin mating in December. A male may stay with a mate for a week or so before wandering off to find another.

Gestation lasts about sixty-three days, during which time the female makes a nest of leaves in a hollow tree, a fallen log, or a rocky crevice. Up to seven young—called cubs or kits—are born, with three to four being the usual number. Their eyes open at about three weeks old—by then, their ears are already open. At ten weeks old, they are making short trips with their mother, and a week or two later they join her on all her forays. Weaning takes about four months; males are mature at about two years old, but females may become pregnant at only a year old.

COMPETITION

Females generally accept only one mate per season. In their quest for a partner, males (above) may travel far from their usual home range and can be unusually fierce toward rivals.

Coatis and ringtails

Between February and March, a male coati wins his way into a group of females by grooming them submissively. Soon after mating, the females chase him away again. Although coatis are generally active by day, mating usually occurs at night.

Gestation is about seventy-seven days, and a few weeks before the birth, each female leaves the group to build a lone nest in a tree. She stays with her litter of four to six young, leaving them only briefly to forage, until they are active at about five weeks old. By then they have at least trebled their weight to about 17 oz (500 g), and are ready to join the group.

A kinkajou (below) weighs up to 7 oz (200 g) at birth. It may open its eyes after just a week.

Carol Farneti/Natural Science Photos

Ringtails mate between February and May, giving birth in April to July. There are usually two to four in a litter. Born in a cozy den, the 1-oz (28-g) newborns have fuzzy white hair and stubby tails. Their eyes open at about five weeks; by this time they are taking solid food and have begun to grow an adult coat. The males help rear the young, bringing solid food to the den. At two months old, the young begin to forage with their parents, and at four months they can hunt independently. They usually disperse by the onset of winter.

INDEPENDENCE

Some young leave the mother and go off to find a home range of their own in the late autumn (above). Others will stay with her through the winter, sharing her den, before dispersing at the beginning of spring, by which time the mother is usually busy preparing for a new litter.

Kinkajous and olingos

In their more tropical environment, both kinkajous and olingos can give birth at any time of the year. The kinkajou's gestation lasts up to 118 days—the

GROWING UP

The life of a young raccoon

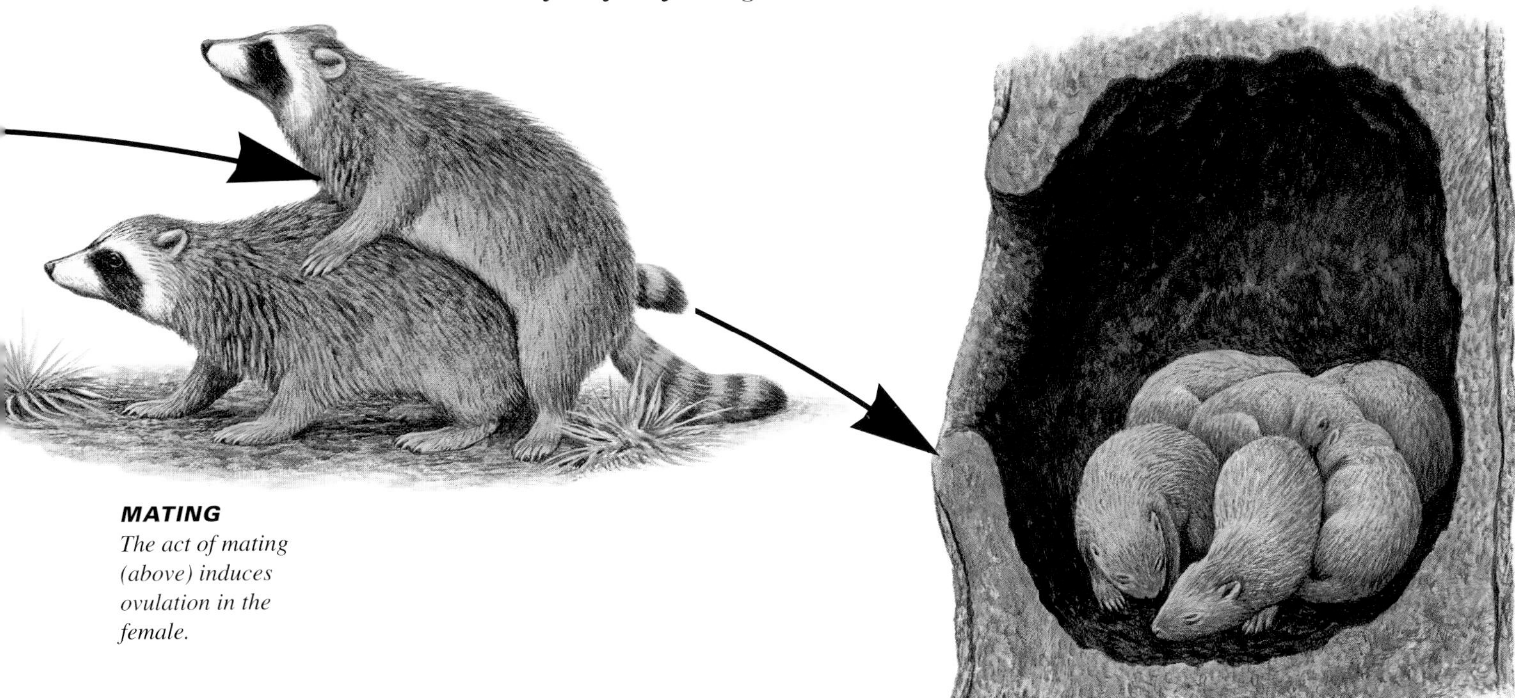

MATING
The act of mating (above) induces ovulation in the female.

TUCKERED OUT
The female becomes increasingly lethargic during her gestation; she gives birth between April and June. The kits are blind and helpless at birth, but they develop quickly.

NIGHT SCHOOL
By the time they are twelve weeks old, the kits accompany their mother wherever she goes, learning the skills they will need for survival by watching and imitating her.

longest of any procyonid—while that of the olingo is about seventy-three days. Both of these animals usually give birth to a single offspring. By the time the young kinkajou is seven weeks old, its tail has become prehensile. Unlike the raccoon, the males become sexually mature first, at eighteen months old, while the females do not begin to breed until they are over two years old.

The olingo's single young weighs 2 oz (55 g) at birth and does not open its eyes until it is nearly four weeks old. Both sexes reach sexual maturity a little before they are two years old. ■

FROM BIRTH TO DEATH

COMMON RACCOON

MATING SEASON: FEBRUARY TO MARCH, SOMETIMES LATER
GESTATION: AVERAGE 63 DAYS
NO. OF YOUNG: 2–7, USUALLY 3–4
WEANED: BY 4 MONTHS
SEXUAL MATURITY: FEMALE 1 YEAR, MALE 2 YEARS
LONGEVITY: OFTEN NO MORE THAN 5 YEARS IN THE WILD; UP TO 20 IN CAPTIVITY

COATI

MATING SEASON: FEBRUARY TO MARCH
GESTATION: AVERAGE 77 DAYS
NO. OF YOUNG: 4–6
WEANED: APPROXIMATELY 4 MONTHS
SEXUAL MATURITY: FEMALE 2 YEARS, MALE 3 YEARS
LONGEVITY: 15 YEARS OR MORE IN CAPTIVITY; LESS IN THE WILD

Illustrations Simon Turvey/Wildlife Art Agency

RAT KANGAROOS

Once a female rat kangaroo reaches sexual maturity, at about one year of age, reproduction becomes an almost constant part of her life. With just a few exceptions, such as the musk rat kangaroo and some populations of the burrowing bettong, breeding is nonseasonal and females can breed at any time of the year. Moreover, the phenomenon of embryonic diapause (see right) means that as soon as a female's pouch becomes empty another birth is already approaching. Not surprisingly, rat kangaroos tend to produce more than one offspring a year, and a female brush-tailed bettong, starting in some cases as early as six months of age, may give birth to three consecutive young per year for several years of reproductive life.

Male rat kangaroos tend to reach maturity shortly after their female counterparts and invest much less time and energy in producing offspring. By visiting females neighboring his home range, a male finds out which are coming into estrus and, unless driven off, lingers nearby until potential partners are ready to mate. Usually courtship approaches are simple, although musk rat kangaroos may court for several days, facing each other standing upright and gently pawing each other's head and neck.

in SIGHT

DIAPAUSE

In most kangaroos, a process of delayed birth, known as embryonic diapause, can take place. Female rat kangaroos often mate soon after the birth of an offspring—in some cases on the same night. Should the resulting embryo develop as normal it would be born before the pouch is vacated and ready for it. Instead, its development is delayed; the embryo is held in limbo and its growth is not resumed until the pouch is empty. This overlap between offspring ensures the mother can breed rapidly: In the Tasmanian bettong, a female may give birth on the same night as her previous young ends its pouch life. Should the first offspring perish, the delayed embryo will resume development at once.

RAT KANGAROOS *are energetic breeders. Having found a female nearing receptivity, the male follows her persistently until she is prepared to mate (above right). If she is not ready for him, she growls, rolls over, and lashes out at him.*

GROWING UP

The life of a young honey possum

HONEY POSSUMS *are mature at about six months of age, and adults (above) may mate in any month of the year, although the lack of food in summer means that births are few at that time of year.*

THE NEWLY EMERGED YOUNG *are soon able to ride around on their mother's back as she forages (below). A full litter is too much for her to bear for long, however, and shortly before they are weaned the young follow her on foot.*

UP TO FOUR YOUNG *are born in each litter and all of them may find their way to the pouch; they are the smallest newborn young of any mammal. As they suckle (right), they increase five times in weight before leaving the pouch at about two months of age.*

GROWING UP

The life of a rufous rat kangaroo

FAST BREEDER

The female gives birth to her tiny, embryonic offspring, which crawls through her body fur from the birth canal to the pouch (right). Within hours, she is ready to mate again.

THE YOUNG RAT KANGAROO

clings steadfastly to a teat for its first two months, but within four months of birth it has left the pouch for good. Its mother will send it off to cope for itself when her next offspring develops (below).

After mating, all the hard work is left up to the female. Following a gestation period ranging from twenty-one days in bettongs to thirty-eight days in the long-nosed potoroo—one of the longest gestations for a marsupial—a single young is born. Twins are usual in the musk rat kangaroo, but in all other species if two young emerge only one will survive in the pouch.

For the first few weeks of life, young rufous rat kangaroos seek the shelter of the nursery nest, and their mother returns periodically to suckle them (below).

The minuscule, grublike young, about 0.6 in (15 mm) in length, attaches itself to one of four teats in the pouch and grows fast, nourished on its mother's milk. As early as seven or eight weeks it is ready to release the teat and soon starts to make its first trips outside the pouch. Pouch life finally ends at three to four and a half months.

In the Tasmanian bettong, the last two weeks of pouch life are characterized by ever shorter stays in this "mobile home," until a stage is reached when the young seeks its safety only when startled. A few nights later, the mother's pouch muscles dramatically tighten and the youngster is forcibly and permanently evicted, although the mother continues to suckle the offspring for several more weeks until weaning is complete. ■

R. J. Allingham/ANT/NHPA

FROM BIRTH TO DEATH

	RUFOUS RAT KANGAROO	MUSK RAT KANGAROO
BREEDING:	THROUGHOUT THE YEAR	FEBRUARY–JULY
GESTATION:	22–24 DAYS	NOT KNOWN
LITTER SIZE:	USUALLY 1	2 OR 3
NO. OF LITTERS:	UP TO 3 PER YEAR	ONE PER YEAR
WEIGHT AT BIRTH:	LESS THAN 0.03 OZ (1 G)	LESS THAN 0.03 OZ (1 G)
LEAVES POUCH:	16 WEEKS	21 WEEKS
WEANING:	22 WEEKS	22–23 WEEKS
SEXUAL MATURITY:	11–13 MONTHS	12 MONTHS
LONGEVITY:	6 YEARS OR MORE	NOT KNOWN

Illustrations Carol Roberts

RED FOXES

Once she is sexually mature, a red fox vixen is receptive once a year, for as little as two or three days. Hormonal rise begins several days before she is ready to mate and her scent marks declare the fact to the local males. Accordingly if any male feels he has a claim on a female—usually the dominant vixen sharing his territory—he has to beware of rivals who might sneak in under his nose.

MATE GUARDING

As the winter breeding season approaches, therefore, a male pays close attention to his intended. They still tend to forage alone, but they may rest or travel together for several hours each night. This "mate guarding" is crucial to the dog fox, for he will shortly invest a lot of time and energy in bringing food to the vixen and her cubs, and he clearly does not want to support the cubs of another male. The female may at first reject the male's advances, spitting and snarling at him despite all his attentions, but persistence usually pays off.

Having mated, the male is likely to slip off in search of other receptive vixens during the 53-day gestation period. But since he can rarely care for more than one brood at once, he may have to use the very trick he was trying to prevent by mate guarding and foist his own offspring onto an unsuspecting male. Not surprisingly, relations between neighboring males reach a low ebb at this time and fights are frequent.

AT THE DEN
The dog fox is kept busy bringing food to the vixen and her hungry litter (right).

In the United States red fox cubs are born from late February to June, usually in a nursery burrow or earth but occasionally in a tussock of grass or a hollow tree. There may be up to twelve of them, but four to eight is usual. These blind bundles of chocolate fur depend fully on the mother for about four weeks; during this time the male brings food to her. At about one month old the cubs leave their nursery at night to explore; at this time, too, they eat their first solid food and their coats start to redden. By about two months old they have their adult color.

At eight to ten weeks they are weaned, but the parents have to bring their food to the den. Among group-living foxes it is normal for all the adults to bring food to the cubs. At about twelve weeks old the cubs begin to forage with the adults, and the nursery is abandoned. This is a period of intense learning for the cubs. They learn about food; how to avoid their

Wayne Lankinen/Aquila

Helpless at birth, red fox cubs can soon fend for themselves, even at the expense of their siblings (left).

CUB CALENDAR

DECEMBER
MATING SEASON STARTS; FOXES BECOME MORE TERRITORIAL

JANUARY
THE MAIN MATING PERIOD IN NORTHERN EUROPE

FEBRUARY
PREGNANT VIXENS LOOK FOR SUITABLE NURSERY DENS

MARCH
CUBS ARE BORN TOWARD THE END OF THE MONTH; MALE BRINGS FOOD FOR NURSING VIXEN

APRIL
CUBS MAKE FIRST FORAYS ABOVE GROUND; VIXEN MAY MOVE THEM ELSEWHERE IF SHE FEELS INSECURE OR THE DEN IS TOO SMALL

MAY
CUBS START EATING SOLID FOOD AND FIGHT AMONG THEMSELVES FOR DOMINANCE

JUNE
FULLY WEANED CUBS LEAVE THE DEN AND FOLLOW ADULTS AS THEY FORAGE

JULY
CUBS BEGIN FORAGING FOR THEMSELVES

AUGUST
CUBS BECOME INCREASINGLY INDEPENDENT, ALTHOUGH THEY ARE STILL SEQUESTERED WITH A PARENT DURING THE DAY

SEPTEMBER
CUBS FULLY GROWN; DOMINANT CUBS EXERT PRESSURE ON MALE UNDERDOGS TO LEAVE

OCTOBER
START OF DISPERSAL PERIOD. YOUNG FEMALES MAY REMAIN WITH THE FAMILY GROUP

NOVEMBER
DISPERSAL CONTINUES THROUGH TO THE END OF THE YEAR AND THE START OF THE NEXT MATING SEASON

enemies, and how to use the terrain to their advantage. They already know who is boss, for red fox cubs establish a pecking order by fighting in the nursery. These fights are in deadly earnest and can even prove fatal. As they mature they employ more subtle tactics, grooming each other selectively to exclude the underdogs, which may eventually be the first to leave the family group. These refugees are also smaller than the young foxes that remain, suggesting that they have been denied their full share of the food brought back by the adults.

By the end of summer the cubs are fully grown and may eventually seek out territories of their own. This is a dangerous time for a fox: As it moves through unknown terrain it is likely to run into trouble as it trespasses on the territories of other foxes or attracts larger predators and humans. Among urban foxes some 55 percent die in their first year before they get the chance to breed, but some lucky survivors may breed for eight seasons in a row before dying of old age. ■

Illustration Guy Croucher/Wildlife Art Agency

RHINOCEROSES

Rhinos live long lives, maturing slowly and progressing steadily through life's stages. The rearing of young is no exception.

The rituals of rhino courtship are prolonged, complicated, and sometimes violent, none more so than that of the Indian species. The female will ward off the approaching bull with a charge, slashing her sharp incisor teeth at him. Only when she has fought with him to the point of exhaustion will mating take place.

CONFLICTING INTERESTS

Rhinos commonly spend more than an hour mating, during which time the male is mounted on the female's back. Rhino males are renowned for their astonishing sexual staying powers—probably the source of the mythical aphrodisiac power of the rhino's horn. By this time, the cow seems surprisingly unconcerned, walking around and feeding while the bull tries to maintain the coupling.

MATING BETWEEN RHINOS IS PROLONGED, AND THIS MAY HAVE LED TO THE MYTH THAT THE HUMAN MALE CAN IMPROVE HIS SEXUAL PROWESS WITH RHINO HORN

Rhinos rarely give birth to more than one calf—only white rhino twins have been observed. Births take place at any time of the year, but, for African rhinos at least, the peak is reached at the beginning of the dry season.

The prospective mother usually finds some dense cover in which to give birth, always keeping a sharp ear and nose out for lions or hyenas if it is an

NEWBORN *rhinos are at the most risk from predators, even though they can get to their feet almost immediately.*

SNIFFING IN *the scent of a female's urine, the male rhino can gather information about her sexual receptivity.*

PLAYTIME *often involves mother and baby rubbing their horns together.*

Illustrations John Cox/Wildlife Art Agency

in SIGHT

BORN LEADERS

Black rhino calves run behind their mothers, whereas the young of the white rhino tend to trot along a few steps ahead. This is thought to be because of habitat differences: A black rhino predator usually hides in ambush, so the mother will meet it first, while, in more open grasslands, predators such as hyenas are likely to chase prey from behind.

Mark Boulton/ICCE Photo Library

GROWING UP

The life of a young black rhino

THE YOUNG CALF
will continue to suckle its mother's milk for about eighteen months, though it will start to eat grasses and leaves when it is a few weeks old.

KEEPING CLOSE
to its mother, a baby black rhino will follow a few paces behind when accompanying her on her travels.

FROM BIRTH TO DEATH

BLACK RHINO
GESTATION: 15 MONTHS
LITTER SIZE: 1
BIRTH INTERVAL: 3 YEARS
WEIGHT AT BIRTH: 48–100 LB (22–45 KG)
WEANING: 18 MONTHS
INDEPENDENCE: 2–3 YEARS
SEXUAL MATURITY: FEMALES 4–5 YEARS, MALES 6–7 YEARS
LONGEVITY: 40 YEARS

WHITE RHINO
GESTATION: 16 MONTHS
LITTER SIZE: USUALLY 1, BUT OCCASIONALLY 2
BIRTH INTERVAL: 4 YEARS
WEIGHT AT BIRTH: 185 LB (84 KG)
WEANING: BETWEEN 1 AND 2 YEARS
INDEPENDENCE: 2–3 YEARS
SEXUAL MATURITY: FEMALES 4–5 YEARS, MALES 6–7 YEARS
LONGEVITY: 45 YEARS

INDIAN RHINO
GESTATION: 16 MONTHS
LITTER SIZE: 1
BIRTH INTERVAL: 3 YEARS
WEIGHT AT BIRTH: 120–145 LB (54–66 KG)
WEANING: NOT KNOWN IN WILD
INDEPENDENCE: 2–3 YEARS?
SEXUAL MATURITY: FEMALES 5 YEARS, MALES 7–9 YEARS
LONGEVITY: 45–50 YEARS

African species, tigers if it is Asian.

The newborn baby's weight will be about 4 percent of its mother's, which differs among the species. For the first couple of days the mother suckles the calf every hour or two, but the calf only sucks for two to three minutes at a time. As it gains strength, the feeding bouts become longer and less frequent. The young calf will drink up to 35 pints (17 liters) of its mother's rich milk every day.

A CALF WILL STAY WITH ITS MOTHER UNTIL A NEW CALF IS BORN, OR FOR UP TO FOUR YEARS. A CLOSE BOND DEVELOPS BETWEEN THEM DURING THIS TIME

Black rhino calves may nibble at solid foods at only nine days old and will supplement their mother's milk regularly after one month. White rhino calves don't try their first grass until they are about two months old. Though they are weaned at about eighteen months, youngsters will not usually become independent until they are two or three years old.

Late developers

Female African rhinos reach sexual maturity after four or five year, and will have their first calf by the age of six or seven. Though they are sexually mature at seven or eight, males are unlikely to breed until they have proved themselves in combat with older males. This rarely happens before they are at least ten years of age. This is not a problem, however, since rhinos can live for up to forty years. ■

RORQUALS

As with other aspects of behavior, more is known about courtship and mating in humpbacks than in other rorquals.

Every year, each humpback returns to its habitual breeding ground. The males arrive first and begin singing. They hang in the water 65–165 ft (20–50 m) down in a characteristic pose with head angled down and huge flippers dangling and announce their presence by song. When a female arrives, the closest male is attracted to her, then other males come, too, and they struggle and jostle to lie next to her.

Gradually more females arrive. Rival males threaten each other by slapping the water with their flukes or flippers. They also rear up from the water, blow massive bubbles, and even lunge at competitors with their mouths or tail flukes, sometimes causing injuries.

Courtship in other rorquals seems to be much less sophisticated—or it has simply not yet been observed.

MATING
The pair of mating humpbacks come together upright in the water, belly to belly and flippers clasping the partner, with most of their heads above the surface.

STAYING CLOSE
By the time the mother and calf return to the summer feeding ground, the calf is weaned, but it may continue to swim close to its mother.

Breeding cycle

The breeding cycle of the rorquals is closely linked to their migratory habits. The general pattern is that calving usually takes place in the warmer waters of the subtropics. Females who gave birth in the previous year, and whose calves are now weaned and independent, mate around the same time. Since the gestation period is about eleven months in most species, calves are born on return to the wintering areas in the following year.

The mother rorqual gives birth, usually to a single calf, in the usual mammal way. The mother suckles her newborn, using her abdominal muscles

- **The blue whale calf is the world's biggest animal baby, at 23 ft (7 m) long and up to 3.3 tons in weight.**
- **Even as it grows in the womb, it puts on 2.2 tons in the last two months of pregnancy.**
- **After birth this big baby suckles about 100 gallons (almost 400 liters) of high-fat, high-protein mother's milk every day and puts on 175 pounds per day—the weight of a fairly large man, and the greatest growth rate of any mammal.**
- **By seven months of age, when a human baby weighs some 17 lb (8 kg), the young blue whale weighs 2,000 times more and has reached 42 ft (13 m) in length.**

Color illustrations Barry Croucher/Wildlife Art Agency

GROWING UP

The life of a young humpback

GIVING BIRTH
The mother rorqual gives birth, usually to a single calf. The calf emerges headfirst, and she may nudge it to the surface so that it can take its first breaths.

FEEDING
As soon as the single calf is born, it fastens on to its mother's nipple (left), which protrudes from folds of skin on her underside, called the mammary slit.

FROM BIRTH TO DEATH

BLUE WHALE	HUMPBACK WHALE
GESTATION: 11–12 MONTHS	**GESTATION:** 11–12 MONTHS
NUMBER OF CALVES: 1	**NUMBER OF CALVES:** 1
LENGTH AT BIRTH: 23 FT (7 M)	**LENGTH AT BIRTH:** 13–16 FT (4–5 M)
WEIGHT AT BIRTH: 5,500 LB (2,500 KG)	**WEIGHT AT BIRTH:** 2,800 LB (1,300 KG)
SEXUAL MATURITY: 6–12 YEARS	**SEXUAL MATURITY:** 5–10 YEARS
LENGTH AT SEXUAL MATURITY: 72–75 FT (22–23 M)	**LENGTH AT SEXUAL MATURITY:** 36–39 FT (11–12 M)
LONGEVITY: 65–75 YEARS	**LONGEVITY:** 70–80 YEARS

to speed up the process of pumping milk into its mouth. Whale milk is exceptionally rich in fats, which the calf's body burns to provide body warmth and lays down as fatty insulating blubber under the skin.

The mother protects her baby, who continues to feed for six months, while the pair return to their summer feeding ground. It is then weaned.

Bryde's whales feed for most of the year in their subtropical and tropical waters and do not have the regular migrations of other rorquals. Their breeding season is similarly ill-defined, and they can mate and give birth at any time of year.

With this breeding cycle, the large rorquals produce a calf every other year. However, there is evidence that some females are reproducing every year. They give birth, then mate shortly afterward. The reason may be that their numbers are lower since commercial whaling began, and so there is more food available and less competition for it.

MATURING EARLY

Another effect of the low population, and greater food supplies, is that juveniles are reaching sexual maturity younger. Whales tend to mature at a certain body length, not at a set age; so if they can eat more and grow faster, they can breed younger. For example, it is estimated that in the past 50 years, the average age of sexual maturity in minke whales has fallen from 13–14 years to 6–7 years.

Both of these effects—breeding more frequently and at a younger age—may help the whale populations increase more rapidly. ■

Kevin & Cat Sweeney/Tony Stone Worldwide

A humpback and nursing calf (right). The mother and calf have a very close bond with one another.

SHREWS

In temperate climates, shrews breed from March to November. In the Tropics, the breeding season extends throughout the year. This is the only occasion in which shrews deliberately seek out each other's company. In the buildup to mating, shrews find suitable mates largely by scent. Then the male follows the female, chasing her and sniffing her until they finally mate. If the female is not ready to mate, she squeaks loudly and bites the male until he is driven away.

In most shrew species, the male plays no further part in the birth or care of the young after mating. He simply wanders off to find other mates. In a few species, however, the male not only helps the female to build a nest, but guards the litter while she is out on hunting trips. The breeding nest is larger and more elaborate than resting and sleeping nests. It is made from grass, leaves, and moss and may be situated in an underground chamber, in a clump of grass, or under a log.

A PRECARIOUS START

Gestation in the European common shrew lasts for about twenty-four days. Usually five to seven young are born, and a female may have two or even three litters in a season. There may be as many as fifteen young in the litters of water shrews. The newborn are naked, blind, and helpless. Some of the litter inevitably perish, often because the mother simply has too few teats to cater to all. Depending on the species, female shrews have between six and ten teats.

THE ADULT *female is receptive only for a few hours in each estrous cycle, and the brief act of mating induces her to ovulate.*

UPON REACHING *independence (twenty-five days), the young are driven away aggressively by the female, who will soon be preparing for her next litter.*

A CARAVAN OF SHREWS

Young shrews use a most effective method of staying in touch with their mothers on foraging trips, or if they are forced to abandon their nest. The first youngster grips the fur on its mother's rump in its teeth. The next baby grabs hold of the first, and before long there is a wriggling line of shrews. However fast the mother runs, the young keep up and keep in step. If the coast is clear, the shrews soon scatter to forage. But if danger appears, they form a line again and dash for safety.

YOUNG SHREWS *on the move grip on tight; if the mother is picked up they come, too, still hanging on to her rump.*

Illustrations Simon Turvey/Wildlife Art Agency

GROWING UP

The life of a young shrew

GESTATION
lasts about three weeks, and the young remain in their burrow nest for five to eight weeks. If they stray, the mother picks them up with her mouth and carefully returns them.

AT THREE WEEKS
of age, the young are encouraged to leave the burrow on short foraging trips.

The youngsters develop very quickly. For the first week of their lives, they suckle their mother's milk. After about ten days, their fur has started to grow, and from two weeks old their eyes open. They remain in the nest, crying out to the female when hungry. She guards them closely, fending off intruders or moving to a new location if danger threatens. At the age of about eighteen days, the young shrews leave the nest for the first time. A week later, they are fully weaned and completely independent. They must then establish their own territories and forage for food by themselves. Their mother drives them out if they are unwilling to go, since she needs the nest for her next litter.

Most shrews are born in June, July, and August. They start looking for a mate the following spring, but by autumn they will die. One of the shortest lived of all mammals, most shrews live for only a year or so in the wild, although some species can live for up to four years in captivity. Some fall prey to predators, such as foxes, or owls and other birds of prey. Others starve as their teeth wear down, and a few are killed in the violent fights over territories. But a few simply die of old age and the chill of autumn.

Solenodons have a low rate of reproduction, producing perhaps two litters in a season with one or two young in each. The female gives birth in a nest burrow, where she suckles and keeps guard over her offspring. The young remain with their mother for several months; among insectivores, this represents a remarkably long period of parental care. ■

FROM BIRTH TO DEATH

EUROPEAN COMMON SHREW

BREEDING SEASON: MARCH–AUGUST
GESTATION: 24–25 DAYS
LITTER SIZE: USUALLY 5–7
NUMBER OF LITTERS PER YEAR: 1–2
BODY LENGTH AT BIRTH: 0.6 IN (15 MM)
WEIGHT AT BIRTH: 0.018 OZ (0.5 G)
EYES FULLY OPEN: 16 DAYS
WEANING: 25 DAYS
SEXUAL MATURITY: 4–6 MONTHS
LONGEVITY: 12–13 MONTHS IN WILD; UP TO 18 MONTHS IN CAPTIVITY

in SIGHT

TEAT TRANSPORTATION

Until they are about two months old, young solenodons accompany their mother on her evening hunting trips. They travel by an unusual manner, hanging on to her teats with their mouths. The female's teats are situated on her rump, and, to begin with, she simply drags her charges along with her. Later, they walk by her side, learning to recognize good foraging routes and to find food for themselves. The female will also use teat transportation if her nesting burrow is disturbed and she needs to move the vulnerable young to a safer site.

SLOTHS

In keeping with their relaxed attitude to life, sloths seem equally unspecific when it comes to breeding. It is difficult even to determine the sex of a sloth, since the male's scrotum is not externally visible. There does not seem to be a fixed mating season in sloths—births of two-toed sloths have been recorded in all months of the year except April, September, and November—and it is thought likely that scent plays a role in attracting a mate. It is also believed that a system of delayed implantation may operate, a system that allows the single young to be born when there is an abundant supply of food.

The mating process is a simple affair; the partners hang from a branch by their arms and turn to face each other to copulate. The gestation period varies between genera; in the case of three-toed sloths it lasts about five months. Among two-toed sloths, however, the full term may be around twice as long—which is comparable to many whales.

A CAPABLE INFANT

The single young is born up in the canopy; often the female giving birth will hang at full length, anchored only by her arms. The infant is born headfirst, and at once it climbs up onto the mother's breast using its claws to clamber through her fur. The female then bites through the umbilical cord to release her baby.

MATING, *like all other aspects of sloth life, is an arboreal affair (right). The courtship is cursory, although copulation demands some fairly impressive gymnastics.*

BRANCHING OUT *As it nears a year in age, the young sloth starts to feed itself among the branches (right). Gradually the female loses interest in her charge, even acting aggressively toward it.*

A baby sloth is a perfect miniature of its parents. Having reached the safety of the mother's chest fur, it is most reluctant to relax its grip (below).

Michael Fogden/Oxford Scientifc Films

Illustrations Joanne Cowne

The newly born young is precocial—fully formed at birth with ears and eyes open—and is covered in woolly fur. It is also born with a full set of brownish teeth. Despite its advanced features, however, a newborn sloth is a true miniature: It only weighs about 5 percent of the mature adult's body weight. This is significantly low compared with most other mammal species, particularly considering that the sloth bears only a single young. This low birth weight is probably explained by the sloth's arboreal existence and the relatively lean diet.

GROWING UP

The life of a young three-toed sloth

GIVING BIRTH
Gestation may last over eleven months in the two-toed sloth. The female is rewarded after this phenomenal length of time with a highly developed infant (right) that can soon take care of itself.

HOLD ON TIGHT!
Although it is weaned after only a month or so, the tiny youngster clings to its mother for several months longer. During this period of dependency (above), the female feeds it on prechewed leaves.

The birth of such a well-developed young after such a long period of pregnancy has evolved as a strategy to reduce energy needs. The long gestation avoids a rapid drain on energy, and the reduction in the duration of lactation (milk secretion) again conserves energy.

During the first four weeks of its life, the baby remains hidden within the fur of the mother, who remains faithful to a small area during this period. Gradually the youngster begins to show more of an interest in its surroundings; it begins to grasp at nearby branches and sniffs at anything within reach.

A baby sloth is weaned at about one month old. At this age, it begins to take leaves that have been chewed first by the mother to reduce them into more manageable portions. At about ten weeks old, the offspring takes leaves from branches adjacent to the ones from which the mother is eating, stretching out for those it can reach from the safety of her belly. But at all times it remains close to her body, clinging to her by its legs. If for any reason the youngster is separated from its mother at this early stage in life, it gives plaintive bleating calls until they are reunited.

There are, however, rare occasions when it takes its own course in the canopy. The mother is apparently a careless climber, leaving the youngster little clearance room against the rough branches. Therefore, the infant detaches itself from its mother as she approaches obstructive branches; skirting the limb, the youngster leaps nimbly back onto the transport—nimbly, at least, for a sloth.

By nine months of age, the young sloth becomes increasingly independent and is then able to hang by itself from branches. At about this age, the mother loses interest in her offspring and will resist its approaches, even attempting to bite it if it continues to persist in its attentions. However, the young of Hoffmann's two-toed sloths have been known to associate with their mothers for up to two years after birth. The male sloth is not known to play any part in helping to rear its offspring. ■

FROM BIRTH TO DEATH

HOFFMANN'S TWO-TOED SLOTH

GESTATION: 345 DAYS
LITTER SIZE: 1
ADULT WEIGHT: 200 LB (91 KG)
WEIGHT AT BIRTH: 12–16 OZ (350–454 G)
WEANING: 3–4 WEEKS; RELIES ON MOTHER FOR 5 MONTHS
SEXUAL MATURITY: FEMALE 3.5 YEARS, MALE 4–5 YEARS
LONGEVITY: 30–40 YEARS IN WILD

BROWN-THROATED THREE-TOED SLOTH

GESTATION: 175 DAYS
LITTER SIZE: 1
ADULT WEIGHT: 100 LB (45 KG)
WEIGHT AT BIRTH: 7–9 OZ (198–255 G)
WEANING: 3–4 WEEKS; RELIES ON MOTHER FOR 6 MONTHS
SEXUAL MATURITY: 3–4 YEARS
LONGEVITY: 30–40 YEARS IN WILD

SPERM WHALES

The great sperm whale is a seasonal breeder, although matings and births are spread over a few months. In the Southern Hemisphere matings are in December and January. The females are pregnant for about fourteen months, so they give birth in February or March of the following year. In the Northern Hemisphere these dates differ by about four to six months.

After the calf is born, the mother feeds it on milk for two years or more, then rests for a year or two. The average young female produces a calf every four or five years. This is one of the slowest reproductive rates of any mammal.

At mating time, male sperm whales often battle with each other for the right to mate with the

All illustrations Philip Hood/Wildlife Art Agency

Godfrey Merlen/Oxford Scientific Films

AGGRESSIVE MALES

At breeding time bull sperm whales often clash. They head-butt each other with tremendous dull thuds. Sometimes they try to slash and bite with their lower jaws. They may damage or lose their teeth, and even crack and break the long, slim jawbone.

Male narwhals also fight by jousting with each other using the extraordinary "tusk," often inflicting serious damage.

MATING
When sperm whales mate (top left) they do so belly to belly with the female on top and the bull supporting her from below.

PODS
Female sperm whales live in groups with their calves and juveniles.

females. After mating, the baby develops in the female's womb. It is born tail first, as in other whales, and at once follows its instincts to swim to the surface and breathe through its blowhole. The mother may initially support the new calf and nudge it to the surface, since it takes some practice to coordinate swimming, surfacing, and breathing.

The mother's mammary glands are contoured into her underside, for streamlining. The nipples protrude through long folds of skin, called mammary slits, only when the baby is feeding. The milk is squirted out by the mother, rather than being sucked in by the youngster. The newborn sperm whale is a big baby with an appetite to match, drinking 45 lb (20 kg) of milk daily.

The dwarf and pygmy sperm whales follow similar life cycles, although, being much smaller, the timings are relatively shorter. Gestation is about nine and eleven months respectively.

Belugas mate in late winter or early spring, and the calves are born fourteen months later, in the next summer. Belugas gather in shallow bays and estuaries to give birth. The mother leaves the main group for a week or two to produce and nurse her offspring. She may be accompanied by a younger female, probably a daughter from a previous mating. Young belugas swim so close to their mothers for the first year or two that the two almost seem to be joined together. The mother is very protective and charges at predators or intruders. The average time between calves is three years.

Narwhals follow a similar breeding pattern to belugas, but they do not seek shallow water, producing their calves in deeper inlets and fjords.

Breeding information for beaked whales is scarce. It seems that northern bottlenose whales have a pregnancy of around one year. New calves are 10–11.5 ft (3–3.5 m) long, arrive in early summer, and are weaned after about a year. Females produce a calf every two or three years, between the ages of about 10 and 25 years. ■

FROM BIRTH TO DEATH

SPERM WHALE

GESTATION: 14–15 MONTHS
NUMBER OF YOUNG: 1
LENGTH AT BIRTH: 13 FT (4 M)
WEIGHT AT BIRTH: 1.1–2.2 TONS (1–2 TONNES)
WEANING: UP TO 2 YEARS
SEXUAL MATURITY FOR FEMALE: 7–12 YEARS OR 26–30 FT (8–9 M) IN LENGTH
SEXUAL MATURITY FOR MALE: 17–20 YEARS OR 40 FT (12 M)
LONGEVITY: UP TO 60–70 YEARS

BELUGA WHALE

GESTATION: 14–15 MONTHS
NUMBER OF YOUNG: 1
LENGTH AT BIRTH: 5 FT (1.5 M)
WEIGHT AT BIRTH: 88–175 LB (40–80 KG)
WEANING: UP TO 2 YEARS
INDEPENDENCE: 3–5 YEARS
SEXUAL MATURITY FOR FEMALE: 4–7 YEARS
SEXUAL MATURITY FOR MALE: 7–9 YEARS
LONGEVITY: 25–40 YEARS

TASMANIAN DEVILS

Most marsupial carnivores breed once a year, in winter or spring, although dunnarts produce two litters each year. The Tasmanian devil usually breeds at the end of its second year, although most other dasyures breed in their first year. The female devil produces two young in the first season, and three or four annually for the next three years or so. Dunnarts may produce twenty young each year.

In March, the female devil's pouch enlarges. By April, males and females pair up. The male keeps the female in his den for about two weeks before they mate. In some dasyures, copulation lasts several hours. The pair may stay together until the young are independent.

THE FEMALE PHASCOGALE WOULD SEEM TO BE UNIMPRESSED BY COPULATION: SHE IS LIKELY TO FALL ASLEEP DURING THE ACT!

Most dasyures have a gestation of 21–28 days; in the dunnarts it is only 12 days. Gestation in the devil is 31 days, after which usually four young are born. They are each the size of a baked bean; only the forelimbs are well developed, with claws to crawl to the four teats in the pouch. The young devils stay attached to the teats until 13 weeks old. By this time they are furred and their eyes are open.

By late September the young have outgrown the pouch, so the adults build them a grass nursery nest in a sheltered spot. The male helps to defend the nest and brings food to his mate, but he ignores

IN LATE SPRING *the male and female come together to mate. It is an aggressive affair, but the male often assists the female for several months.*

AT TWO YEARS *the devil is sexually mature; now it starts to seek out a mate.*

Andrew Henley/Biofotos

The brown antechinus, like most dasyurids, is nocturnal. It spends the day resting in a nest, usually inside a hollow log (left).

GROWING UP

The life of a young devil

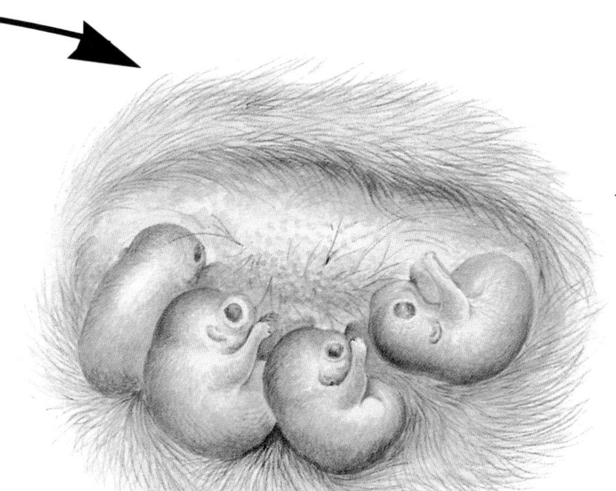

THE NAKED
newborns are tiny, with outsized heads. Having found a teat, they hang on tight for about three months.

FULLY FURRED
at fifteen weeks, with their eyes open, the young start to investigate their surroundings but remain safely under cover.

AT TWENTY WEEKS
the devil is fully weaned and capable of feeding on carrion.

FROM BIRTH TO DEATH

TASMANIAN DEVIL	COMMON DUNNART
GESTATION: 30–32 DAYS	**GESTATION:** 12–14 DAYS
LITTER SIZE: 3 OR 4	**LITTER SIZE:** UP TO 10
SIZE AT BIRTH: 0.4–0.6 IN (10–15 MM)	**SIZE AT BIRTH:** 0.2–0.3 IN (5–8 MM)
EYES OPEN: 10–13 WEEKS	**EYES OPEN:** 3–4 WEEKS
WEANED: 5 MONTHS	**WEANED:** 9 WEEKS
INDEPENDENT: 6 MONTHS	**INDEPENDENT:** NOT KNOWN
LONGEVITY: 7–8 YEARS	**LONGEVITY:** 1–2 YEARS

his offspring. The young stay and play at the nest while their mother forages. They are weaned after five months, but they continue to follow the mother, hanging on to her fur or heels, until November or December, when they become independent.

QUOLLS AND PHASCOGALES

Quolls mate between April and June; the gestation period is sixteen to twenty-one days. The female has only six teats, yet may give birth to up to thirty young. The babies are attached to the teats for seven weeks. They begin to leave her and start to play at thirteen weeks, and they are independent at eighteen weeks.

The phascogales also have a winter courtship. Like many dasyures, the female lacks a proper pouch, but has folds of skin around her eight teats, which enlarge during the thirty-day gestation period. More than eight young are born, so some die at once—a strange feature common to several species, including the quoll. The surviving youngsters stay attached to the teats for forty days, then the mother makes a nursery nest, where they are based until weaned at five months. The juveniles may stay in the nest until the next breeding season, when they are fully grown and sexually mature. ■

AMAZING FACTS

DEATH FROM MATING

In many of the antechinuses, the male searches frantically for a suitable female. Competing males battle strenuously to win a mate. Mating, too, is action packed, taking twelve hours as the male bear-hugs the female and grips her neck in his teeth.

Stressed by searching for a mate, fighting off other males, and copulating endlessly, nearly all males die after mating. This means that hardly any male antechinuses live for more than one year. It also leaves the females and young with no local competition for food.

Robin Budden/Wildlife Art Agency

GROWING UP

The life of a Bengal tiger

TIGERS

Tigers will mate at any time of the year, whenever the female is in season. Female tigers remain in season for only between three and seven days, so they must attract a mate during this time.

A male senses if a female is in season by her scent and will follow her, usually advertising his presence by calling. The female replies and the two tigers eventually meet in the dense undergrowth.

When the tigers meet, they make a facial expression known as the *flehmen* reaction. This is a kind of open-mouthed lip curl, where the tiger wrinkles its nose and sticks out its tongue. The potential mates then indulge in some courtship-playing, which involves mock chases and vicious swipes with the forepaws.

No one has ever seen tigers mating in the wild, but several people have heard them. The female tiger roars and grunts, while the male emits high-pitched squeals and long moans. The actual mating is short, lasting only about 15 seconds, but they may mate as many as 20 times a day, and the courting couple remain together for three to five days.

Once the mating period is over, the tigers separate and the male takes no interest in finding food for the female or helping her raise the cubs.

Gestation lasts for between 95 and 112 days. The tigress continues to hunt almost until the moment of birth, which is generally at night. She finds a quiet spot in dense cover and gives birth very quickly. Then, exhausted, she rests on her side while her cubs begin to suckle.

Tigers can give birth to between one and six cubs, although an average litter is more generally three or four. From this it is usual for one or two cubs to survive to maturity. Tiger cubs measure from 12 to 14 in (30 to 35 cm), with a tail length of about 6 in (15 cm). They are born blind and helpless and are completely dependent on their mother.

Cubs' eyes open after about a week—at about the time when hunger compels the female to leave them to hunt. She leaves at night, hunts quickly, gorges herself, and returns to her young. During the day, the female remains with the cubs. At first, as much as three-quarters of the day is spent suckling the young, but this gradually lessens and they are weaned at five to six months. They cut their milk teeth at the end of the second week; their permanent

THE BIRTH
After a gestation period of about 103 days, the female gives birth to three or four cubs.

MATING
After mating, the male and female remain together for three or four days.

GROWING UP
The cubs remain dependent on their mother for food until the age of eighteen months.

A. & M. Shah/Planet Earth Pictures

A family drink (above). The cubs will not leave the mother's home range until they are about two years old.

AMAZING FACTS

• The Siberian tiger is unique among tigers in that it develops an insulating layer of fat, sometimes as much as 2 in (5 cm) thick, on its flanks and belly to protect it against the extreme cold.

• Sometimes porcupines cause the deaths of tigers. The quills embed themselves in the tiger's feet and legs, rendering the tiger incapable of hunting.

• Siberian tigers often become infected with tapeworm, while most Bengal tigers are infested with ticks.

teeth come through after about a year.

After about one month, the mother eats more than she actually needs at a kill. Returning to her cubs, she regurgitates some of the food in a partly digested form for them to eat. By the beginning of the third month, the female brings small chunks of meat back with her for the cubs.

Newborn cubs already have stripes, but the background color of their coats is lighter than that of the adults. Adult coloration comes through at three to six months.

When the cubs are about six months old, the female takes them with her on a hunt. Hiding them in the undergrowth, she makes the kill. Then she calls the cubs to join her and allows them to feast before she feeds herself. By watching her, they learn how to hunt.

MOVING TIME
Sometimes the mother moves her cubs to a new den. She carries them gently by the scruff of the neck.

Leaving home

The affectionate bond between cubs and mother remains intact and the young stay with her until they are about two years old—longer for Siberian tigers. Male cubs tend to be the first to leave the family unit. When all the cubs have left, the female will come into season again.

When they are first on their own, the young tigers have to find their own hunting grounds. Although other adult tigers will tolerate them passing through their territories, they will attack if they stay too long or if the two come face to face. After a few months, the young tiger will have established its own territory. At four years old it is sufficiently mature to raise cubs of its own, although it is not generally fully grown until it is five.

Most tigers can live up to fifteen years in the wild, although Siberian tigers seem to live longer, sometimes up to twenty years. ■

FROM BIRTH TO DEATH

BENGAL TIGER

MATING SEASON: USUALLY SPRING
GESTATION: 95–112 DAYS
LITTER SIZE: 2–4 CUBS
WEIGHT AT BIRTH: 33–42 OZ (925–1,195 G)
EYES OPEN: 10–14 DAYS
FIRST LEAVE DEN: AT ABOUT 2 MONTHS
INDEPENDENCE: 2 YEARS
SEXUAL MATURITY: 3–4 YEARS
LONGEVITY IN WILD: UP TO 15 YEARS

SIBERIAN TIGER

MATING SEASON: ANY TIME
GESTATION: 95–112 DAYS
LITTER SIZE: UP TO 6 CUBS (AVERAGE 3–4)
WEIGHT AT BIRTH: 28–53 OZ (785–1,500 G)
EYES OPEN: 10–15 DAYS
FIRST SOLID FOOD: 14 DAYS
WEANING: 5–6 MONTHS
INDEPENDENCE: 2–3 YEARS
SEXUAL MATURITY: 3–5 YEARS
LONGEVITY: UP TO 20 YEARS

M. Donnelly/Wildlife Art Agency

TREE SQUIRRELS

The timing of breeding in most squirrels is geared to the availability of food. Some tropical rain-forest squirrels can breed at any time of the year; but even in this comparatively nonseasonal environment, most species have their breeding peaks during the periods when certain key foods—especially fruit—are most abundant. In northern latitudes reproduction is concentrated in early spring and summer, when warmth and plentiful food is assured, though mild winters can trigger breeding too.

The breeding behavior of temperate tree squirrels has been most closely studied, but observations of other species' habits indicate that they have much in common. Male squirrels, and in some species female squirrels, tend to be promiscuous. During the breeding season, a female coming into estrus will soon attract a group of males from the vicinity that follow her as she moves around in her home range. Casual following turns into more vigorous mating chases, with as many as ten males vying to keep as close as possible to the female. In

LIFE IN THE NEST

Nourished by their mother's milk, infant squirrels develop fast. After a few weeks the young are covered in fur and their teeth start to develop. And from about six weeks they start the switch to solid food. Once they have reached independence, they try to establish space for themselves in the neighborhood, but the unlucky ones have to face the perils of dispersing farther afield.

Liz & Tony Bomford/Ardea

JUVENILES

Once they have gained independence, juveniles (below) usually try to establish a small territory near their birthplace.

FIRST FORAYS

When they are around seven weeks old, the young are ready to take their first faltering steps onto the branches outside the drey. Soon they begin to play and start foraging for themselves.

GROWING UP

The life of a young red squirrel

COURTSHIP

When a female red squirrel is ready for mating (usually twice a year), males will gather around her and chase her until one of them is allowed to mate.

NEST-BUILDING

After mating, the female prepares a nest for her young, lined with soft plant material. She becomes very protective of her nest-tree, driving any intruding squirrels away.

HELPLESS LITTER

A litter of young is born in the drey after some thirty-eight days. The tiny pink infants emerge naked and helpless, with no teeth and their eyes and ears closed.

most cases it is the dominant males that accompany her most closely. At this time, she takes pains to keep the males a modest 3.3–6.6 ft (1–2 m) away, but when she is ready for mating she lets the closest approach with little courtship ritual.

In the gray squirrel, the males gradually disperse after one has mated—including the successful male, who rarely takes a further role in the rearing of his offspring. But in some squirrels, among them species of beautiful squirrels, the female may mate with a succession of up to six males in a mating bout lasting an entire morning.

After mating, the female prepares her nursery drey and the males retire either back to their home ranges or to pursue another female in the vicinity. After three to six weeks, depending on species, the female gives birth to a litter of naked, helpless young. A red squirrel litter usually contains several young, while that of a giant squirrel consists of just one or two. But the latter may compensate for this by producing multiple litters during the year, while the red squirrel manages at best two. ■

Illustrations Simon Turvey/Wildlife Art Agency

FROM BIRTH TO DEATH

RED SQUIRREL

BREEDING: USUALLY 2 SEASONS SPANNING JANUARY–MARCH & MAY–JULY
GESTATION: 38 DAYS
LITTER SIZE: 3–8
NUMBER OF LITTERS: 1 OR 2 PER YEAR
WEIGHT AT BIRTH: 0.3–0.4 OZ (8–12 G)
EYES OPEN: 3 WEEKS
WEANING: 8 WEEKS
SEXUAL MATURITY: 11 MONTHS
LONGEVITY: USUALLY 2–3 YEARS, BUT UP TO 5

SOUTHERN FLYING SQUIRREL

BREEDING: USUALLY 2 SEASONS SPANNING FEBRUARY–MAY & JULY–SEPTEMBER
GESTATION: 40 DAYS
LITTER SIZE: 1–6
NUMBER OF LITTERS: 1 OR 2 PER YEAR
WEIGHT AT BIRTH: 0.07–0.1 OZ (2–3 G)
EYES OPEN: 3 WEEKS
WEANING: 8–9 WEEKS
SEXUAL MATURITY: 9 MONTHS
LONGEVITY: NOT KNOWN

TRUE SEALS

Among marine mammals, only whales and dolphins have become sufficiently specialized for aquatic life to breed at sea. The seals are forced to give birth and, in most species, suckle their pups on shore or on floating ice. Since true seals have become highly adapted to the water in every other way and cannot move efficiently, find food, or even see particularly well on shore, this biological constraint presents them with a problem.

They have tackled the problem in two ways: They choose secluded or remote breeding sites where their onshore vulnerability puts them at less risk, and they have acquired a number of adaptations that reduce the time on shore to a bare minimum. Typically, a female may spend some three weeks ashore during the breeding season, during which she will give birth, suckle her pup to the point where it is weaned, and mate. The record for a quick turnaround is held by the common or harbor seal. When the birth of her pup is imminent, she hauls out on a tidal sandbank or among rocks below the high-water mark and usually produces her pup within a few minutes of arrival. By the time the returning tide reaches them, both mother and newborn pup are ready to go to sea. Unlike most other species, she suckles the pup in the water until it is capable of feeding itself.

Each male may mate with several females, but his interest in them extends no further, and by the time his pups are born he may be far away. This is hardly surprising, for the pups are not born until a whole year later. The actual gestation—the period

JOSTLING FOR POSITION

About a year after mating, the females are ready to give birth. They haul themselves out onto the pack ice and aggressively set about securing a place on the crowded breeding ground.

MATING

During the breeding season males lie in wait beneath the ice floes, ready to mate with females as they enter the water after weaning the newborn pups (above).

SNOW-CAVE NURSERIES

While the harp and hooded seals breed on the unstable pack ice, raising their pups in record time, the ringed seal has its pup on thicker, often permanent or land-fast ice and suckles it in a lair beneath the snow for at least six weeks. The pregnant seals exploit the weaknesses around pressure ridges in the sea ice, digging upward with their foreflippers to create breathing holes. The holes emerge beneath the snow, which often forms deep drifts around the pressure ridges; and each seal hollows out a nursery lair, or often several lairs, beneath the snow cover. The snow shelters the newborn pup from the Arctic windchill and provides some protection against the polar bears and arctic foxes.

A Weddell seal and her newborn pup (right). Weddell seals both breed and give birth on the fast ice around Antarctica.

B/W illustrations Ruth Grewcock

GROWING UP

The life of a young harp seal

BIRTH
Harp seals, like most ice-breeders, are born with a white lanugo or birth coat, which will eventually be molted.

WEANING
takes place when the pup is between ten and fourteen days old, after which it is abandoned by its mother.

MOLTING
The pup's woolly coat must be molted before it can leave the ice to begin its independent life, foraging at sea.

FROM BIRTH TO DEATH

HARP SEAL

GESTATION: 7.5 MONTHS, AFTER 4 MONTHS DELAYED IMPLANTATION
LITTER SIZE: 1
BREEDING: FEBRUARY–MARCH, ON PACK ICE
WEIGHT AT BIRTH: 26 LB (12 KG)
WEANING: 10–12 DAYS
WEIGHT AT WEANING: 73 LB (33 KG)
FIRST ENTERS WATER: 26 DAYS
SEXUAL MATURITY: 5.5 YEARS
LONGEVITY: 30 YEARS OR MORE

HAWAIIAN MONK SEAL

GESTATION: 7.5 MONTHS, AFTER 4 MONTHS DELAYED IMPLANTATION
LITTER SIZE: 1
BREEDING: MOSTLY MARCH–MAY
WEIGHT AT BIRTH: 37 LB (17 KG)
WEANING: 40 DAYS
WEIGHT AT WEANING: 140 LB (64 KG)
FIRST ENTERS WATER: SOON AFTER BIRTH
SEXUAL MATURITY: 4 YEARS
LONGEVITY: 30 YEARS OR MORE

Illustrations Simon Turvey/Wildlife Art Agency

Rick Price/Survival Anglia

when the pup is developing in the womb—lasts some seven to eight months, but development is suspended at an early stage and the fertilized egg floats freely within the womb instead of becoming attached to the uterine wall. After three to four months, the egg implants and the embryo begins to grow in the normal way. This mechanism, known as delayed implantation, enables the females to take advantage of predator-foiling synchronized birthing and allows both sexes easy access to each other at the pupping sites.

Among many seals the timing of the birth is crucial. Species that breed on the pack ice, such as the harp seal, often start breeding as the weather improves, both to spare their pups the rigors of an Arctic winter and to take advantage of the channels of open water that begin to open up between the ice floes. Before long, however, the spring thaw causes the complete breakup of the ice, destroying the breeding habitat.

There is also every incentive to wean the pup as soon as possible, since in all species except the common seal the pup is suckled out of the water. In the harp seal the pup is suckled for some 10–14 days before being abandoned by its mother; in the hooded seal, which breeds farther offshore on drifting, unstable ice floes, the pup is suckled for an average of only four days—a record among mammals. ■

WEASELS

Compared to larger carnivores such as dogs and bears, all weasels and polecats are fast breeders. The smaller they are, the faster they breed: A female least weasel is sexually mature at three months and is likely to breed in her first summer. She may also have a second litter later in the year, by which time the females in her first litter may themselves be breeding. Since a least weasel averages six kits in each litter, she has the potential to generate 30 descendants in her first year of life: two litters of six each, plus a brood of six apiece from the three daughters in her first litter (her male offspring are unlikely to breed quite so rapidly).

Steve Downer/Aquila

A polecat-ferret with her young (above). Albinos and white or pale fur are common among ferrets.

THE PACE OF LIFE

This cracking pace is partly a consequence of the least weasel's fast metabolism. This animal races through life and is generally dead within the year; as a result everything happens quickly. A fast metabolism is not the sole reason for fast breeding, however. Like all animals, the weasels and polecats have developed breeding strategies that are defined partly by biological constraints such as metabolic rate and partly by the circumstances in which they live. In the case of the least weasel, evolution has tailored it to exploit the burrowing rodents of the tundra: the voles and lemmings. For reasons that are not entirely clear, these animals undergo roughly four-year cycles of population boom and crash: On any acre of Alaskan tundra the brown lemming population may proliferate to 100 or more, crash to less than a couple within two years, then build up to 100 again. Such wild fluctuations favor predators that can match the pace by breeding rapidly to exploit temporary gluts in the prey supply, and the least weasel fits this specification perfectly.

The stoat also hunts on the tundra, and although its slower metabolism prevents it from breeding quite as fast as the common or least weasel, it has developed a couple of tricks that help it make the most of "lemming years." The first is the disposable litter. An ovulating female produces an average of

BIRTH BURROW

A stoat with her young in an underground burrow (below). The babies are born blind and covered with fine down. Their eyes open at five to six weeks, and they are fully furred at about eight weeks.

Color illustrations Peter David Scott/Wildlife Art Agency

LEAVING HOME

When young weasels and polecats reach the age of independence, they tend to move away to find feeding territories of their own. Females do not move as far as males, and among a population of stoats studied in Sweden, the immature females tended to settle on or near their mothers' territories. Among such short-lived species, the female often dies within a few months of giving birth, enabling one of her daughters to inherit her territory.

In the Swedish study, the males tended to linger in their mothers' territories throughout the autumn and winter, then set off on extensive travels.

ten eggs, and in a poor year most of these are either not fertilized, are aborted, or die at the suckling stage. Only the strongest survive, and ultimately this is to the good of the species. In a "lemming year," however, when the tundra is teeming with prey, the extra nutrition enables the mother to bring all the embryos to term, suckle them all, and rear them all to take advantage of the abundant food supplies.

The other trick involves delayed implantation, in which the true gestation starts several months after mating. This in itself is of little value, but the female stoat capitalizes on it by mating while she is still a suckling infant—often with the male that has just mated with her mother. Hormones in the mother's milk probably activate her daughters' reproductive systems to make this possible. The development of the young female's litter is delayed until early spring, when she is old enough to bear young and when the lemmings are just starting to multiply.

Mating and Birth

Courtship and mating are rough and prolonged in weasels and polecats. This is because ovulation is triggered by the mating act, and if it is over too quickly, ovulation may not be activated. The male has a well-developed penis bone or baculum, which he uses to good purpose while grabbing the female by the neck with his sharp teeth and dragging her around; a polecat will often draw blood. The whole business lasts for up to an hour in the case of polecats; captive black-footed ferrets may keep going for up to three and a half hours.

The kits are born blind and covered in fine down. For the first few weeks they are totally dependent on their mother, who rears them alone, without any assistance from the male. This can be hard work, for once they are weaned—at three to six weeks in common weasels—she has to keep them supplied with freshly killed prey; the small size of the female can be a mixed blessing here, since although it reduces her own food requirements, it also puts a limit on the size of prey she can carry back to the nest. At six to eight weeks, young weasels can kill their own prey, but they generally hunt in family groups for some weeks before branching out on their own; this enables them to polish up their predatory skills and sometimes overpower relatively large animals that they would be rash to tackle alone. ■

ON THE MOVE
If threatened or if hunting is bad, the mother will move her young, carrying them by the scruff of the neck.

HIGH JINKS
Adolescent polecats play-fighting (below).

WILDCATS

When breeding time comes, it is usually the female of wildcat species that advertises her receptivity by calling in a particular way and indulging in scent marking—rubbing against the ground and various objects. In this way she soon attracts the attention of a male. Sexual encounters are markedly friendly. As the male approaches, the female may roll over on the ground in a submissive manner. She may also rub against him, and the two rub necks together. Vocalizations during courtship and mating are gentle and inviting—usually soft meows and loud purring.

INVITATION

Living alone, the female wildcat must make an effort to attract a mate. She does this by calling (right) and by leaving sexual clues in her scent deposits.

Seasonal breeding

Breeding among most small cats occurs once a year, although second or even third litters may occur in temperate areas. The European wildcat in Scotland, for example, mates mainly in March; in other parts of Europe and Asia mating may occur anytime from January to March. Asiatic golden cat kittens are born in February. Lynx in Spain mate mainly in January, while leopard cats in Siberia generally mate in the spring. In most species, if a female loses a litter for any reason, she is likely to come into estrus again and will resume the search for a mate.

LESSONS IN HUNTING

The young gain hunting skills when their mother brings them live prey for practice (right).

Terry Whittaker/Frank Lane Picture Agency

Although their weapons are pin-sharp from the start, they need protection for several months (left).

Gestation periods and litter sizes vary. The European wildcat typically has two to four kittens about sixty-six days after mating. For the lynx, gestation may be a few days longer, and there can be up to five kittens in a litter—although in Spain two or three is more common. For Pallas's cat, litter size is generally five or six. Jungle cats are thought to produce two litters a year in some parts of their range, and there may be as many as seven in a litter. Gestation in these cats is about eight weeks.

Although in most instances a male cat has nothing more to do with the female after mating, it may assist in raising the young in some species; for example, in the leopard cat. Male fishing cats have been known to help care for the young in captivity, but it is uncertain whether they also do so in the wild. The

GROWING UP

The life of a young wildcat

SECRET BIRTH
The female prepares a special nursery den where her young will be protected from predators. She licks the afterbirth from the newborns as they are born (left).

FEEDING
The tiny, sightless kittens can do little except suckle. They knead the female's abdomen (above) to stimulate the flow of milk — a habit that is displayed even by mature domestic cats when they find a soft rug or sweater.

European wildcat may be monogamous on occasion—the same pair breed year after year, even if they do not spend their entire lives together. The male may bring food to the den after the female has given birth, although the female is likely to chase him off if he comes too close to her kittens.

All kittens are born blind, deaf, and helpless—unable to walk or do anything except suckle. Their one action is to knead their feet against the mother's body close to a teat to stimulate the flow of milk. Births always occur in a sheltered den established in advance by the female: possibly an old burrow, in a hollow under some rocks, or deep within dense vegetation. Kittens are fully furred, some in a similar pattern to adults, others showing different markings. Those of the jungle cat, whose adult coat shows very little in the way of markings, are born with distinctive tabby patterning, which may help camouflage them; they are usually born in reedbeds. Pallas's cat kittens have thick, woolly coats at birth, but the white tips that give the frosted appearance in adult cats do not appear until later.

DEFENSIVE MOTHERS

A female is ferocious in defense of her young. At first she spend most of her time in the den with the kittens, feeding and cleaning them. By licking them she encourages them to excrete waste matter, which she consumes; this helps to prevent predators from sniffing out the hiding place. Most kittens open their eyes when they are about ten days old, but they rarely make their first foray outside the den until they are a month or so old. Then they begin to play with one another, chasing and mock-fighting while the mother goes hunting. If, on her return, she finds they have strayed too far from the den for her liking, she either calls them to her or gently carries them back to the den in her jaws.

European wildcat kittens are fully weaned at about four months. Also around this time they start to climb and the mother begins teaching them to hunt. She may start by lying close and twitching her tail to attract them, encouraging them to jump on it and pin it to the ground with their paws.

At two to three months old, the kittens have learned enough to accompany the mother on hunting trips to improve their skills. At around five months old, each young cat disperses to establish its own territory. At this time the adolescents are easy prey for predators, including larger adult male cats, but their births have usually been timed to ensure that other prey is abundant. In temperate areas, by the time the winter comes, the young cats have established their home ranges and honed their hunting skills, so they are better able to survive the harsher conditions. In most species they will be ready to breed themselves the following year; the lynx, however, does not reach sexual maturity until nearly two years old in females and a year later in males. ■

FROM BIRTH TO DEATH

EUROPEAN WILDCAT

GESTATION: AVERAGE 66 DAYS
LITTER SIZE: 2–4
WEIGHT AT BIRTH: 1.4 oz (40 g)
EYES OPEN: 10 DAYS
WEANED: FROM 7 WEEKS; FULLY AT 4 MONTHS
INDEPENDENCE: 5 MONTHS
FULLY GROWN: 10 MONTHS
SEXUAL MATURITY: 1 YEAR
LONGEVITY: 15 YEARS IN CAPTIVITY

LYNX

GESTATION: 9–10 WEEKS
LITTER SIZE: UP TO 5, USUALLY 2–3 IN SPANISH SPECIES
WEIGHT AT BIRTH: 7 oz (200 g)
EYES OPEN: NOT KNOWN
WEANED: 5 MONTHS
INDEPENDENCE: 8 MONTHS
SEXUAL MATURITY: MALES 33 MONTHS, FEMALES 21 MONTHS
LONGEVITY: 26 YEARS IN CAPTIVITY

Illustrations Robin Budden/Wildlife Art Agency

WILD CATTLE

Wild cattle give birth to coincide with the most favorable natural conditions. Depending on the species and the location, this may be during the rainy season or the months with the most favorable temperatures. The bulls join the females as the latter become sexually receptive, but there is often fierce competition between bulls for females; usually there is a dominant bull who fights any others that try to lay claim to a female, and he certainly has the first selection of cows.

Gestation periods vary between species. The anoa may give birth after only 275 days, while the African buffalo gestates for roughly 340 days. Calves may be born within the herd—in the African buffalo —or the female may give birth on her own and rejoin the herd later; this is the case with the gaur.

CALVING

The calf is highly developed at birth and is up on its feet soon after birth. In some species, however, such as the African buffalo, it is some hours before the newborn can follow the female and it remains fairly uncoordinated for many weeks. This can be a problem when a herd takes flight from a predator; the mother usually drops out of the herd to hustle her calf along, but she may be forced to abandon it.

The mother licks the calf vigorously after birth, and thereafter may strengthen the bond by licking it on its head and neck. The first drink the calf takes from its mother is full of substances that help to give it immunity from disease.

TESTING FOR READINESS

The bull assesses a cow's sexual condition by sniffing her urine (above), then curling his lip to drive the scent back to his Jacobsen's organ, a sensory organ in the snout.

SEPARATION

As they mature, the young bulls draw away to live alone (above right), while the cows herd together (right).

Martin Harvey/NHPA

SACRED CATTLE

Any visitor to India will have seen the huge cattle that walk the streets of towns and villages, untroubled by people or traffic. And woe betide anyone who harms them, for these animals are sacred to Hindus. According to the Hindu mythology, the milk of a cow once saved the life of one of the gods, Krishna, who was being persecuted at the time. Seen as an incarnation of Vishnu, the universal God, Krishna is the most revered Hindu deity, and the cow has become the life-giving "mother" of all Hindus. The meat must not be eaten, and should anyone harm a cow, the act is considered a mortal sin, more serious than the murder of a fellow human being.

GROWING UP

The life of a young anoa

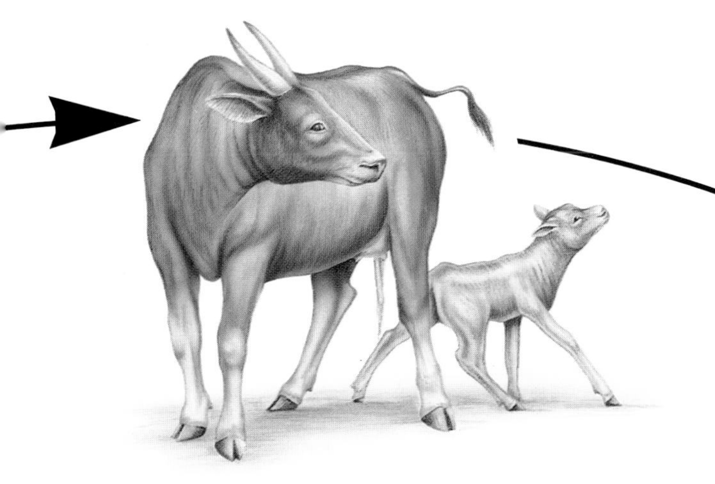

EARLY TO RISE

Almost as soon as it is born, the calf staggers to its feet on wobbly legs (above). The mother licks it clean, then nudges it gently toward her udders.

HEALTH DRINK

The calf's first drink is rich in vitamins and protective bacteria. During the course of the day, the calf suckles from each teat in turn (right).

MOTHER LOVE

The cow's close bond with her calf remains strong, at least until she gives birth again, and the two graze side by side (left).

Nursing takes place at irregular intervals during the day and may continue for anywhere from three to ten minutes. In most instances the calf is weaned after six to nine months, although it may go on suckling up to within two or three months of the next calf's birth. During this time, a cow keeps in contact with her young with various calls. In spite of the bond between mother and calf, however, when a new calf is born, the female takes no further interest in her older offspring. Nevertheless, they generally stay nearby for another year or so. As they grow, the calves spend more time in each others' company; they indulge in play sessions, practicing dominance displays, fighting, and other social gestures.

In general, females can breed two or more years before males. For example, African buffalo cows first calve at about five years—although they are able to do so a year or two earlier—while males may not mate for another three to four years. In most other species, sexual maturity comes earlier. ■

Joanne van Gruisen/Ardea

From the start, the mother forms a strong bond with her calf, nursing and watching over it (left).

FROM BIRTH TO DEATH

AFRICAN BUFFALO	WATER BUFFALO
GESTATION: ABOUT 340 DAYS	**GESTATION:** 300–340 DAYS
NUMBER OF YOUNG: 1, RARELY 2	**NUMBER OF YOUNG:** 1, RARELY 2
WEIGHT AT BIRTH: 77–110 LB (35–50 KG)	**WEIGHT AT BIRTH:** 77–88 LB (35–40 KG)
WEANED: UP TO 9 MONTHS	**WEANED:** 6–9 MONTHS
SEXUAL MATURITY: 3.5–5 YEARS	**SEXUAL MATURITY:** 2 YEARS
LONGEVITY: 18 YEARS IN THE WILD	**LONGEVITY:** 25 YEARS IN THE WILD

Illustrations Richard Tibbits

WILD PIGS

The courtship and mating cycle of wild boars has been more thoroughly studied than other species, but most wild pigs follow a similar pattern. Adult male boars that have led a solitary life during the past year join the sounders of receptive females at the beginning of the rutting season, which in temperate climates occurs once a year and in tropical climates may occur at any time. The boars may have to travel long distances in order to reach the herd, often arriving exhausted and hungry. Where there are young boars present that have not yet left the mother the older male's first act will be to send them off.

Both wild boars and warthogs will persistently follow a female and drive her around in circles, all the time uttering a strange noise, which has been described as sounding like a "clattering motor." At the same time, the male will repeatedly nudge the female, massage her roughly with his snout, and attempt to rest his snout on her rump. The latter action has the result of making the female stand still. Mating occurs several times, and at the end of the rutting season the male leaves the herd to pursue his solitary life again.

SUCKLING
The warthog sow has four teats, but the piglets have solid food after one week. The mother leaves her young for long periods during the day.

BUILD UP TO MATING
The male lets out rhythmic grunts and attempts to rest his snout on the female's rump. This brings her to an immediate standstill.

A WARTHOG'S DEN

The female warthog gives birth in a den (perhaps an abandoned aardvark's nest) that she has lined with leaves and other plant material. She may also use stems and branches to construct a rough canopy over the nest. In cold weather, the piglets benefit from this extra protection because they have only a small amount of hair at birth.

GROWING UP

The life of a young warthog

FOLLOW ME

Adult warthogs always run with their tails held vertical so that they act as a visible guide to the young, even in long grass.

ROUGH AND TUMBLE

Young warthogs and wild boars indulge in playful fighting and biting.

Illustrations Toni Hargreaves

FROM BIRTH TO DEATH

WILD BOAR

GESTATION: 170–175 DAYS
LITTER SIZE: FIRST LITTER, 3–4; SUCCEEDING ONES UP TO 12
BREEDING SEASON: SEASONAL IN TEMPERATE ZONES, NONSEASONAL IN TROPICS
MAMMAE: 6 PAIRS
EYES OPEN: AT BIRTH
FIRST SOLID FOOD: 14 DAYS
WEANING: 12 WEEKS
INDEPENDENCE: 2 YEARS
SEXUAL MATURITY: 18–24 MONTHS
FULL ADULT SIZE: 5–6 YEARS
LONGEVITY: 15–20 YEARS

WARTHOG

GESTATION: 170–175 DAYS
LITTER SIZE: 1–8, USUALLY 2–4
BREEDING SEASON: SEASONAL
MAMMAE: 2 PAIRS
EYES OPEN: AT BIRTH
FIRST SOLID FOOD: 7 DAYS
WEANING: 21 WEEKS
INDEPENDENCE: 12 MONTHS
SEXUAL MATURITY: 12–20 MONTHS
FULL ADULT SIZE: 5–6 YEARS
LONGEVITY: 12–15 YEARS

The female remains in the herd until she is ready to farrow (give birth). She then leaves and finds a suitable place to make a nest—somewhere quiet that is hidden by dense plant cover.

The piglets are small and rounded in shape. Wild boar piglets have a striped coat, warthog piglets are grayish pink and not striped. The piglets begin to crawl about as soon as they are born and scramble to suck at the teat. The female wild boar has twelve teats and the warthog four. If more piglets are born than there are teats, all may still survive if the female is well fed.

Both wild boar and warthog piglets remain in the nest for some time. The wild boar sow stays with her young most of the time and only leaves for short periods. When she does so, she will often cover the piglets with nesting material. The warthog sow leaves her young for long periods during the day, returning at intervals to suckle them and returning at nightfall. After a week the piglets leave the nest and begin to follow the sow, but for some time they continue to return to the nest at night. Although they begin to eat some solid foods within the first few weeks of life, the piglets continue to suckle for about three months. Once the piglets have been weaned, the sow returns with them to the herd.

MANY WILD BOARS DIE BEFORE THE AGE OF TWELVE MONTHS. THE CAUSES INCLUDE DISEASE, COLD, AND PREDATORS

The young males leave their mother when they are about twelve months old, or before the sow has her next litter. However, females may stay with the mother until they are eighteen months old. Although males are sexually mature by two years they are not usually able to compete successfully for the females until they are five years old. ■

WOLVERINES

Eero Murtomaki/NHPA

Mother and young share a reindeer carcass (above).

Sparsely distributed in their bleak northern habitats, roaming over vast tracts of forest and tundra, male and female woverines rarely encounter one another and are often hostile when they do. Outside the breeding season, they may barely recognize a member of the opposite sex. As the pace of life quickens in April, however, an adult wolverine's instincts send it in search of a mate. The quest may be a long one, because the animals are so sparsely distributed. A male cannot simply go up to a female and court her favor; he must hope to pick up her scent and track her down. Luckily wolverines possess musk glands capable of laying an enticingly fragrant scent trail, rich with information about the animal's sexual status, so there is little risk of the male's being led astray.

A SPRING BIRTH ENABLES THE MOTHER TO FIND FOOD NEAR THE NURSERY DEN; THIS IS ESSENTIAL, AS SHE CANNOT ROAM FAR

Most matings occur from late April to July, but the implantation of the fertilized egg in the wall of the uterus is delayed by several weeks to extend the gestation to about nine months. By this means the birth of the young is postponed until the following spring, when food is beginning to become plentiful again after the rigors of winter. In normal circumstances, a mature female breeds every other year, but she may not breed at all after a poor feeding season; conversely, if food is particularly plentiful, female wolverines breed annually.

Two to four young, called kits, are born in a den dug into a deep snowdrift or nestled among boulders. Although fully furred at birth, they are helpless and do not open their eyes for three or four weeks. Their mother suckles them for about ten weeks, and in that time she may change dens several times—either to avoid flooding by spring meltwater or as a precaution against human persecution.

The kits leave the den in early May, but they stay with the mother throughout the summer and autumn, sharing her prey and learning the arts of hunting and scavenging. During the winter the young males disperse, but the females may stay within their mother's home range indefinitely.

MATING MADNESS

In skunks, the breeding season varies from region to region. Among spotted skunks, for example, the

SKUNK KITS *play under the watchful gaze of their mother (right).*

populations in the southeastern United States mate in March and April, and the young are born 50–65 days later. There is some delay in the implantation of the egg, but this amounts to only 14–16 days. By contrast, spotted skunks in the western states mate in September and October, but implantation is delayed until the following spring and the young are born from April to June. In both species the development of the embryo within the uterus, once implanted, takes only a month or so.

A male becomes much more active as the mating season approaches, extending his daily range and vigorously defending his territory (which encloses those of several females). According to some observers, he may also suffer a kind of "mating madness" that leads him to attack—and spray—animals of other species (including humans) that stray through his patch. The mating itself is often a rough affair, with the male chasing the female, grabbing her by the scruff of the neck and pulling her off her feet. Having mated, the two usually part for good. The male plays no part in raising his young, and indeed the female may have to defend them from aggression on his part.

Janet Haas/Natural Science Photos

Young skunks stay together until they are about five months old (above).

Illustration John Morris/Wildlife Art Agency

The kits are born naked and blind, and their eyes open at twenty to thirty days. They are suckled for six to ten weeks, depending on the species. By the time they are weaned they can already use their spray defenses, and they will have accompanied their mother on a few hunting forays. The family unit remains together through the summer, but by early autumn the young skunks will have dispersed to acquire their own territories. ■

in SIGHT

ROGUE MALES

A male wolverine can do little to benefit his kits, since the female supplies their every need. So his best chance of ensuring the survival of his line is to generate as many offspring as possible by mating with several females, a strategy typical of mustelids.

The males of some species monopolize groups of females within breeding territories. The striped skunk uses this tactic, but the wolverine cannot rely on it because the home ranges of the females are so large. Instead, he seems to mate promiscuously over a large area, hoping to "stake his claim" ahead of any nearby rivals.

WOLVES

In wolf packs, mating is limited to one breeding pair—usually the alpha male and female—although in smaller packs there may only be one pair mature enough to breed anyway.

During a four-week period in the spring, all the adult females in the pack are able to mate so the alpha pair assert their breeding rights over the rest of the group. The alpha female will aggressively force the other females temporarily from the pack.

ALTHOUGH THERE IS ONLY ONE BREEDING PAIR IN THE PACK, ALL THE ADULTS HELP REAR THE PUPS

Tensions run high as the alpha male dominates the other males to prevent them from mating with her. Eventually the alpha pair mate, and peace returns to the pack.

The male wolf's penis contains a bony structure called the "baculum." After mating, the male and female turn to face in opposite directions, but this has the effect of locking the two animals together for up to a half hour or more. They remain like this until the blood vessels trapped in the swollen baculum can return to normal. No one knows for certain why this happens, although it may help to create a "pair-bond" between the male and female.

After about six weeks, the pregnant female will prepare a den for the pups. In the late spring, after a gestation period of sixty-three days, she settles alone there to give birth to a litter, typically of five or six pups. The newborn pups are blind, deaf, and helpless and can do little but wriggle and squirm and suck their mother's milk.

FROM BIRTH TO DEATH

GRAY WOLF

GESTATION: 63 DAYS
LITTER SIZE: 5–6 PUPS
WEIGHT AT BIRTH: 1 LB (450 G)
EYES OPEN: 2–3 WEEKS
FIRST WALKING: 3 WEEKS
WEANED: 7–8 WEEKS
LEAVE DEN: 8–10 WEEKS
HIERARCHY: TOP PUP ESTABLISHED AT 12 WEEKS
FOLLOW THE PACK: 3–5 MONTHS
INDEPENDENCE: 10 MONTHS
FULLY GROWN: 18 MONTHS
SEXUAL MATURITY: 2 YEARS (FEMALE); 3 YEARS (MALE)
LONGEVITY IN WILD: 15–16 YEARS (UP TO 20 YEARS IN CAPTIVITY)

RED WOLF

ALTHOUGH THE RED WOLF IS SMALLER AND LIGHTER THAN THE GRAY WOLF, THE LIFE CYCLE DETAILS ARE THE SAME.

CONCEPTION
The parent wolves mate in the spring, after several days of tension within the pack.

INDEPENDENCE
Eventually the young wolves leave the pack to mate and claim territories of their own.

ADOLESCENCE
As they grow the young wolves learn to assert themselves, laying the foundations for their future role in the pack.

GROWING UP

The life of a young wolf

BIRTH
Blind, deaf, and helpless, the pups are born in a secure den in the heart of the pack territory.

INFANCY
At first the pups rely on their mother's milk, and depend on her to keep them safe from other predators.

WOLVES' DEN

A. Wolfe/ZEFA

A typical wolf den is made by a pregnant female in a sandy hillside where the ground is easy to dig and well-drained. It is usually close to a supply of drinking water from a spring, river, or lake. The pregnant wolf sometimes adapts an old porcupine den or badger sett, digging under tree roots or rocks for extra protection. In the Arctic, the wolf den is often a protected hollow in the ground.

The burrow is usually about 16 in (40 cm) high and 26 in (65 cm) wide. Inside, 6 ft (1.8 m) from the burrow entrance is a sharp turn with a rounded hollow where the mother sleeps. The burrow then slants slightly upward for about 6 ft (1.8 m), to a snug chamber where the pups stay until they begin venturing out after four or five weeks.

After two or three weeks they can see and hear, and a week or two later they emerge from the den for the first time. They soon begin to play the puppy games, which have their serious side—practicing hunting skills, learning wolf body language, and understanding the social relationships of the pack structure. The pups stay near the den, and in large packs other wolves look after the pups as "helpers" when the parents are away from the den.

Soon the pups are too big for the den and the family moves to a "rendezvous site" for the rest of the summer. This is an area of about half an acre (1,000 square meters) where the pups can play safely, and to which the adults return every day.

At ten months the pups join in hunting, acting as observers on their first few expeditions. At eighteen months, they are adult size. When they reach sexual maturity in their second year, some will leave the pack and travel as lone wolves until they find a mate. Males often remain in the pack longer than their sisters.

A wolf can live for nine to ten years if it survives the threat of human hunters, starvation, or aggression from other wolf packs; though as it reaches old age, its teeth become worn, and it is a less efficient hunter.

Sometimes an old wolf is fed and protected by the younger pack members, who rely on its experience of territory and prey. Old and sick animals may, however, be treated as outcasts of the pack when they have outlived their usefulness. ■

WOMBATS

Marsupial reproduction depends heavily on the weather. In wet areas—such as tropical rain forests—females can breed all year-round; in drier areas they time births to coincide with maximum food abundance. Bilbies, for example, breed mainly from March to May (the southern autumn), when rainfall is highest.

In dense vegetation, expectant long-nosed bandicoots construct a mound of twigs, leaves, and earth and give birth in a hole in its center. In more open areas, however, they will excavate a nest chamber, line it with plant fibers, and then cover this with a twiggy mound. In areas where mound making is difficult, bandicoots nest in abandoned rabbit burrows, rock piles, and hollow logs.

BANDICOOTS AND BILBIES HAVE THE SHORTEST REPRODUCTION CYCLES OF ANY MAMMAL SPECIES

Having mated in her burrow, a female bilby gives birth to one to three young after a pregnancy of some twenty-one days. She possesses eight teats in a rear-opening pouch. The newborn young attach their mouths firmly to the teats and do not vacate the pouch until seventy to seventy-five days later. Some fourteen days after that, they are weaned. During this time, they will still try and leap into the pouch if danger threatens. A female long-nosed bandicoot will not be receptive again for about two months after giving birth, though this still means that she can produce three to four litters in a season.

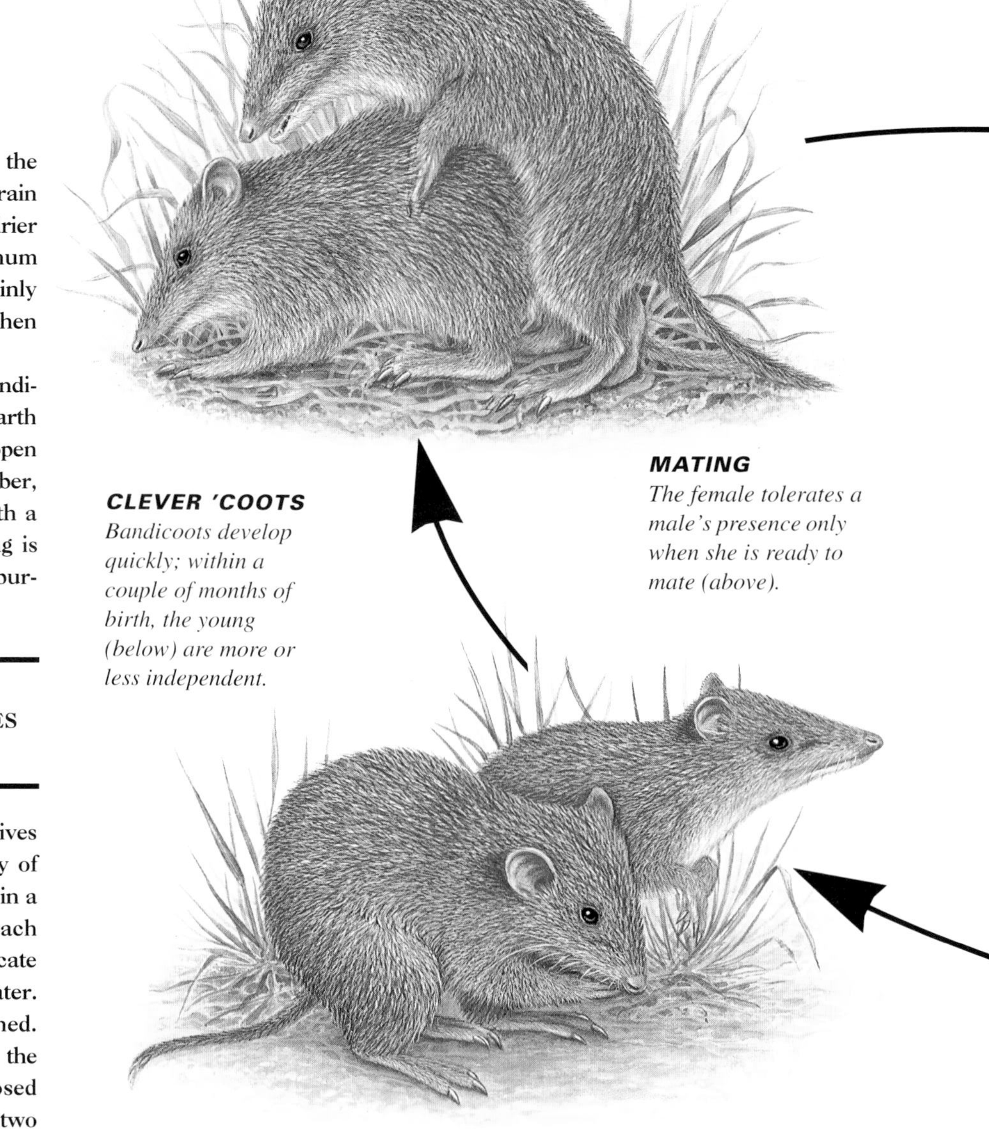

MATING
The female tolerates a male's presence only when she is ready to mate (above).

CLEVER 'COOTS
Bandicoots develop quickly; within a couple of months of birth, the young (below) are more or less independent.

POUCH VARIATIONS

In most marsupials the pouch opens forward. Female wombats, however, are one of the few marsupials that have the opening to the pouch facing backward. This shields the baby while the mother is moving underground and prevents earth from entering the furry nursery and possibly smothering the infant. An even more extreme development is found in the South American yapok. This stream-loving opossum has a ring of sphincter muscles around the mouth of the pouch, which close it off like a duffel bag every time the yapok enters the water—so preventing the enclosed babies from drowning.

B/W illustrations Ruth Grewcock

Color illustrations Wayne Ford/Wildlife Art Agency

GROWING UP

The life of a young golden bandicoot

WALK OF LIFE

A newborn bandicoot crawls from the birth canal to the pouch (left). In many species, newborns are born with special claws for this purpose; these are later shed.

RAPID GROWTH

When it first grips a nipple in the pouch (right), each newborn is smaller than a bean. By the time the young are ready to emerge, the female is having trouble walking (below).

FROM BIRTH TO DEATH

COMMON WOMBAT	LONG-NOSED BANDICOOT
MATING: ANYTIME	
GESTATION: 20–22 WEEKS	**GESTATION:** 12–13 DAYS
NO. OF YOUNG: 1, RARELY 2	**NO. OF YOUNG:** 1–5
WEIGHT AT BIRTH: 0.07 OZ (2 G)	**WEIGHT AT BIRTH:** NOT KNOWN
TIME IN POUCH: 6–7 MONTHS	**TIME IN POUCH:** 48–53 DAYS
WEANING: 8–9 MONTHS	**WEANING:** 59–61 DAYS
SEXUAL MATURITY: 23 MONTHS	**SEXUAL MATURITY:** 3 MONTHS IN FEMALE, 4 MONTHS IN MALE
LONGEVITY: 6–10 YEARS IN THE WILD, UP TO 27 YEARS RECORDED IN CAPTIVITY	**LONGEVITY:** 3 YEARS OR MORE IN CAPTIVITY; UNKNOWN IN WILD

Bandicoots have eight nipples, but usually raise three or four young at a time. This is because each new litter is generally born just as the previous one is weaned. Nipples used by the previous litter swell up as the babies develop, and would be too large for the newborns, but because there are four spare nipples, the new young are assured a source of milk. Meanwhile, the nipples unused in this reproductive session slowly diminish in size, getting ready to feed the next batch of babies.

Hairy-nosed wombats give birth in the spring (October–January), if there has been sufficient rain. Common wombats have no such complications: Their young can be born at any time of year.

A female wombat usually gives birth to a single young weighing 0.07 oz (2 g) and measuring 0.9 in (22 mm). The baby stays in the pouch for six or seven months. Weaned at eight or nine months, it leaves the mother soon afterward. It becomes sexually mature at twenty-three months in common wombats, and at eighteen months in hairy-nosed wombats. ■

Two young northern brown bandicoots head for the warmth and safety of their mother's pouch (below).

ANT/NHPA

in SIGHT

BABY FACTORY

The golden bandicoot has the briefest gestation of any mammal: just twelve days. The tiny newborns enter the pouch and suckle for seven weeks; the pouch expands as they grow until it almost brushes the ground. Ten days after the young emerge, they are weaned and on their own as their mother ceases to care for them. Within three months the new females can start families of their own. This rapid cycle allows the golden bandicoot to exploit new sources of food and to respond quickly when bushfires decimate the population.

ZEBRAS

Female zebras are receptive every few weeks, but births are generally timed to coincide with the rainy season, when grass is most abundant. Since gestation takes roughly a year, mating also occurs at this time. It suits the zebra herd to foal in unison, as lone foals are so vulnerable to predators. Despite this, however, births among plains zebras seem to continue at a peak for about six months.

In plains and mountain zebras, a herd stallion identifies the receptive mares by sniffing at their urine. It may be a few days before the mare is fully receptive, during which time the two will indulge in nibbling and mutual grooming. Mating is generally repeated every few hours over a 24-hour period. In Grevy's zebra, where a stallion mates with mares as they cross his territory, the courtship may be violent. The stallion herds the mare by chasing and nipping her, and repeatedly tries to mount her; if she is not ready she lashes out with her hooves.

Zebras give birth to a single foal lying down, often in the open. In the case of the plains and mountain zebras, the herd is generally nearby, with the stallion being highly vigilant. In Grevy's zebras, birth is a more solitary affair. Grevy's zebra foals are usually brown and black with a crest of longer hairs extending right down the body to the tail. Adult coloration develops at about four months of age.

A foal is up on its feet within about ten minutes, breaking the umbilical cord as it rises. The mare licks its anus to encourage it to defecate. Within an hour the foal is walking, and shortly afterward can trot and canter after the mare.

Initially, newborn foals are so leggy that they have to splay their forelimbs to reach the ground, but they grow into proportion. They are playful, particularly the colt (male) foals. Later on, bachelor herds of young males spend a lot of time indulging in mock fights and general "horseplay," presumably rehearsing for when fighting will be more important to establish their adult role.

Foals stay reasonably close to the mare, however, for some time, and are weaned at about eight to ten months old, even though they have been nibbling grass since about a week after their birth. Young males generally leave a herd at two to

RIVALRY FIGHTS *between stallions look very violent, although bloodshed is usually avoided. The biting, hoof-pounding, and whinnying unsettle the herd, until eventually the victor drives away his adversary and claims his "ownership" of the females (below).*

A PATTERN FOR SURVIVAL
Unlike the zebra's stripes, those of a tapir are designed to conceal and protect the tiny offspring.

three years old, teaming up with others of the same age. Fillies usually stay with the herd until abducted by a stallion. Mares begin to come into season when they are a year or two old but generally do not begin breeding for another year. Stallions are five or six years old before they begin forming a herd of their own and mating successfully.

TAPIR REPRODUCTION

Tapirs, too, can reproduce year-round but may well time births to coincide with the monsoon rains. Males track down receptive females by their scent, and courtship is a noisy affair with lots of wheezes and whistles. Mating is accompanied by biting and sometimes occurs in the water. After this point the male loses interest in the female, and she gives birth to a single young after 55–59 weeks. The baby is small but well formed, with eyes already open. The female licks it to encourage it to stand, at which time she lies on her side and nudges it toward her teats. For a week or so the baby lies low in the bushes, later accompanying its mother on her foraging trips. Its baby coat of white stripes and spots begins to fade at about five months old, and by the time it is ten months it has its full adult coloration. Soon after, it leaves its mother. ■

FROM BIRTH TO DEATH

PLAINS ZEBRA	MALAYAN TAPIR
GESTATION: 360–396 DAYS	**GESTATION:** 390–403 DAYS
NUMBER OF YOUNG: 1	**NUMBER OF YOUNG:** 1
WEANED: 8–11 MONTHS	**WEANED:** NOT KNOWN
INDEPENDENCE: 2–3 YEARS	**INDEPENDENCE:** 10–11 MONTHS
SEXUAL MATURITY: 4–6 YEARS IN MALES; 3 YEARS IN FEMALES	**SEXUAL MATURITY:** 3–4 YEARS
LONGEVITY: UP TO 40 YEARS IN CAPTIVITY; SELDOM MORE THAN 10 YEARS IN THE WILD	**LONGEVITY:** 35 YEARS IN CAPTIVITY; NOT KNOWN IN THE WILD

Born in the open, the Grevy's zebra foal must be able to run with its mother within hours of birth. It suckles for up to eleven months, growing rapidly on her rich milk (below).

E. Dragesco/Ardea

CLASSIFICATION

The following lists the genuses of the mammals detailed in this book.

ARTIODACTYLA	camel, deer, gazelle, giraffe, goat antelope, hippopotamus, impala, prong–horn, warthog, wild cattle
CARNIVORA	african wild dog, american black bear, badger, brown bear, cheetah, dhole, giant panda, hyena, jackal, jaguar, leopard, lion, meerkat, otter, polar bear, puma, raccoon, red fox, serval, tiger, weasel, wildcat, wolf, wolverine
CETACEA	gray whale, humpback whale, sperm whale
CHIROPTERA	fruit bat
EDENTATA	anteater, armadillo, sloth
INSECTIVORA	hedgehog, mole, shrew
LAGOMORPHA	hare
MARSUPIALIA	bandicoot, kangaroo, koala, opossum, rat kangaroo, tasmanian devil
MONOTREMATA	platypus
PERISSODACTYLA	horse, rhinoceros, zebra
PINNIPEDIA	eared seal, true seal
PRIMATES	capuchin, chimpanzee, galago, gibbon, gorilla, lemur, marmoset, orangutan
PROBOSCIDEA	elephant
RODENTIA	beaver, capybara, deer mouse, hamster, porcupine, prairie dog, tree squirrel
SIRENIA	manatee

INDEX

Page numbers in **bold** indicate the main entries for an animal.